FROM SILENCE TO SILENCE

FROM SILENCE TO SILENCE

A BENEDICTINE PILGRIMAGE TO GOD'S SANCTUARY

FATHER FRANCIS BETHEL, OSB

Foreword by Joseph Pearce

Be still, and know that I am God.
—Psalm 46

TAN Books
Gastonia, North Carolina

From Silence to Silence: A Benedictine Pilgrimage to God's Sanctuary

All biblical quotations are taken from the Revised Standard Version, Second Catholic Edition, 2001, unless the line from the Bible is in the interior of a quotation from another author.

Cover design by Jordan Avery

Cover image: *Monks in the Cloister of the Church of Gesù e Maria, Rome* by François Marius Granet. Public domain, via Wikimedia Commons

Library of Congress Control Number: 2025935981

ISBN: 978-1-5051-2987-8
Kindle ISBN: 978-1-5051-2988-5
ePUB ISBN: 978-1-5051-2989-2

Published in the United States by
TAN Books
PO Box 269
Gastonia, NC 28053
www.TANBooks.com

Printed in the United States of America

To the Sunday night class

Contents

Foreword

THERE IS SOMETHING paradoxically perplexing about feeling honoured and humbled at the same time. The feeling of being honoured seems to be a temptation to the sin of pride, whereas feeling humbled is the experience of humility, the very antithesis of pride and the antidote to its poison. This perplexity of apparent contradictions was what I experienced when Father Francis Bethel asked me whether I would be willing to write a foreword to his book on silence. I was both honoured and humbled in equal measure that he should feel that I was worthy of such a task. In response, I can only say that I feel towards this wonderful Benedictine monk what G. K. Chesterton felt about the great Dominican, Father Vincent McNabb, that he "is walking on a crystal floor over my head" or what T. S. Eliot said about the great poet, Dante. Referring to an article that he had written on "Dante as a Spiritual Leader" for the *Athenaeum* on April 2, 1920, Eliot had informed a friend that "I feel that anything I can say about such a subject is trivial. I feel so completely inferior in his presence [that] there seems nothing to do but to point to him and be silent."

It is delightfully apt that my response to a book by Father Bethel on silence is the desire to point to him and be silent. Were I to do so, however, I would fail to fulfill Father Bethel's request. I will therefore venture to say something in the hope that it will not be trivial in comparison with the wisdom to be found in the rest of this volume.

I will approach Father Bethel's wonderful meditation on the connection between silence and sanctity by following his approach to the theological virtues. In Part III, "Approaching the Sanctuary: The Theological Virtues", he precedes the three separate chapters on faith, hope, and charity with a chapter on humility. In doing so, he is following other great thinkers of the Church, including St. Thomas Aquinas, in insisting that humility is the beginning of wisdom because it is the necessary prerequisite for our eyes being opened to reality. One who has humility will have a sense of gratitude for his own existence and for the existence of others. This gratitude enables him to see with the eyes of wonder. The eyes that see with wonder will be moved to contemplation on the goodness, truth and beauty of the reality they see. Such contemplation leads to the greatest fruit of perception, what St. Thomas calls *dilatatio*, the dilation of the mind and soul. It is this dilation, this opening of the mind and soul to the depths of reality, which enables a person to live in communion with the fullness of goodness, truth and beauty. To summarize what I like to call the five metaphysical senses: *humility* leads to *gratitude,* which sees with *wonder*, prompting the *contemplation* that leads to the *dilation* of the mind.

It is little wonder that Father Bethel should have this wonder-filled approach to reality, considering that he studied under John Senior in the celebrated Integrated Humanities Program at the University of Kansas, a program which sought to show students the great texts of civilization in the light of the goodness, truth, and beauty of the cosmos.

Father Bethel and the other students in Senior's Integrated Humanities Program did not only look down at the text on the page but also cast their eyes upwards at the stars in the sky, seeing the former in the light of the latter.

The one thing that is equally necessary for the reading of books or the reading of the stars is the gift of silence, which might be defined as the absence of distraction.

The gift of silence is difficult to attain in our techno-addicted culture in which we are being incessantly tempted to distraction. Techno-addiction lulls the mind into a comfort zone of banality, narcissistically self-centred and self-gratifying, disconnecting us from the reality that surrounds us. At the same time, even as it lulls us from reality, it agitates us into a state of restlessness, which is one of the defining traits of addiction. Thus, we find ourselves in a state of soporific agitation, unable to awaken ourselves from virtual reality to veritable reality and yet unable to find any rest in our narcissistic escapism.

This modern obsession with technological media might be seen as an infernal inversion of the true order of perception, predicated on humility. If humility opens our eyes to reality, pride shuts them, blinding and binding us with the arrogance of our own ignorance. Pride, or narcissism, sees only itself, or more correctly, it sees everything in the light or darkness of its own self-centredness. It is myopic. It cannot see beyond its own self-centre of gravity. It lacks gratitude. Such ingratitude leads to the cynicism which cannot experience wonder nor see the beauty inherent in reality. The lack of wonder makes contemplation on the goodness, truth and beauty of reality impossible and therefore makes *dilatatio* unattainable. To put the matter succinctly, pride leads to ingratitude which lacks wonder, preventing contemplation and therefore the closing instead of opening, the mind.

Another way of saying the same thing is to say that humility *takes* time while pride merely *wastes* it.

Truly humble souls, filled with gratitude and wonder, *take* the time to stop in the midst of a busy day to sit in the presence of beauty. They open their eyes to the glories of God's Creation and to the reflected and refracted glories of man's sub-creation in art and literature, or else they close their eyes from all distraction so that they can listen to the singing of birds or the singing of choirs, or the saying of prayers. Such time *taken* is the most joyful part of the day, a time when the mind communes with the reality of which it is a part.

Prideful souls, lacking both gratitude and wonder, *waste* their time with mindless distraction after mindless distraction, filling the vacuum that their mindlessness has created with whatever trash and trivia that their fingers or thumbs can deliver on the gadgets to which they are chained. For such people, these gadgets have become godgets, pathetic and petty gods which command their attention and rule and ruin their lives. Such people spend much more time with their godgets than with their God.

If we wish to have minds open to the presence of God, we need to *take* time and not *waste* it. We need to take time in the silence of prayer or the silence of poetry. We need more time with trees and less time with trash and trivia. A tree, or a flower, or a sunset are priceless gifts for which a lack of gratitude is a sin of omission. We cannot ever be *wasting* time when we're *taking* it in wonder-filled contemplation.

To be or not to be. That is the question. To be alive to the goodness, truth, and beauty which surround us, or not to be alive to it. To delight in the presence of Creation so that we might dilate into the presence of the Creator, or to distract ourselves to death.

Father Bethel once asked me for some suggestions on great poetry which offered the gift of silence by inviting the reader to plunge into the tranquility of quietude. As a means of contributing something to Father Bethel's own wisdom on the subject of silence, I'll conclude my introduction to his deeper musings on the topic with a few poetic pointers of my own.

The first poem I suggested was Wordsworth's "Daffodils", with its unforgettable and unmistakable opening line: "I wandered lonely as a cloud." This poem, which is wonderful in the literal sense of the word, being full of wonder, engages silence in two ways. The first half engages silence in the moment of experience; the latter half in the memory of experience. The poet is wandering alone in the hills when "all at once" he sees a field of daffodils "dancing in the breeze". He is astonished at the swaying sea of gold and finds his breath taken away by the sheer beauty of the gift of the moment. Yet the deeper gift was not the astonishment of the transient moment, but the lingering contemplation in moments of solitude of the memory of the gift:

> For oft, when on my couch I lie
> In vacant or in pensive mood,
> They flash upon that inward eye
> Which is the bliss of solitude,

And then my heart with pleasure fills,
And dances with the Daffodils.

The next poem I selected as a celebration of silence was "The Lime-Tree Bower My Prison" by Wordsworth's collaborator and fellow Romantic poet, Samuel Taylor Coleridge. As with "Daffodils", this poem also engages silence in both the moment and the memory, but it does so in very different circumstances. Coleridge finds himself unable to go walking through the beauty of the countryside with his friends because of an injured foot. Forced to sit beneath the shade of a solitary lime-tree, he uses his memory of previous wanderings through the vistaed landscape in which he knows his friends are walking to imagine himself being with them and enjoying the same views; then, however, he is drawn to the beauty of the present moment in the beauty of his present surroundings. Unable to experience with his friends the telescopic splendour of the panoramic panoply of a sprawling landscape, except in memory, he contemplates the microscopic splendour of the few things he can see from his imprisoned and stationary perspective in the present moment. He notices the individual leaf, "broad and sunny . . . dappling its sunshine". Later, as the blaze of the day gives way to the gloaming of the day's end, more solitary pleasures are bestowed on him:

. . . now the bat
Wheels silent by, and not a swallow twitters,
Yet still the solitary humble-bee
Sings in the bean-flower!

In another Coleridge poem, "Hymn Before Sunrise, in the Vale of Chamouni", the poet finds himself in the presence of that moment which is given as a free gift every single day, inviting silence and the contemplation which is its fruit. Every rising of the sun, and every setting, is a unique work of art, inviting the heart and soul to dilate into the glory it presents. In his "Hymn Before Sunrise", Coleridge gazes at the majestic alpine peak of Mont Blanc and is moved to meditation:

> O dread and silent Mount! I gazed upon thee,
> Till thou, still present to the bodily sense,
> Didst vanish from my thought: entranced in prayer
> I worshipped the Invisible alone.

The poet, wrapped in the moment and enraptured by the experience, is prompted by the beauty of art to sing a hymn of praise to the Artist:

> Thou too, hoar Mount! With thy sky-pointing
> peaks . . .
> Rise, O ever rise,
> Rise like a cloud of incense, from the Earth!
> Thou kingly Spirit throned among the hills,
> Thou dread ambassador from Earth to Heaven,
> Great Hierarch! tell thou the silent sky,
> And tell the stars, and tell yon rising sun,
> Earth, with her thousand voices, praises God.

Many will be reminded in reading these lines of "The Canticle of Brother Sun" by St. Francis of Assisi who speaks of the beauty, radiance and splendour of the sun as "a sign that tells, All-highest, of you". If we have the humility of the saint and the eyes of the Romantic poet, we will be grateful for the gift of beauty, being rendered speechless in its presence, that we might hearken to the silence and its visual music. It is through this silence, born of wonder, that we are moved to the contemplation that opens us into a closer communion with God.

—Joseph Pearce

Preface

Two Silences and the Path

"And as we talked and panted for [eternal wisdom], we touched just the edge of it by the utmost leap of our hearts; then, sighing and unsatisfied, we left the first-fruits of our spirit captive there, and returned to the noise of articulate speech, where a word has beginning and end."

—St. Augustine[1]

I VIVIDLY REMEMBER my first visit to the Benedictine abbey of Notre Dame de Fontgombault in France. I had been told that Fontgombault had ancient, beautiful buildings, but, as that information had not entered my imagination, I was surprised as the taxi pulled alongside the ten-foot stone wall that enclosed the abbey grounds and then drove around to the grand portal of the twelfth-century abbey church. My three companions and I went in and were instantly captivated by a place drenched with centuries of prayer and silence, vaulted high and arched, shadowed in mystery.

We arrived just in time for Vespers and sat down in the front row. The stillness of the place enveloped us. Suddenly,

[1] St. Augustine, *Confessions*, trans. Mary Boulding (San Francisco: Ignatius Press, 2012), IX, ch. 10, no. 24.

a monk appeared in the sanctuary and grasped a rope that reached all the way up to the lofty bell tower. He began pulling the rope, and we heard the calm sound of a bell ringing regularly and slowly: bong . . . bong . . . bong. A long line of eighty monks entered the sanctuary two-by-two, serenely, graciously. The bell eventually stopped, the monks knelt for a moment, and then, all together in one movement, quietly got to their feet. Next, rising out of the silence, I heard for the first time a single voice chant: "*Deus, in adjutorium meum intende*." Eighty voices responded: "*Domine, ad adjuvandum me festina*." Then the psalmody began.

Here were men accomplishing what is essential for human life, praising God, unperturbed by the tumult of the world. I especially remember the refrain of psalm 136 jumping out at me, echoing in my heart: "For His merciful love endures forever." The silence continued to underlie the singing of the calm, simple, attractive Gregorian melody. At the end, when the singing was over, the silence had become palpable, enriched somehow.

Afterwards, we were shown our rooms. In mine, I found on the wall a little engraving of the Blessed Virgin holding a finger to her lips; it was titled *Notre Dame du silence*—"Our Lady of silence." The title intrigued me, and it still does. Soon, we were ushered to dinner in the monks' refectory. Things remained quiet, with the monks in service smoothly accomplishing their tasks, and the only vocal sound being that of a monk reading out loud from the life of a saint. Lastly, we experienced the serenity of Compline in the dark church, lit by only a couple of lamps. At the end of the office, a monk lit also two candles in front of a statue of Our Lady, and the monks sang the *Salve Regina* to her.

When the last words had been sung, a bell peacefully sounded again in the silence, this time for the Angelus. Then all was quiet for the night, as if all the singing and praying had been building up to that silence. I tiptoed up to my room; it felt like the whole monastery was dripping with a silent presence. I remember hearing the church bell ringing the hours during the night, rising out of the silence then fading back into it. This only increased the feeling of a dense presence. That was my first experience with silence, you might say. I entered Fontgombault a year later in order to enter more deeply into that mystery. Twenty-five years later, Fontgombault began our monastery here in Oklahoma, Our Lady of Clear Creek.

There were two silences in my experience that first evening at Fontgombault. The first was the monks' attention, which I am going to call here subjective silence. The second was what they were attentive to, an objective silence, one might say. Singing the psalms, ringing the bells in that magnificent church, all was ordered to a contact with God's mysterious presence.

Subjective silence, an attentive receptivity, is essential for a truly human life. To observe events, to listen to a lecture, to read a book, to speak with a friend, we must not be distracted by noise, especially by interior noise—that is, extraneous preoccupations and wayward imaginings. We need to cultivate a certain interior calm beyond the hubbub of superficial impressions and drives if we are going to really reflect, make personal decisions, and be able also to give ourselves to others instead of blindly following egotistical impulsions. We need an interior place of silence to receive Our Lord's word.

Entering into *objective* silence is the main purpose of the subjective one. We need to recollect our faculties around more important thoughts in order to be attentive to what really counts in life. Now, what really counts in life are mysteries, such as friendship, love, beauty, and, most of all, God. A mystery is not merely something that we have not figured out. Rather, it is something we do know but only obscurely and will never get to the bottom of. Knowledge of mystery is like being plunged into the ocean: the mystery penetrates us, surrounds us; we know we are in it, but we cannot embrace it all. Mysteries are thus imbued with a sort of silence, something beyond our clear knowledge.

Msgr. Romano Guardini stresses the importance of interior silence to hear the objective one: "Silence or stillness is the tranquility of our inner life, the quiet at the depths of its hidden stream. It is a recollected, total presence, where one is all there, receptive, alert, ready. It comes only if seriously, earnestly desired. We must be willing to give something in order to establish a quiet area of attentiveness in which the beautiful and the truly important reign. Once we have experienced it, we will be astounded that we were able to live without it."[2]

He speaks of beauty and truth. By Christian revelation, we know even more tremendous mysteries: the incarnation

---

[2] Romano Guardini, *Meditations Before Mass*, trans. Elinor Briefs (Westminster, Maryland: Newman Press, 1956), 3–4.

of Our Lord, the Redemption, His presence in the Holy Eucharist, the Church, Our Lady, and most of all, the ultimate mystery, infinitely greater than all created mysteries, than the entire universe, that of the most holy Trinity. To participate in the silence of the Blessed Trinity is the ultimate goal of our interior silence, as St. John of the Cross intimates in a famous text: "The Father spoke one Word, which was his Son, and this Word he speaks always in eternal silence, and in silence must it be heard by the soul."[3] During the course of this book, we will try to understand better what St. John is saying here.

Subjective silence itself is not emptiness. It is attention and receptivity. It is also a light, for the soul is ordered to objective silence, to great mysteries in which we participate. Cultivating interior silence consists, firstly, in taking away obstacles that distract our attention from that light. Secondly, we enrich this interior silence with all we have learned that attunes us to the mysteries. For example, we learn about the mystery of beauty, we acquire a sense of it, and become able to enter into it. Ultimately, our understanding of beauty points us toward God's inconceivable Beauty.

The epigraph of this introduction evoked the two silences and the path from one to the other. Concerning his famous ecstasy at Ostia with his mother, Monica, St. Augustine described how, through a meditation, the two rose to a great concentration and contact with God's eternal Mystery, His

---

[3] St. John of the Cross, "Sayings of Light and Love," no. 100, in *The Collected Works of Saint John of the Cross,* trans. Kieran Kavanaugh and Otilio Rodriguez (Washington: Institute of Carmelite Studies, 1991), 92.

Silence. The meditation, like the meditation of the psalms, by the Fontgombault monks and the praying of the psalms, caused a certain enriching that attuned to the great object.

We monks enter the monastery to cultivate interior silence in order to participate better in God's silence. Not only monks, but everyone must make space in themselves to give place to God. A deep, rich silence, receptive to truth, goodness, and beauty, has never been easy. But special reflection and deliberate effort for it are required today, because our world is a culture of noise, both interior and exterior. It fosters diversion from God, from the true meaning of things, and from our authentic selves. A century ago, it was said that the modern world is a conspiracy against contemplation, against silence. And even two centuries ago, during a time which seems peaceful and silent to us, Soren Kierkegaard describes what corresponds amazingly well to our situation. The world has simply gone further in the same direction:

> Create silence. Ah! everything is noisy; . . . everything in our day, even the most insignificant project, even the most empty communication, is designed merely to jolt the sense or stir up the crowd—noise! And man, this clever fellow, seems to have become sleepless in order to invent ever new instruments to increase noise, to spread noise and insignificance with the greatest possible haste and on the greatest possible scale. Everything is turned upside down. Communication is brought to its lowest point with regard to meaning, and simultaneously the means of communication are

> brought to their highest with regard to speed and overall circulation. O! create silence![4]

I invite the reader to join in the adventure of silence. I propose that we make a pilgrimage together to the Sanctuary of Silence, where Our Lord dwells. I have called this book *From Silence to Silence*—that is, establishing interior silence and then proceeding toward contact with God's silence. I will begin with considerations on how to cultivate the first silence: an interior, receptive calm. Then we will be ready for a second stage, in which we will meditate on some mysteries that advance us toward God's infinite and silent mystery. Lastly, we will try to see how we can reach His silence through the theological virtues of faith, hope, and charity, which ultimately means through prayer.

In the text above, Augustine referred to normal speech as noise in comparison with God's transcendent silence. The dictionary defines noise as an unpleasant or undesired sound, as an annoying, irregular one. Noise, for us in this book, will be whatever is disharmonious with our deep life, whatever at some level impairs our attention to great truths, and, in the last analysis, anything that hampers our progress toward God.

We will keep in mind Our Lord's silence. During His earthly life, in the bottom of His soul, He was in silent communion with His Father. He spent most of that life in the quiet home of Nazareth, began His public life with the

---

[4] Quoted in *The Power of Silence* by Robert Cardinal Sarah, trans. Michael Miller (San Francisco: Ignatius Press, 2017), 86. The cardinal's book is a treasure of wonderful quotations on silence.

silence of the desert, and even during those three years of preaching would regularly sneak off to be alone with the Father. He was mostly silent during His passion. Finally, He returned to the silence of the Father.

We will also think of Mary's silence when she bore Jesus in her womb and waited to see His face, of her adoring silence at Bethlehem, the silence of the separation during Jesus's public career, her silent pondering of her son's words and the events around Him, the awful silence at the cross, the silence of Holy Saturday in a calm expectation of her son's resurrection, and then after the Ascension, the silent waiting in her heart for Him to come to take her.

I subtitled this book *A Benedictine Pilgrimage to God's Sanctuary*. I have not, in view of this book, done research on the Benedictine tradition concerning silence, nor will I particularly comment on the Rule of St. Benedict. I simply put forward my meditations, the fruit of almost half a century of Benedictine life. I have been formed in the great Solesmes tradition, especially through Dom Paul Delatte's writings and through my master of novices and later abbot, Dom Antoine Forgeot, to whom I will often refer in these pages.[5]

I address primarily the lay faithful and families, but I hope that priests and those of the consecrated life, especially contemplatives, will be able to find some nourishment in this writing. My reflections mainly aim at fostering our life of prayer. I am not on the summit next to the sanctuary, beckoning to those below; I am, rather, on the slope with

[5] Other Benedictine authors I have frequented are St. Bernard, St. Gertrude, Blessed Columba Marmion, Dom Prosper Guéranger, and Lady Abbess Cécile Bruyère.

the others, striving to put one foot forward at a time. I have, nevertheless, thought deeply and at length on what I write here, and hopefully, have put it to the test in my life.

I want to thank those who have looked over this manuscript: Anne Calovich and Galina Bedyulina, plus a couple of monks here at Clear Creek. I thank Joseph Pearce for his foreword and Jason Gale of TAN Books for his great patience with me.

Let us ask Our Lady to show us the way and accompany us on our journey. Let us also pray to St. Joseph, that man who silently served his two beloved companions. I entrust this work especially to the prayers of that other man of silence, our Blessed Father St. Benedict.

Introduction

Taking Stock for the Journey

"A person possesses absolute dignity because he is in direct relationship with the realm of being, truth, goodness, and beauty, and with God, and it is only with these that he can arrive at his complete fulfillment. His spiritual fatherland consists of the entire order of things which have absolute value, and which reflect, in some manner, a divine Absolute superior to the world and which have a power of attraction toward this Absolute."

—Jacques Maritain[1]

St. Benedict opens his Rule with the words "Hearken, o my son . . . that you may return . . . to Him from whom you had departed."[2] Our unique goal in life is to return to the Father; that is the one thing necessary. In this introduction, I want to consider how the culture of silence fits into that journey back to God. We need to understand our basic condition before we depart on our pilgrimage.

---

1 Jacques Maritain, *Education at the Crossroads* (New Haven: Yale University Press, 1943), 8–9.

2 All quotations from the Rule of St. Benedict are taken from *A Commentary of the Rule* by Dom Paul Delatte, trans. Dom Justin McCann (London: Burns and Oates, 1921).

The paradox of man

Pascal wrote: "By space the universe encompasses and swallows me up like an atom; by thought I comprehend the world."[3] The greatness of man is not in size and strength. In the epigraph above, Jacques Maritain told us that we are at home in the realm of the absolute, above the ups and downs of this world. The human soul is, in a way, larger than the universe since it is open, by its intellect and will, to more than anything creation can provide. Man naturally reaches beyond the world both in thought and desire.

Indeed, since the intellect is ordered to truth as such, it tends farther than theh things we encounter, for they do not completely explain themselves; they do not provide the full truth. We realize that this changeable, limited world cannot suffice as the ultimate truth. The mind naturally rises to the first truth upon which all other truth depends—that is, to the cause of this world, the first being.

Similarly, since our will is ordered to the good, it cannot be satisfied with a limited good. When we perceive something good, it stimulates in us a desire for something better, even of an absolute, pure good. Our mediocre happinesses stir up in us a yearning for happiness without limit, for all possible happiness. We witness this in the book of Ecclesiastes, where King Solomon, who had drunk from all earthly pleasures, concludes that all is vanity. He had everything, yet his heart was unfulfilled; it needed more.

---

3 Blaise Pascal, *Thoughts*, trans. William Finlayson Trotter (New York: Collier and Son, 1910), 120.

Only God, who is truth and goodness, perfection and beauty, can adequately correspond to this ordering of both the intellect and the will to the absolute. We are made in the image of God, launched toward Him. We naturally desire God; we unconsciously seek Him in the sense that our intellect and will are inherently aiming in His direction. The *Catechism of the Catholic Church* tells us that "the desire to see God is our deepest desire."[4] In Him alone can we find ultimate, total rest. There alone is silence for our soul.

Our natural strength, however, does not suffice to reach God. We are finite, and He is infinite. This is the paradox of human nature: only God can fulfill our intellect and will, yet He is out of proportion to them. We can admire Him as the cause of the universe, but He is too far above us and our natural faculties for us to directly know Him or be in loving communion with Him. Trying to reach Him would be like jumping to the moon: we are propelled in the right direction but are unable to arrive at the goal.

It might seem, therefore, that we would have to resign ourselves to a life of limited happiness. We would have to consider our reaching the Sanctuary of Silence as only a sad, impossible wish. In fact, however, God has graciously elevated our quest for truth and happiness so that we may attain Himself, absolute truth and goodness.

---

4 No. 2557. All quotations from the *Catechism* will be from the second edition, 1997.

Communion with God in Christ

Divine Revelation informs us that our first parents, Adam and Eve, were gratuitously lifted up into friendship with God. He proportioned them to Himself—their jump to the moon was carried all the way to the target. Human history thus began in personal communion with God. This divine friend even gave Adam and Eve a special gift, what is known as Original Justice, which is the full submission of the inferior parts of the soul to the superior part. Their sensible faculties were in complete harmony with the spiritual. In terms of this study, Adam and Eve were in contact with God's silence and also possessed an interior, lower silence, so that they could be attentive to God's.

There was, however, noise already present in creation. In the midst of the beautiful music of the angels, Satan had inserted discordant notes. He wanted to make himself the end, instead of moving harmoniously with the rest of creation toward God. He desired to twist reality so that it no longer led others to God, no longer glorified Him. C. S. Lewis, in his *Screwtape Letters*, has Satan give as his fundamental project to "make the whole universe one big noise."[5]

Consequently, the devil told Adam and Eve that God is a liar and put before them the dream of becoming like God, of deciding for themselves what is good and what is evil. They listened to him and turned their desire toward the forbidden fruit. They sought happiness in a perverted way, by grasping for it rather than receiving it as a gift in trust and

---

[5] C. S. Lewis, *The Screwtape Letters* (New York: Macmillan, 1961), 103.

love. They did not want to receive from God truth, goodness, and beauty, but they wanted to create their own. They sought to be in charge, autonomous. Thus, our first parents broke off from their divine friend and, by the same token, lost God's special gift of Original Justice. Their minds, deliberately turned away from God, no longer held full dominion over the inferior parts of the soul, and the body was given over to its natural corruptibility. Noise, thus, broke out also on our planet.

Since, in its representative head, the human race had fallen, Adam and Eve passed on a humanity that is in rupture with God, a state we call Original Sin. Man, made for God, was now congenitally turned away from Him. We have become prodigal children in exile. The human nature we all receive is also deprived of Original Justice; its inferior powers are strongly and unreasonably attracted to limited and especially sensible goods. That is, man, having forfeited his contact with God's silence, consequently lost his interior silence.

God, however, did not abandon mankind. Eventually, He sent His Son Jesus Christ who, by His death and resurrection, reopened the path to the Father, building a bridge for all of us to take. Or rather, He is the bridge. Christ is the way, the truth, and the life. To follow Him on the path to the Father, we must be united to Him. Christ instituted the sacrament of Baptism as the means of our vital insertion in Him.

St. Paul taught that at Baptism, we die and rise in Christ: we die to the world of sin, and we rise to the life of a child of God. Like adopted children in a family, we are not naturally members of the Blessed Trinity but act and are treated as though we were. We have received, as a gift from God, the power to live as His children. The Spirit of sonship enables us to cry to God from the bottom of our hearts, "Abba, Father." Nevertheless, we are not yet in heaven, as we have all noticed. We do not have clear, jubilant, and permanent possession of our heritage. We have a pilgrimage to make.

We Christians are, through and in Christ, on the road to the Sanctuary of Silence. But Baptism does not give us back Original Justice in the full sense. The divine life is grafted on our weak and disordered nature. We have especially an unruly sensibility that hinders our intellect and will. We are still sheep lost in the noisy valley of the shadow of death. We, too, tend to want to create our own happiness outside of God. There are noise and battles in us, because we are made for the absolute and yet stop at less, making idols out of creatures.

We, therefore, have some rough going in our pilgrimage. Christians participate in Christ's victory over sin. They belong by right to a world without sin, a kingdom of life and light, but they live in a corrupt world and bear in themselves a certain complicity with evil. There is noise around and in us. We must establish harmony and silence in us in order to connect with God's silence. By God's gift, we have turned back to Him. We are fundamentally rectified, but we must perfect that basic justice. God first takes hold of the high point of our soul, so to speak, but we need to collaborate with Him in converting our whole self to Him so that we think, will, and love in union with Him, until we enter into our ultimate life toward which Baptism launched us, into the full life in the Trinity as the full fruit of the Redemption.

This voyage consists in cultivating receptive silence and entering more and more into God's silence.

Supernatural equipment for the journey

The spiritual life, all the way to heaven and the Beatific Vision, is an unfolding of the powers given to us at Baptism. What establishes us as children of God is sanctifying grace, a quality inserted in the depths of our being that furnishes us with what we need to actively participate in the intimate life of the Trinity, to live as a child and friend of God.

In itself, grace is a participation in divine life, but in fact, in God's plan, in the present economy, it is a "Christic" grace, an extension to us of Christ's grace. It reproduces the filial character of His grace. Our union with God is accomplished in Christ, according to Christ. Our Christian life is a communion in Christ's personal life, in intimate and constant dependency on Him. Our Lord infuses His vital strength and light into us, touching our soul in its depth. "It is no longer I who live, but Christ who lives in me," wrote St. Paul (Gal 2:20). We are holy in the measure that we live of His life, of His filiation.

Grace, then, is the radical principle of our supernatural activity. Its potentialities flow out into the intellect and will in the theological virtues of faith, hope, and charity. These virtues are what immediately give us the capacity to behave as children of God. They produce supernatural acts that have God as their formal object: I believe Him and in Him, I hope for Him and by Him, and I love Him. They are ordered to Him as eyes are to light and ears to sound. We participate through them in God's own knowing and loving.

The essence of the spiritual life consists, therefore, in the exercise of the three theological virtues that alone bear directly on our end, God in Himself. We call moral virtues those that have for their object regulating our relations with created things. They serve the theological virtues. They help cultivate silence in the soul so that we can better believe, desire, and love God. For example, the virtue of temperance governs our sensible desires according to reason. It keeps us from being distracted and pulled in all directions toward lesser things so that we can, by the theological virtues, hear God's calls and taste His goodness and beauty. We are like candles. The wax is our body, and the wick our soul. They exist for the flame, which is the high point of our soul, in communion with God by grace and the theological virtues. All our faculties and all our activities should work together for the perfection of our faith, hope, and charity.

Grace also provides us with the gifts of the Holy Spirit, dispositions given at baptism that help achieve the exercise of the theological virtues. They liberate these virtues from the weight of our earthly ways. By the gifts, we act according to a more supernatural and filial modality, as St. Paul wrote: "Who is moved by the Holy Spirit, those are the sons of God" (Rom 8:14). They make us sensitive to the Holy Spirit's promptings and lights. From the point of view of the gifts, our spiritual life can be compared to a boat: We row under the regime of reason and will, but we have sails that can move us along by the wind of the gifts, under a more direct intervention of God. The Spirit blows when, where, and how He wills, but we need to have the sails of the gifts ready to receive His impulsion. The gifts, by their higher modality, more directly under divine influence, especially bring us into God's mystery and silence.

In conclusion, we are ordered to God's silence but are full of noise. Our pilgrimage aims to diminish that noise and fill the place with God's riches in order to ultimately enter into His silence. Knowing now what it is all about, having appreciated our strengths and weaknesses, we can begin walking, by God's grace, toward the Sanctuary of Silence. The first objective will be to cultivate a receptive, interior silence.

C | S
P | B

Part I

First Steps: Cultivating Receptive Silence

"Human beings are called to live in their inmost region and to have themselves as much in hand as possible from that centrepoint."

—St. Teresa Benedicta of the Cross[1]

In part i, we want to consider how to foster a calm and deep interior life for an attentive receptivity to God's word and action. We have to discipline ourselves so that we are not like a reed that blows in the wind or a computer that functions mechanically, but a responsible person who chooses the true and the good. We want to be silent interiorly so that we can hear the calls of truth, goodness, and beauty. The three major domains of effort for this are our exterior environment and senses, our interior faculties, and our speech.

I do not mean to say that the spiritual life begins with this discipline of interior silence. We have first to know and be attracted to Our Lord if we are going to take up spiritual combat. Then, we can exercise ourselves in interior silence, as well as in the other parts of this book, learning about the

1 St. Teresa Benedicta of the Cross (Edith Stein), *The Science of the Cross,* trans. Sr. Josephine Koeppel (Washington, DC: Carmelite Studies, 2002), 160.

Christian mystery and prayer. These efforts are simultaneous, but the first focus can be interior tranquility.

Chapter One

Exterior Silence

"The silence of nature is permanent; it is the air in which nature breathes. The motions of nature are the motions of silence; the pattern of the changing seasons is covered by silence. The silence of nature is the primary reality. . . . Things of nature are full of silence, they are reserves of silence."

—Max Picard[1]

The first context for the culture of silence is the exterior world. We are rational beings, but the spiritual in us is incarnate, deeply rooted in sensible reality. What is in the imagination issues from sense perception. So, discipline begins by regulating your eyes and ears. Furthermore, harmonious sounds and sights favor our psychological balance and recollection, whereas disordered, unpleasant, and unfitting ones agitate us and disturb our ability to focus.

Our Lord chose to be born in a quiet, little village near a beautiful inland sea with hills round about, in a peaceful home into which telephones, television, and internet did not invade. It was in the Galilean countryside that He

---

[1] Max Picard, *The World of Silence,* trans. Stanley Godwin (Wichita, Kansas: Eighth Day, 2002), 137.

experienced the lilies of the field under the Father's loving care, as well as the shepherd with his flock, an image of that care.

I was born and raised in the city. My family played sports rather than hunt or fish. Our backyard was my forest when I was little; later, the nearby creek became the Mississippi. I did, as a boy, have some contact with larger nature on a few vacations in the mountains and, in later years, camping out with friends. These momentary, special experiences and the memories of them have been very important for me, both for finding God and cultivating interior peace. One of my attractions to the monastery was to be nearer to nature and its harmonious silence.

In this chapter, I want to consider how the sensible harmony of the natural world fosters interior attention and intimates God's silence, then consider what we can do to promote a culture of sensible silence.

The pacifying silence of nature

As Max Picard told us in this chapter's epigraph, and as we all can still experience in the countryside or a secluded park, the overall atmosphere in nature is silence. He spoke of "the motions of silence." Spring blossoms suddenly unfurl and fruits grow, the clouds come in, the birds fly over, the snow falls, all in silence. There are, of course, plenty of sounds in nature, as dogs bark, bees buzz, the wind gusts, but silence is first; it is "the primary reality"—natural sounds seem to be part of it. The sounds themselves usually converge in a soothing concert, like an evening when the crickets chirp in chorus, the air breathes gently through the boughs of trees, and water gurgles in the nearby stream. This sweet harmony of sounds has a parallel in the sight of the layered landscape of green grass and blue sky, with brown tree trunks and all the colors of the flowers. There are, however, startling sounds, such as a violent storm, and ugly sights as when one animal mangles another. Nevertheless, these are momentary events that even bring out, by contrast, the underlying harmony.

The lovely, tranquil rhythms of sights and sounds favor interior calm and silence. When we live in this exterior order and beauty, we naturally and peacefully enter into their rhythms, and our minds quiet down. We are able to reflect more deeply. A poem from Yeats imparts the experience of the pacifying effect of nature's rich concord, if you read it slowly and receptively, and read it again:

> I will arise and go now, and go to Innisfree,
> And build a small cabin there, of clay and wattles
> made:
> Nine bean rows will I have there, a hive for the
> honey-bee;
> And live alone in the bee-loud glade.
> And I shall have some peace there, for peace comes
> dropping slow,
> Dropping from the veils of morning to where the
> cricket sings.
> There midnight is all a glimmer and noon a purple
> glow
> And evening full of the lynnet's wings.
> I will arise and go now, for always night and day

I hear lake water lapping with a low sound by the
  shore;
Whether I stand on the road or on the pavement
  grey,
I hear it in the deep heart's core.

The world's silence points to God's

The natural world, by its harmonious stillness, not only assists peace but also teaches us about what I have called objective silence. When we interact with nature, we learn about mystery, beauty, and the deep silence of things. Most of all, we are taught about God and His silence.

Picard spoke of things being "full of silence . . . reserves of silence." We can consider a flower, see its colors and shape, feel its texture, and inhale its fragrance. These exterior manifestations fit with one another, and by the very fact, point to something deeper, toward the flower's silent depths and the mystery of its being. The flower also is interdependent with the objects around it, with the tree, the stream, the soil, and the bees. That mutual fitting also points to a mystery, a common silence for these various things. We perceive a certain oneness of nature beyond them. The silent depth and order of things direct us to a Maker. There is a mystery beyond this universe, from which the universe came. There is an intelligence behind the order of this world.

This ascension in silences seems to be what Simone Weil had in mind when she wrote: "Silence is not the absence of sounds, but something infinitely more real than sounds and the centre of a harmony more perfect than anything which a combination of sounds can produce. Furthermore, there are degrees of silence. There is a silence in the beauty of the universe which is like a noise when compared with the silence of God's."[2]

Thus, being close to nature cultivates our interior silence and also leads to objective silence. The world expresses some of the fullness of God's silence; that is, the various creatures speak of His ineffable riches. As St. Paul wrote: "Ever since the creation of the world [God's] invisible nature, namely his eternal power and deity, has been clearly perceived in the things that have been made" (Rom 1:20). God charged the world with the task of relating Him, and He gave men the ability to read its message. The *Catechism* teaches that "each creature possesses its own particular goodness and perfection. . . . Each of the various creatures, willed in its own being, reflects in its own way a ray of God's infinite wisdom and goodness."[3]

We need the visible creation to know and love God since we do not perceive Him directly. We draw our ideas of God from our experience of things. We need to taste the goodness of things in order to have some sense of God's goodness, as John Senior explained: "A child can't honestly admire the Maker until he first honestly admires the things He made. It's an insult to ignore the artist's work while praising him on hearsay. 'Taste and see.' This thing is good; it couldn't make itself; therefore we know He who made it is good. . . . If you jump from rocks to God without a long, sensible,

---

[2] Quoted in *The Twelve Degrees of Silence*, by Sister Marie–Aimée de Jésus, ed. Lucinda Vardey, trans. François Reuter (Toronto: Novalis Publishing, 2012), 6.

[3] No. 339.

emotional, willful, thoughtful intercourse with them, your understanding and love of His goodness and greatness will be proportioned to the meager experience."[4] The world serves our meditation, passing from silence to Silence.

Contemporary challenges

Things of experience foster our recollection and help us look toward God's plenitude, but there are hindrances to our contact with these things. Many of us have lost sight of the world as pointing toward God. In fact, we no longer even have much experience of natural things. These are the two negative aspects of our modern relationship to creation: our mental attitude causes us to miss the meaning of God's handiwork, and our technology even cuts us off from that handiwork.

Our mental attitude toward creation

There is no need to spell out how progress in knowing and dominating the physical world is extremely useful. Science also has discovered many wonders that point to God. It detects ever more the intricacies of creation, notably in the so many systems and cycles that collaborate to make life possible on our planet. They say that the simplest living cell is as organized as New York City.

Nevertheless, although our modern physical and mathematical sciences are efficient and fascinating, they analyze only what they can measure. This has led modern man to focus on superficial aspects of reality. The prodigious success

---

4 *The Restoration of Innocence* (mss, 1994), 79.

of modern sciences has produced a general atmosphere of positivism that only accepts as sure what can be proven in a mathematical way or through experiment. This tendency has been seconded by a parallel utilitarian approach. Things of nature are regularly considered merely as objects to use for power and as a source of a sense satisfaction, to be greedily seized for maximum gratification at minimum cost.

The ascendency in our society of such views cultivates mental habits that cause us to lose the sense of the rich and silent mystery of things. The visible world has become mute for our intellect, as if it had nothing to say. Its manifestations seem to be empty noise which points nowhere. Wordsworth lamented the modern reductive gaze in his poem "The world is too much with us":

> Getting and spending we lay waste our powers:
> Little we see in nature that is ours;
> We've given our hearts away, a sordid boon! . . .
> The winds that will be howling at all hours,
> And are up-gathered now like sleeping flowers;
> For this, for everything, we are out of tune;
> It moves us not.

Cut off by technology

Even if someone has a healthy, respectful attitude in regard to natural reality and its mysterious, silent depths, it is with difficulty that he could find that reality anymore. Our experience is separated from God's creation. The sensible world is now largely mediated to us through technology. To know the weather, to find our way around town, to do most of our ordinary daily tasks, we attend only to electronic devices that tell us about reality. We know nature through our screens.

Or rather, even more often, technology does not mediate but instead puts up a wall between us and God's direct work. The sounds we hear, what we see, most things we touch, the scents are not only man-made but also disjoined from creation. We no longer see, feel, and smell fire; we experience only light bulbs. We do not hear the gentle breeze because of rumbling cars. We cannot perceive the stars due to the dominance of electric lights. We no longer live in a world of plants and animals but of cement and plastic, of computer screens and cell phones. I remarked earlier that the sounds of nature arise from silence. Today, however, silence in our experience is rather a momentary interruption of noise. Noise is omnipresent as the continual backdrop of our lives. It has broken into what used to be havens of silence, notably the home. Contact with the silence of natural things is rather a vacation from everyday life.

Why are these artificial sounds and sights not as fitting, not as beneficial for us? First of all, the continual screeching of machines and the buzzing of devices are not harmonious. What they emit is not only loud but also grates on our nerves. These sounds fulfill the dictionary definition of noise. Sights also have their noise. Our roads are plastered with aggressive billboards and flashy lights that clutch our attention.

Secondly, artificial instruments do not point as readily to God as does nature. Our cars, our airplanes, and our devices rely ultimately on the First Cause, but they direct the mind before all to man who invented them. When we wonder at the sight of an airplane flying above, it is rather to glorify man.

Furthermore, this unrelenting noise and these dazzling lights train us not to really listen or to look, incline us not to pay attention. Our senses are overwhelmed and overstimulated, as when our cars charge down the road, we cannot see anything in particular, there are just too many images going by too fast. Often, there is not much to see anyway, with bland, purely functional, machine-made things all around. We develop lazy eyes and ears.

Technology thus dulls our senses. It also takes away our ability to concentrate as we are tossed to and fro by the frenzy of modern life. We are pulled away from what we are doing as our phones chime in our pockets. We check text messages while we are in conversation or while we are reading. We become addicted to this stimulus. We develop an artificial need for these images and noise. Furthermore, there is so much good information, that we hardly have time for anything but a cursory run-through. We take in more than we can reflect on. There is no space, no leisure for calm, purposeful reflection. We end up living on the surface of reality and of ourselves, never building up an interior life.

The continual excitement and all these possibilities do not fulfill us and only make us restless. We easily pass from one stimulation to another in a feverish quest for sensations and news—that is, for noise. Our sensuality and curiosity overpower us. We are scattered, fragmented, according to impressions and impulsions in all directions.

What to do

In response to the challenges of a mental and technological separation from natural reality, in view of acquiring an interior silence opening toward God's silence, I would recommend four efforts: cultivating a contemplative gaze toward the underlying silence of reality, disciplining our use of technology—especially media devices—supervising our exterior senses, and fostering silence in our human environment.

Contemplative gaze

It is easy to realize that the modern "scientific" mentality is inadequate. We cannot reduce all knowledge to what we can measure or even to what reason can fully grasp and manipulate. We must foster a humble, wondering look on visible creation, one that is receptive to the silence in the depths of natural things. We have to rediscover the beauty and appeal of mysteries.[5]

For a contemplative listening to the underlying silence, we must learn another language than that of numbers and even of clear ideas. Robert Frost, in his poem "Choose something like a star," puts forward, on one hand, scientific information and, on the other, a more mysterious and patient and receptive type of learning, a listening. Speaking to a star, he first asks for its exact measures:

> Talk Fahrenheit, talk centigrade,
> Use language we can comprehend,
> Tell us what elements you blend.

[5] Permit me to send off to my book, *John Senior and the Restoration of Realism,* which deals very much with wonder, especially in chapters seven through nine.

Then he refers to a different gaze on the star, one that does not seek to explain but listens to the star's silence, waiting for it to speak in its own way. This listening is, in fact, a higher attention:

> It gives us strangely little aid,
> But does say something in the end.
> And steadfast as Keat's eremite,
> Not even stooping from its sphere,
> It asks a little of us here.
> It asks of us a certain height.

We need, therefore, to cultivate a reverence for God's creatures, not considering them firstly as problems or as objects to exploit, but rather attending in awe to their beauty, to the very mystery of their existence. We cannot force the silent depth in things. To respect and listen to it, we must not be in a hurry, not always seeking excitement. It is not a waste of time to watch the stars, giving them the opportunity to teach us, or to sit by a lake in the afternoon, soaking up its beauty and peace. Louis Lavelle wrote that to be attentive, we must attain "a state of trust and abandon that prepares us to receive. This state . . . is in regards to the universe humility, an expectation, and at the same time an appeal."[6] We are in correspondence with reality and so can "trust" with a "humility" and an "appeal" that recognizes we are to receive, that this knowledge is a gift.

We must let ourselves be astonished, as Joseph Pearce tells us, speaking of the poet Gerard Manley Hopkins:

---

[6] Louis Lavelle, *Conscience de Soi* (Paris, Grasset, 1933), 58. The translation is mine.

> Every time we see a tree, resplendent in countless shades of green and washed in sunlight, we see the presence of the goodness, truth and beauty of God. . . . Hopkins' greatest gift is the way that he shows us the grandeur of God in creation, teaching us how we are meant to see, with eyes wide open with wonder. . . . When Hopkins looked up, he did not just see stars, he saw the "moth-soft Milky Way" with its "belled fire" ringing forth God's glory, calling us to prayer and praise. . . . We are in the presence of a miracle, of which we are ourselves a miraculous part.[7]

My godfather and former professor Dennis Quinn presents the ancient Greeks as a model: "[Greek wonder] accompanies the most ordinary acts of life. Eating and drinking and dressing are all accomplished with effortless but intense attention . . . always fully alive and present to immediate experience. . . . How is it that these beings are able to sustain this keenness of experience? I ascribe it to a pervasive recognition that the world and human experience are at once strange and familiar, mysterious and intelligible."[8] Quinn is here commenting on the scene of Telemachus's last evening in his home before setting out in search of his father. About to leave, the young man feels a mystery in the little common activities and things of his home. He was so used to these things, but now that he may never see them again, they

---

[7] Joseph Pearce, *Literature, What Every Catholic Should Know* (San Francisco: Ignatius Press, 2019), 113–114.

[8] Dennis Quinn, *Iris in Exile: A Synoptic History of Wonder* (Lanham, MD: University Press of America, 2002), 60. Dr. Quinn condensed into this book years of meditation on wonder.

touch him, and he considers them more closely. They are old and yet, somehow, new.

Paintings can teach us to appreciate the hidden mystery of concrete things, of a tree by the waters, of a peasant's wooden clogs, of a family harvesting hay. But in view of cultivating a contemplative gaze on reality, with Dr. Quinn, I want to especially mention here wholesome, usually older, literature. Stories, poetry, and songs are needed to form the wondering gaze; they can train us to look beyond the superficial, quantitative order. All good literature drawn from experience outside of an industrial context conveys a sense of the common mystery of reality, of a silence behind all things and ourselves. Such writing touches and expands our souls, teaching us that there is something more than getting and spending. We learn to listen to the voices of silence.

For example, Willa Cather, in *My Antonia*, instructs our gaze by her description of the homely Nebraska prairie. She discloses a radiance of something higher than the sensible world. The scene is "strange and familiar." The "burning bush" is, of course, an allusion to God's presence, but more generally, it refers to the presence of a mystery overriding everything.

> We drifted along lazily, very happy, through the magical light of the late afternoon. All those fall afternoons were the same, but I never got used to them. As far as we could see, the miles of copper-red grass were drenched in sun light that was stronger and fiercer than at another time of the day. The blond cornfields were red gold, the haystacks turned rosy and threw

> long shadows. The whole prairie was like the bush that burned with fire and was not consumed. That hour always had the exultation of victory, of triumphant ending, like a hero's death—heroes who died young and gloriously. It was a sudden transfiguration, a lifting-up of day.[9]

Miss Cather speaks of a "transfiguration." Christ's transfiguration, in fact, revealed His true depths. Perhaps this view of the prairie likewise is a deeper, more real one. Each day is glorious in its way. Its end is a celebration. This ending reveals the hidden glory of all the day.

Among this good literature is, of course, the Bible. Its reading will educate us in looking on creation in God's light, as God's work. "O LORD, our Lord, how majestic is thy name in all the earth! . . . I look at thy heavens, the work of thy fingers, the moon and the stars which thou has established" (Ps 8:1, 3). "The heavens are telling the glory of God" (Ps 19:1). If I am gazing at the stars, I enjoy their beauty, but I need to remember Who made them, to be grateful for this gift, and dream how beautiful He must be. One can ponder how Jesus and Mary must have gazed on the stars together of an evening in Nazareth.

Disciplining our technology

Although our technology impairs our exterior silence, it does not escape Divine Providence. The contemporary world remains in God's hands. God has chosen this period for us

---

9 Willa Cather, *My Antonia,* (New York: Dover, 1994), 22.

to live in, with its advantages as well as its poorer aspects. Nothing is perfect here below; there is no return to Eden in this life.

Thus, one should not be tense about the noise around us. Interiorly fighting it and getting angry will only bother that much more our recollection. There is a certain relativity in our experience of material silence. A friend of mine's grandmother lived near a train station, and when she visited her son's family, she could not sleep because she was used to the clamor of trains! One prays well, they say, in the noise of the battlefield. I remember a high school "study hall" that was, instead, more a riotous game room, but I simply accepted the chaos and relaxed and was able to focus on my reading.

Nevertheless, as Our Lord's servants, in our little place, we need lucidly to offset technology's disadvantages as we are able. We should humbly, patiently, and gently strive to make conditions favorable for interior silence and contemplation, doing what we reasonably can in our context to cultivate quiet and beauty for ourselves and others.

First, our habitual environment itself should be appropriately natural because our experience of creation needs to be part of our everyday life, not just a visit to the zoo once a year. If we live in town, we can try to inhabit a peaceful, usually older, and rather rustic neighborhood, maybe visit old parks regularly. One could have a place to get away to in the country, for vacations or in visits to cousins and friends who live in a rural area. Youth can belong to scout troops and take some camping trips in the wilderness.

Secondly, we should lean toward selecting what cultivates nature rather than crushes it; for example, drinking from a ceramic cup rather than a plastic one, using physical books instead of a screen. Utensils, furniture, and other objects around us ought to be attractive and interesting, pointing beyond the utilitarian. It is beneficial to exercise some handiwork with natural material, perhaps gardening or woodworking. When buying new machines, we need to take into account sight and sound.

Thirdly, it is do-or-die to bridle our use of electronic devices so that they do not dominate us but instead serve our humanity, our deeper self. We need to realize that this media is largely fabricated to seduce us, to provoke our cravings. The internet is seeking our money by appealing to our lower instincts. It does not want our good, just our billfolds. Furthermore, online images are powerful, and one can blatantly stare as long as one desires. We become physically addicted to screens.

Media plays a significant part in forming our minds, so we must deliberately determine to what we open ourselves, just as we choose the friends to whom we give access to our minds. We should engage our gadgets only in the measure that they are indeed useful. Even when dealing with valuable and healthy content, we need to restrict usage. We must mortify our yearning to see and hear, to be totally informed, to be continually excited by this electronic world—otherwise, we will have no interior life with Our Lord. If we realize that God abides in silence, we will more easily choose to remain with that silence rather than click a button to fulfill a curiosity.

In view of this discipline in the use of media devices, it is necessary to set up some rules for ourselves and our families. It would be good, for example, to restrict to certain moments plugging into news. We could avoid getting on the computer in the evening, perhaps also in the early morning. We ought to give ourselves only a precisely defined length of time for shopping online—we do not need to exhaust every possibility in order to find the "perfect" item. One could probably have a simpler cell phone and avoid carrying it all the time. One should usually turn off its warning noises and notifications so that one is not constantly on edge for a call.

Custody of the senses

Governing the use of electronic instruments is only part of controlling data that enters us via our senses. We are to be generally moderate in the use of our hearing, touch, taste, smell, and especially sight. We must not let greedy eyes go in all directions, trying to drink in everything. Whatever may be our milieu, we need to guard the very entrances to the soul. One does not open the home to all comers. If we are careful about what we eat, what we let into our stomach, all the more should we filter what we let into our soul. St. Bernard tells us that it is no use sweeping up the inside if you leave the doors and windows open to dust coming in from the outside.

We do need to know how to look closely at something when it is useful and proper to do so, but if we look at most everything that comes in our path, we will not be able to think about important things, we will not be attentive to the silence of reality, to the presence of God in the depths of our soul. We need to know how and when to stop, even in the use of good things.

Silence in the home

If we cut out time chasing after superficial information, we will be able to find more leisure for quiet moments with the Lord as well as with our family and friends. We will be able to read and pray and have interesting conversations and healthy recreation with our loved ones. With less input from screens and devices, with some habit of silence, we begin noticing so much more of the wonder that is right in front of us, and we will be more attentive to those around us. And of course, we are able to remember God, to listen to Him and His will. We more easily recognize Him silently and lovingly at work.

It is much better to read aloud as a family in the evening or sing around the piano than watch television. A few years ago, an ice storm knocked out electricity in our area for about a week. Several of our neighbors told me what a refreshing time they had as a family gathered for an evening around the fire, talking, reading, and singing together. That is more in harmony with human nature, does not overload the senses or deaden the imagination, and it does not introduce unhealthy images and scenarios into the sanctuary of the home, into the sanctuary of minds.

Along these lines, we can remark how an orderly day fosters focus and calm. There should be quiet times. Mothers could perhaps set aside short periods each day for silence so that the children become habituated to it and acquire a taste for it. Once in a while, for an hour in the afternoon, all could be still, perhaps with everyone alone reading in different rooms. Also, one should regularly take family and friendly walks outside, where one can leisurely look and listen. We monks are taught to walk lightly, shut doors softly, and govern the tone of our voices. Even in a home with children, one can learn to be attentive to these little activities.

All this effort to discipline our exterior has interior silence as the immediate goal—that is, our interior faculties in peace and order, receptive to God's mystery, nourished by His silence.

Chapter Two

Custody of the Heart

"To keep our strength for the Lord is to keep our whole being in unity by interior silence; to collect all our powers, to occupy them in the one work of love, to have the 'single eye' which allows the light of God to enlighten us. . . . A soul which listens to itself, which is preoccupied with its sensibilities, which indulges in useless thoughts or desires, scatters its forces. It is not completely under God's sway."

—St. Elisabeth of the Trinity[1]

Interior silence consists in a certain mastery of our inner life. It allows us to focus on what we are doing but also on what we should be doing. To live deeply, we have to discipline ourselves. This silence is requisite, especially if we are to recognize and be responsive to spiritual realities and to God's presence. Disordered images and greedy quests of selfish desires make it very difficult to heed higher, demanding truths and goals, and to hear the soft voice of the Holy Spirit.

Living in attractive, congenial, and natural surroundings, while keeping a guard over exterior senses, does not suffice to establish a proper interior silence. Effort is also demanded

1 Quoted in M. M. Philipon, *The Spiritual Doctrine of Sister Elizabeth of the Trinity,* trans. a Benedictine of Stanbrook Abbey (Topeka, KS: Christ the King, nd), 41.

to order our inner world. Dom Paul Delatte wrote: "Some souls do not care for external noise . . . and yet they are never in a state of silence . . . there is a continuous hubbub of interior talk, in exact proportion to their unmortified passions. . . . Have we ever tried to review rapidly the infinite variety of objects and pictures which have just occupied the field of our interior vision? Memories, grudges, projects, regrets, vain quests, angry emotions, vexations, scruples—how many winds and waves buffet this world of our secret life!"[2]

In Jesus and Mary's souls, there was no noise, no disordered passions, no vanity, no wild imagination; their attention and wills were given totally over to love of the Father and His work. They were simple and harmonious. All their words and actions proceeded from their depths, where they were with the Father.

We will here examine our various interior faculties of knowledge and love in order to recognize what nurtures harmony and silence in each and in the whole. These faculties are mutually influential, for good and for bad. The study of one overlaps with elements of others, but we will consider successively what especially pertains to a particular faculty. First, however, it would be worthwhile to situate the relationship between God's role and ours in the effort for interior silence.

Asceticism and grace

In this quest for order and silence in our interior faculties, we are aiming at something like a restoration of Original

2 Paul Delatte, *Commentary on the Holy Rule,* 98–99.

Justice, in which the senses were subordinated to the mind and the mind to God. This quest can be called asceticism. Mortification, where we strive to overcome sin and root out sinful tendencies, is the more negative side of the endeavor. Asceticism's positive side lies in strengthening the will and pursuing virtue. The negative and the positive go together, however, like two sides of a coin. We basically become detached from disordered egotistical and sensual impulses in the measure that we are attached to spiritual values.

The goal of this asceticism and interior silence is, nevertheless, union with God through Christ, which can only be an effect of divine grace. Our supernatural life is, most of all, a deification where our activity is lifted up into a participation in God's. Consequently, asceticism, our effort to straighten out our deviated habits, is not the dominant factor, but only a condition for our supernatural life. Our main work is opening to God's action. Most important is putting ourselves directly in contact with God's grace by prayer and the sacraments. Second in importance is our effort to look toward Him, trust Him, and love Him. Third is asceticism and the discipline of our faculties.

Asceticism itself is a cooperation where God's action has the primacy. Grace anticipates, supports, and achieves our activity; it at once heals our action in its own order and lifts it up toward God our Father. Even in these ascetical efforts, we rather strive to show our goodwill to Our Lord. We give ourselves up to His action, putting all our energies in corresponding to His grace. St. Therese of the Child Jesus puts the elements in their proper practical place: "One must do all in one's power, give without counting, constantly renounce oneself, in a word prove one's love by all the works in one's power. But, in truth, since that is very little, it is urgent to put one's confidence in Him who alone sanctifies the works, and to confess oneself to be a useless servant."[3]

Spiritual faculties

Intellect

Sense faculties—sight, hearing, smell, touch, and taste—only receive the *appearances* and impressions of things. It is up to the intellect to judge *what is*. I see brown, hear a bark, smell an odor, and my intellect judges: "This is a puppy." The intellect thus provides the light for the other faculties and is charged with guiding them.

Since its object is truth, order and silence for the intellect consist in adherence to truth, in knowing what is. Seeking truth implies that the intellect does not remain on superficial levels but pursues where these levels lead, all the way to the foundations of what we experience. Things around us present only partial truths, for they do not completely explain themselves. Only the ultimate truth, the final explanation, gives total repose to the mind. Noise for the intelligence, then, will be whatever hinders, in one way or another, the pure and full assent to truth, ultimately whatever thwarts knowing God.

The intellect is not isolated in its quest for truth. The imagination is made to help the realism of our knowledge,

---

3 Quoted in *I Am a Daughter of the Church,* by Blessed Marie-Eugène of the Child Jesus, trans. Sr. Verda Clare (Allen, TX: Christian Classics, 1997), 409.

keeping it in contact with reality, but it can also captivate the intellect in shallow views, distract it from truth. The will and emotions also play major roles in our desire for truth, inclining us to truth as our good or, to the contrary, pushing us to avoid truths that, in some way or other, bother our egoism and sensuality. It is indeed usually because of the difficulty in practice that we turn away from truth. We prefer darkness sometimes so we can follow our preferences and carry on our own little mediocre life. When we shun looking at what really is, truth loses its hold on us. We are less able to know reality. The old, rather humorous prayer conveys this: "Lord, may I act according to what I believe, lest I begin to believe as I act." If we do not conduct ourselves according to what we know, we willingly let darkness in, as Our Lord told us: "Everyone who does evil hates the light." "Walk while you have the light lest the darkness overtake you" (Jn 3:20; 12:35). We must not let our wayward desires drive us from considering the truth.

The intellect itself also forms habits. It notably can tend to seek deep and whole truth or, to the contrary, pursue minor items at the cost of the big questions. One fills oneself with the noise of superficial and superfluous information. We have spoken of the curiosity developed by consuming media, as well as of modern man's proclivity to dwell on what he can measure and control, on what is useful, to the extent that he frequently loses all deep perspective, anything that touches on mystery. E. I. Watkin wrote: "The evils which afflict modern civilization, the ruin of culture, the desecration of beauty, blindness to metaphysical and religious truth, are largely due to lack, often to the willful refusal, of mental leisure. We do not, cannot or will not stop to think."[4]

I might mention four interwoven virtues especially important to counteract bad leanings of the intellect: the cult of truth, intellectual purity, intellectual humility, and detachment. All four include a goodwill, but they directly concern the intellect.

First, the *cult of truth* honors truth as an absolute. One recounts that a Russian under the Soviet regime was imprisoned but was promised freedom if he would simply tell one little lie. He refused and suffered the consequences. He did not believe in God, for he had heard so many stupidities about Him, but he nevertheless knew he did not have the right to lie. He realized that truth was somehow greater than himself.

Some words of Raissa Maritain also illustrate this recognition of the supremacy of truth. She and her future husband, the later famous philosopher Jacques Maritain, were young students in college at the beginning of the twentieth century. Both were agnostic at the time but yearned to find something to live for. They were, however, disappointed in their studies, in which the professors taught them that the basis of reality was merely a mechanical process, a blind evolution, that reality is, in fact, only noise, empty of significance. There remained, nevertheless, hidden under the ashes, a spark of hope in them, as Raissa explained forty years later:

---

[4] E. I. Watkin, *A Philosophy of Form* (London: Sheed and Ward, 1937), 160.

> From instinct we fought against a relativism that led nowhere, against a relationship to nothingness, for no absolute was admitted. Despite all that might have turned us from it, we persisted in *seeking the truth* . . . in continuing to bear within ourselves the hope of the possibility of a full adherence to a fullness of being. . . . The very word "truth" filled my heart with enthusiasm. The beauty of the word shone in my eyes like a spiritual sun dispelling all shadows—those of ignorance, of error, of deceit, even those of iniquity, which is an error of measure or a lie. . . . [This] truth so ardently sought for, so invincibly believed, was still for us only some sort of unknown God. We kept an altar for it in our hearts, we loved it ardently even though we did not know it; we acknowledged beforehand all its rights over us, over our lives.[5]

Second, *purity* belongs to an intellect that gives itself only to truth in what one has called "virginity of mind." We have to be resolved to look only for truth, to consider all things, including ourselves, with absolute sincerity, careful to avoid all compromises in our hearts with half-truths.

This purity concerns not only speculative but also practical truth, not only what is but also what we should do. We must seek truth in all domains—in public and private life, in our work, our prayer, and our relationships. We want to be true in the presence of others but also when alone behind closed doors. The first thing to do when faced with an event

---

5 Raissa Maritain, *We Were Friends Together*, trans. Julie Kernan (Garden City, NY: Image, 1961), 69–71.

is to see clearly. We need to search for the whole truth of the context, enlighten the situation by the truth we know, by God's light.

The third habit, *intellectual humility*, consists in a docile attention to the object. Pride does not want to listen to reality, to be a disciple of reality. To know truth, we must adapt to reality, not adapt reality to ourselves, as Adam and Eve desired to do, and as we do when we sin. We need to put ourselves at reality's feet and let it teach us. Reality is indeed rich and deep, full of nuances, paradoxes, and aspects. As we have seen, wonder is the proper attitude in regards to the mystery in things. We respect the mystery and know that we cannot force it but must be open to its teaching. It is often because we do not realize the value of reality that we do not think deeply and thoroughly. We do not consider it worth the effort, and so we tend to take hasty, superficial glances.

A fourth virtue is *detachment*. We have spoken of how we cannot follow everything that is going on, listen to all the hypotheses by political commentators, and at the same time pay attention to deep truths. We have to restrain our compulsive greed for information. To know great truths, we must be sober in this world of overwhelming possibilities of knowing trifles. As in all domains, we must know how to mortify the superficial and the temporal in view of the substantial and the lasting.

The will

Sensible affectivity is attracted to what *feels* good and runs from what feels bad. The will moves toward what the intellect judges *to be* good. In charge of the inclination to the good, the will has the role of commanding the other faculties. Who holds the will holds the man, they say. I have mentioned its influence on the intellect. The will decides to apply the intellect to this or that. Thus, a will delivered to the good helps render the intellect attentive to truth. Also, because love unites us to the object, it allows us to know the good in a more penetrating and sympathetic way, as if from the inside. In contrast, a diverted will darkens the intellect by leading it to judge as good what is not, in fact, good; it directs attention away from what is.

Silence for the will consists in adherence to its object: the good. What is the good? We could say that it is whatever makes us grow in human perfection. Man is not simply a more cunning animal, wily to catch his prey. The lion's good is the antelope. It loves the antelope in the sense that the ferocious beast desires to eat that handsome animal. We, too, might like to eat the antelope, but we also admire its gracious run and jump. We appreciate the antelope for itself, in itself. We see the stars with the dark mountains in the background, and we repose in this beautiful scene; I delight in what it is. I like my friend and truly want his good, I want him to be happy.

Since the intellect can know things themselves and can judge their real value, the will can adhere to things for themselves, for a value in itself, and not for what we might be able to get out of it. We can give ourselves to the service of the good.

There is an order, a hierarchy in the good. As Maritain told us in the epigraph of the introduction, man belongs to the realm of the absolute; our spiritual fatherland is in great values—truth, beauty, goodness, friendship, God. The more we love these values, the more our soul blossoms because it is ordered to them. We become more human, more ourselves. It is in obedience to our conscience, to the truth, to God, that the will finds itself.

Also, as they become ordered to these values, our faculties begin to collaborate. We develop a harmony between intellect and will, between light and love, and in a measure with our sensitivity. We find interior silence and unity. One can think of the silence of St. Maximilian Kolbe's will. He could have come up with many good reasons not to sacrifice himself at Auschwitz. Notably, he could have told himself how much good he could still do as a priest. He was instead simple and firm in the good and did not hesitate to offer his life.

If, to the contrary, we let our will be swayed by evil, we harden our hearts against the good. We are less sensitive to the appeal of the good. We no longer listen to reality. We close up in ourselves and find only emptiness. We become complicated and noisy as our will is divided between its fundamental orientation to the good and rival impulsive desires. Our conscience rises up against ourselves in the name of truth and goodness. We are torn by discords, by unharmonious movements.

Doing evil is like going down a funnel. When we conform to our egotism and senses, the space is large at first, it might seem exhilarating, but soon we are trapped in our despotic vice. Like drug addicts or alcoholics, we often know we are hurting ourselves, making ourselves and everyone around us unhappy, but we cannot stop. There is a deep, noisy conflict within us. Doing good is like ascending the funnel. Disciplining our superficial desires makes the beginning narrow but after a while, the way to the end opens up. We have to discipline our superficial, sensual spontaneity in order to liberate our deeper, spiritual one. By mastering ourselves, we can adhere to the true and the good and find interior silence, joy, and peace. Learning to give ourselves to the good is a conquest of interior and spiritual freedom. No one is freer than the one who gives himself for a cause or a real being worthy of the gift. What should we do to cultivate silence in the will? The will has bad dispositions. It is weak and wavering, has disordered self-love, egoism, envy. It is often swayed by wild emotions. We will consider later how to discipline our superficial, whimsical, sensual spontaneity. For now, let us underline that, since the will follows thought, we need to think about good things. As St. Paul wrote: "Whatever is true, whatever is honorable, whatever is just, whatever is pure, whatever is lovely, whatever is gracious, if there is any excellence, if there is anything worthy of praise, think about these things" (Phil 4:8). Our effort to silence the will consists largely in keeping our eyes and mind on the good and in letting vain, disordered, egotistical thoughts fade away into oblivion. If we persistently do this, as time goes on, our inclinations to bad images, emotions, and thoughts will weaken.

Sometimes, however, we need to directly fight bad temptations. For example, if I feel envy toward someone, I might remind myself that each has his gifts and his weaknesses and that human beings are complementary. I could consider how it is, in fact, good for me that this person is gifted, also that

I will be happier if I rejoice in his talent. I need to recognize that it is love that counts, and by my envy, I lower myself in love. I should also make an effort to be friendly to this person and do good for him. I pray for him.

In any case, looking at reality in the face, whatever my emotions are, I must will and accomplish the good. I may be solicited by emotions, but I must firmly discern the good and then will it. It is by strong acts of will that we build up the habit of truly seeking the good. We weaken the will when we give in to lower attractions.

The will is made to command our sensible faculties, but there is nevertheless work to be done to win them over. Even when we truly want to correspond to high ideals, the lower man may lean in egotistical and sensual directions and still go his own way. We have to disengage ourselves from inferior appeals.

Sensible interior faculties

Interior silence consists mainly in the control of the imagination, but that control depends on our sensible affectivity. In the preceding chapter, we considered how sensational images and capricious emotions agitate us and do not leave us with the calm needed to reflect in depth. Our interior world can be a wild jungle, as Dom Delatte's description at the beginning of this chapter vividly showed. We fill ourselves with noise. There is often an interior idle chatter going on. We daydream and pursue fanciful pleasures. We worry about the future or fruitlessly relish the memory of past times. We cultivate resentment and anger. Therefore, a steady, persevering work of purifying these sensible faculties lies before us.

Imagination and sensible memory

Our interior senses store and work with what we have received sensibly—that is, with images, by which I mean not just visual ones, but all sensible interior representations: sounds, smells, feelings, touch, and taste.

Images are the intellect's connection to concrete reality, and it is from them that it forms its ideas. Consequently, for good thought, we need healthy images. Also, since they are concrete like reality, images have a powerful influence on our affections, much more than abstractions do. As we all know through experience, the attractive or repulsive power of an image can override our clearest convictions, pulling our actions in its direction. Furthermore, once they are within us, images have a certain life of their own, rising up in our imagination and memory, and awakening other images and emotions, for good or bad. We live very much by our imagination.

The culture of silence in the imagination and the memory means rendering them useful, in harmony with our intellect and will—that is, with the true and the good. We need to discipline and enrich these faculties. We need to clear out the noisy weeds and plant the grass, trees, and flowers of healthy images, thereby replacing the jungle with a peaceful, orderly, handsome park.

Turning from bad thoughts to good ones takes place largely at this level. We need, through our experience, to put good images in our soul and avoid bad ones. We need to remember that whenever we give in to a bad image, it gets stronger. There can be a real tyranny of images that we have great difficulty calming down. As we all know through experience, the attractive or repulsive power of an image can override our clearest convictions, pulling our actions in its direction.

Positively, we need to put good images in our soul. As I said, we want to have a good sensible milieu—a comely countryside, harmonious grounds, gardens, buildings, and healthy art. Secondly, our memory and imagination should be full of Scripture scenes and its stories, as well as the deeds of saints. We should be permeated with experience of radiant, reverent liturgy. We also need wholesome and inspiring literature, poems, and songs. Because we are more passive with movies and other visual media, because they grab our sensibility more directly and strongly, we must be especially careful there about what we let in.

When I first entered the monastery, my interior life actually became noisier for a while. With less exterior input from images, old memories arose, and I tended to chat with myself to fill the void. Immersion in spiritual reading, a general wholesome human environment, and in beautiful liturgy allowed me to forget harmful distractions; I began to have a calm, sensible interior, full of the true, the good, and the beautiful, which I found all around me.

We need to consider our emotions from which the images often arise.

Sensible affection

By sensible affection or emotion, I mean an interior movement toward sensible good and away from sensible evil. Sensible affections have an enormous importance in our life. They pull on our will and intellect and also provoke images. Silence in this domain will be affections helping us both look toward and will the authentic good. Noise will be what hampers those actions.

Our emotions, so touched by sin, are the major immediate source of disorder and noise in us. They often constitute in us a sort of autonomous center of desires, one that is foreign to truth and the real good. Our emotions are easily anarchical, seeking pleasure for its own sake and fleeing what feels bad, whatever the circumstances.

Furthermore, these sensible affections often usurp command and render the spiritual faculties inefficient in their governing role. Strong passions, such as anger and lust, greed and ambition, can overwhelm the intellect and the will. The main cause of their power is the sensible level's immediate, concrete, and striking character, whereas the ethical good seems abstract and distant, not real enough to exert oneself for. The will easily capitulates before the effort needed to go beyond the sensible attraction. And so, we develop bad habits—that is, vices.

In *The Ascent of Mt. Carmel,* St. John of the Cross details the havoc caused in the soul by disordered sensible desires: They weary and torment us, make us their slaves; they darken our knowledge, weaken our will. They are like restless little children and hard to please, who do not really know what they are doing.[6] We all know from experience that if our sensible appetite is not bridled within the measures required by right reason, we do not lead a worthy human life. If we are immersed in our sensible appetites, we lose the taste for spiritual things, we cannot rise to the true, the good, and the beautiful.

Because of the power and instability of these appetites, the Stoics of olden days and Puritans of all times have advocated for the practical suppression of these passions. They think of passions as automatic mechanisms that cannot be integrated into the moral life, as mere impediments to the voluntary character of acts. Yet, Christ was a man of ardent feelings. He experienced joy with His friends, anger at the hypocrisy of the Pharisees, sadness at the death of Lazarus, compassion for souls, fear at Gethsemane. He was moved as He said goodbye to His disciples at the Last Supper before His departure.

These sensible affections are, in fact, a richness of our nature, given to us by God to be used in service of the good. As Benedict XVI wrote: "It is neither the spirit alone nor the body alone that loves; it is man, the person, a unified creature composed of body and soul who loves. Only when both dimensions are truly united does man attain his full stature. Only thus is love able to mature and attain its authentic grandeur."[7] We need emotions to give us zest in loving and pursuing the good, as well as in repulsing evil. Insensibility

---

6 See especially I, ch. 6 no. 6, and III, ch. 19.

7 Encyclical Letter *Deus Caritas Est*, no. 5.

is a defect: to be without emotions is crippling; the apathetic is not inclined to act.

We are then to bring our emotions into our effort for the good. What the *Catechism* describes concerning chastity can be applied to all culture of virtue in the sensible domain: "Chastity means the successful integration of sexuality within the person and thus the interior unity of the man in his bodily and spiritual being." "Chastity includes an apprenticeship in self-mastery, which is a training in human freedom. The alternative is clear: either man governs his passions and finds peace, or he lets himself be dominated by them and becomes unhappy. 'Man's dignity therefore requires him to act out of conscious and free choice, as moved and drawn in a personal way from within, and not by blind impulses.'"[8] The goal is to integrate these powers in our deliberate human activity.

I should mention, that with calm emotions, where one does not treat the sensible as an absolute, one, in fact, better savors the sensible. Striving to draw the infinite from the sensible only makes us feel our emptiness while enslaving us. It has been asked who would more enjoy a glass of beer: St. Francis of Assisi or the local wino. Certainly St. Francis, because he would recognize the limited goodness of brother beer for what it is, praising God for this gift; whereas the alcoholic anxiously tears himself apart as he tries to squeeze the infinite out of the poor creature.

---

[8] Nos. 2337 and 2339. The quotation in the interior was from *Gaudium et Spes,* no. 17.

How, then, are we to bring the emotions under the direction of reason?

We have to be aware that our emotions possess a certain autonomy. Intellect and will cannot command them as they do our arms or legs. We cannot, at will, become angry or afraid. Aristotle compared governing arms and legs to tyranny and governing our passions to working with a citizen who has his own rights and ways.[9]

Nevertheless, our sensible affection is, in fact, made to be regulated by reason's judgment of the good. The powers of the soul are disposed to work together in harmony and according to their hierarchy. To be fully human, to be what they should be, our emotions need to be subordinated to the intellect and will, in service of truth and goodness. With help, they begin to spontaneously move in that direction. Some moralists have compared the intellect and will's direction of emotions as holding back fierce dogs, which one lets loose at the right time to attack prey. I think training these faculties is more like working with a horse: You do not beat it almost to death so that it lifelessly trudges along; you make a friend of it so that it puts all its vigor into your service. The horse enjoys serving a good rider, feels that serving him is its proper place. We thus channel our sensitivity's energies toward the true, noble, and beautiful.

Our task, then, is to cultivate good habits in our emotions, co-naturalizing them to the real good, shaping them from the inside according to the direction of reason. We can develop in our emotions a repugnancy for moral evil

---

[9] See Aristotle, *Politics, 1254b.*

and an attraction to the real good. We can feel like being courageous, be disgusted with our cowardice. St. Teresa of Calcutta spontaneously saw Jesus in the poor man found on the street.

Since two main interior sensible movements impede the will from following the reasonable good, two fundamental virtues are particularly important for this ordered silence of sensible affections. The first likely obstacle is the excessive desire for sensible pleasure, which temperance puts in order to the spiritual. The second is the repulsion we feel when we encounter difficulties, and here, fortitude intervenes in order to overcome that aversion. Here are a few practical remarks on these two.

For *temperance,* we need to reflect sometimes on the fact that these sensible goods are not absolute, that they are limited, that if we become attached to them, they hinder our progress toward what alone will indeed fulfill us. We can use them in a way that helps lift our hearts to God. We strive to love God through His gifts. In just about everything we do, there is something enjoyable that we should use with thanksgiving, and there is also a call to some sacrifice by which we recognize that God is far more beautiful and good than this thing or activity.

Nevertheless, because we are fallen creatures tending to excess, we need to hold ourselves back in regard to sensible pleasure. We should stop before attaining full satisfaction in created, especially sensible, goods, for they are not God. We cultivate our freedom that way. My master of novices, Dom Antoine Forgeot, taught us that we should show our heavenly Father, by our acts, that we are free in the use of His gifts, that He can do anything He wants with us.

We see Our Lord's accomplished temperance. He is like someone who has tasted an exquisite wine, so ordinary wine would no longer move him. Jesus had His eyes and heart on the Father and was totally free with the lesser beauties of creation. He appreciated God's creatures but did not let them divert His attention from the love of the Father.

For temperance in eating, we should know about how much food we need and so not have to think much about it. We eat in order to live; we do not live in order to eat. In principle, if the food is good, so much the better, but we must lift our minds higher. One can eat a bit like an artist, taking some and appreciating the skill of the cook. On special days, the provisions should be a little better and fancier. A meal should be a time of conviviality and conversation. One could imagine Our Lord in Nazareth moderately and simply appreciating the good food His mother lovingly prepared. Nevertheless, we must pull back sometimes, do some fasting, mortify a special taste.

We cultivate chastity in order to love better. We are so weak in this domain of sensual desires that we have to turn away immediately from bad images. In modern times, we are bombarded by sensual images, and our imagination is rather corrupt. I would recommend, especially for youth, frequenting older literature, such as Charles Dickens or Jane Austen, which ushers us into a world of deep but chaste images, a more normal world of modesty and true affection, of "calm desires that asked but little room," as the poet said.[10]

Fortitude does not consist in experiencing no fear but rather in not allowing oneself to be forced by fear into doing evil or turning from the realization of good. Fear has its role for the good, as it renders more acute senses and attention, but it tends to paralyze and distract us. We have to be capable of accepting injury and self-sacrifice for the good. We need to keep our eyes fixed on the true and the good in the present situation and seek them whatever the difficulties. We also must persevere cheerfully and calmly in the good despite renewed obstacles.

During His public career, Jesus was deeply saddened by evil and reacted with anger, but in the desire to redress it. His anger did not disturb His reason, which continued to direct him. He retained perfect control over His speech and His thoughts. His anger conformed to the just order; it gave energy for the good. We see His fortitude especially in the Passion. At the Agony, He said yes to God in spite of His sensitivity being riled up. He was calm throughout the rest of the Passion. There was no trace of an egotistic complaint or any bitterness about unfairness.

We can encourage ourselves also with the examples of courageous saints, of heroic men and women. We notably have many in recent times who were faithful and grew spiritually in the midst of the horrors of Nazi and Communist concentration camps. There exist copious eyewitness and personal accounts.

---

[10] Oliver Goldsmith, "The Deserted Village."

All this order and silence in our faculties cannot come about unless we are attracted to a higher good. The intellect and will do not turn aside from lesser appeals except by the call of higher ones. Mother Abbess Cécile Bruyère describes this union of our powers around our final end. She does not, of course, deny intermediary ends, and love of creatures for God: "[The simple soul has] no discord arising from contradictory elements or rival claims, and thus she regains the primary unity of her being. . . . The simple soul has but one look, one love, one intention, one pretension, one end. One look, she sees but God; one love, she loves but God; one intention, she tends but to God; one pretension, to please God; one end, to possess God . . . in the present moment she sees but the unity of God's good pleasure."[11]

We need, then, to look at Our Lord's beauty and learn to live under His gaze, but first, it would be good to consider another aspect of the culture of our interior silence: the word. How does that fit in? This reflection will also lead us to our meditations of the next part.

---

[11] Cécile Bruyère, *Spiritual Life and Prayer,* trans. Benedictines of Stanbrook (Eugene, OR: Wipf and Stock, 2002), 363.

Chapter Three

Silence of the Lips

"Accept what comes from silence. Make the best you can of it. Of the little words that come out of the silence . . . make a poem that does not disturb the silence from which it came."

—Wendell Berry[1]

The word is a marvelous gift from God and should be used with reverence. Speech is a talent entrusted to us, for which we are responsible, and any bad use of it is a sort of profanation. Our Lord takes our words very seriously: "For out of the abundance of the heart the mouth speaks. . . . I tell you, on the day of judgment men will render account for every careless word they utter, for by your words you will be justified and by your words you will be condemned" (Mt 12:34, 36–37). We are justified or condemned by all our actions, but there must be something special about words in this regard. Jesus seems to explain His warning by the fact that we speak "out of the abundance of the heart"; that is, our words manifest our heart, we put ourselves in our words. We kill ourselves and others by activating bad dispositions through our words, but we open to life when we fulfill our

1 *New Collected Poems* (Berkeley: Counterpoint Press, 2012), 354.

deep, God-given tendencies in them. Our heart forms our words, but our words also form our heart.

Words would seem, rather, to contradict the culture of interior silence because when we talk, we are no longer attentive to receiving. We cannot talk and listen at once. We all have experienced how chattering can be a door to dissipation, to forgetting God and His will.

Yet our words, as everything else, should serve somehow to help us advance in God's silence. A conversation is able to be uplifting and lead to recollection around some beautiful idea. The question here is how to speak without losing our attention to high values and even grow in that attention. To respond to that question, it would be beneficial to reflect first on the relationship between word and silence. That reflection will also provide a foundation for much of the book that follows. After these philosophical considerations, we will be able to take up some practical advice about speaking and listening in communion with God's silent presence.

Philosophy of the word

Man, in his deepest mystery, is intimately linked to the word. He is the animal that speaks. It is amazing how children pick up the complex phenomenon of language as spontaneously as they learn to walk. Animals communicate only through very limited and automatic emotional reactions. A human being, on the contrary, has a deliberate, definite message to get across. The baby, as also the little puppy, cries when it is hungry or angry, but one day the child is able to precisely recognize and express what he wants. He intentionally reflects on the impressions received and forms a concept of reality and then transmits his idea through sounds: "I am hungry; I would like a sandwich."

Through language, we enter into a culture, into an already accomplished assimilation of reality. It is when he begins to speak and understand others' speech that a human being is launched into human life and flies far ahead of animals. All our culture and education, all our social life depend on language.

Man's capacity to speak is based on the fact that he is a spiritual being and so is present to himself, penetrates himself. He possesses a treasure in the memory of what he has experienced, of what he has felt and imagined, what he has read or heard, as well as of his own reflections. Because of his presence to self, he is able to grasp what is in him and express it first to himself in an idea or an interior word. He poses it before himself to consider it, draw out aspects, and link them to other objects. He can eventually communicate what he has discovered to others in an exterior word. Articulating his thought in a sensible word also helps the actualization of his silence. In expressing his thought, he takes possession of it.

This personal expression, furthermore, allows us to enter into relationships with other people. We are able to articulate to others our thoughts and also our affections. Louis Lavelle wrote: "The word is a miraculous path between two beings who until then were closed up in fear and distrust, and who all of a sudden discover one another. Language reveals each one to the other; words touch us because they give us the presence of the other."[2] We rejoice when we together recognize a truth, aspire to a good, admire the beautiful.

Man, nevertheless, develops ideas and words only laboriously. He slowly and gradually draws forth what he has received and can never completely expound the content of his memory. He cannot bring out all of the treasures into ideas and words. This limitation comes partly from the fact that man is not pure spirit but an incarnate being and so is not perfectly present to himself. The angel, a pure spirit, on the contrary, immediately perceives and expresses an adequate idea of himself. He can draw out all the possible objects in him.

It is not only the fact that the aspects of reality are indefinite that renders man incapable of exhausting the riches of his memory. There is also something present in him that leads beyond himself. We know a plant; we recognize the laws of its operations, but there is a silence in its depths, the mystery of growth, of life, of being, of beauty. In all things, man finds a door opening to mystery, in which the object of his consideration only participates. To totally know the plant, we must go beyond it. We can learn about the mystery present to us, but we will never dominate it. It constitutes a domain of silence for us.

Even for the angel, there is a silence, a zone of mystery beyond his idea. The things he knows also point farther. The angel, too, only takes part in being, and thus, cannot express all being. His word is not absolute. God alone expresses

---

2 Louis Lavelle, *La Parole et l'Écriture* (Paris: l'Artisan du Livre, 1942), 98. My translation.

absolute being. His eternal Word is adequate to His silence. Max Picard evokes how God is perfect silence and absolute Word, as He is perfect repose and absolute act: "The silence of God is different from the silence of men. It is not opposed to the word: word and silence are one in God. Just as language constitutes the nature of man, so silence is the nature of God; but in that nature . . . everything is word and silence at the same time."[3] God's eternal Word is the perfect expression of the Father, and so also of all being and perfections. He is the perfect unfolding of God's silence. God is absolutely one in this perfect, eternal, lucid, joyful possession of Himself in His Word.

Angels and men are in the image of God, are in relation to His Word, and in their imperfect words, they endeavor to imitate this absolute Word. Our word is an incomplete, limited manifestation of the Word. God Himself said an imperfect word when He created the universe. We discover this limited word of God inscribed in things, and we learn, little by little, to articulate a finite echo of His Word. Our words can and should advance us in the path from our interior receptive silence to the Word, to God's full silence.

Teaching and learning

How, then, do we grow in the Word while speaking? We all teach and learn in turn when we speak. Both activities should look toward silence. Since our ideas and our words only pinpoint a part of the wealth in us, only isolated aspects, they

[3] Picard, *The World of Silence,* 228.

need to refer to the whole, with its silence and underlying mystery, in order to have their full meaning. There are three types of discourses according to their relation to the silent mystery behind our ideas and words—namely, science in the modern sense of the term, philosophy, and poetry.

If we are affirming something rather scientific, technical, or factual, we seek exact ideas. In mathematics and experimental sciences, mystery and silence may not be referred to explicitly. Mathematics, for example, works fine in itself, without the need to wonder at the mystery of numbers. But as human beings, we should also pose the more philosophical question. The philosopher, dealing directly with mysteries such as the human soul, love, and being, must know how to use words and ideas while referring to the unspeakable realities of which the ideas have a partial grasp. He uses precise analogies that he can delineate. He situates what he says as clearly as possible with the mystery beyond.

A more poetic type of language strives to weave silence into the very expression, to help the listener hear the unspeakable beneath the words. For example, philosophers define love as wanting the good of another. Literature, art, poetry, and songs use metaphors to bring you into the experience of love, to give you a feel for it. In the epigraph of this chapter, Wendell Berry instructed the poet not to cut his words off from the silence from which they come, not to chop up the mystery into rational bits. Plato's dialogues, typically, after expressing clearly what they could, turn to a story where symbols might indicate something beyond ideas, might stretch our gaze toward the mystery.

In both the philosophical and the poetic modes, the teacher needs to keep his attention on this silence so that his thoughts and words flow from reality. Secondly, he must know how to evoke the mystery for his listeners. One can tell the difference between the teacher repeating even very good formulas and the one who is meditating on a reality, striving to convey a sense of the silence.

For his part, the listener of philosophy or poetry should also look toward the deeper reality the other is speaking about—that is, to the silence behind the words. What Dom Augustin Guillerand wrote about reading concerns listening as well: "Books are worth more by what they do not say than by what they say. The reader is like someone who looks on the horizon: he seeks, beyond the lines that he sees, perspectives that he just barely guesses and which attract him precisely by their mystery of which he has some presentiment. The books we like are the ones that make us think. We look for the silence from which these words are born."[4] Teacher and learner should turn together in a gaze on the mystery as they converse. They both are listening.

Silence in our daily conversations

The need to govern our tongue

When we speak, we proffer what is in us, but we can focus on different areas, superficial or deep. We can use the word for various goals. We can try to lead people to Our Lord; we

4 Augustin Guillerand, *They Speak by Silences,* trans. by a Carmelite nun (Kalamazoo, MI: Cistercian Publications, 1996), 5.

can also strive to trick people, speak for our personal advantage. We can twist, consciously or not, what is in us.

We, therefore, must govern our tongue. St. James warns us how important but difficult this is:

> If someone does not stumble by words, that one is a perfect man, capable of bridling his whole body also. . . . The tongue is a little member and boasts of great things. How great the forest set ablaze by a small fire! And the tongue is a fire. The tongue is an unrighteous world among our members, staining our whole body. . . . Every kind of beast and bird . . . can be tamed . . . but no human being can tame the tongue, which is a restless evil, full of deadly poison. With it we bless the Lord and Father, and with it we curse men. (Jas 3:2, 5–9)

We must, of course, avoid evil with our tongue. We may not lie or detract. Such deviations are pure noise, turning ourselves from truth and goodness, from God. As I said, we, in conversing easily, forfeit our attention to deeper reality and values. We let slip our presence to our authentic self and forget our true end; we lose contact with God.

St. Benedict severely restrains monks' speaking to help them maintain a peaceful attention to God's presence and action. Dom Delatte commented: "The fundamental purpose of silence is to free the soul, give it strength and leisure to adhere to God. It sets us little by little in a serene region where we are able to speak to God and hear His voice."[5]

---

[5] Delatte, *Commentary on the Rule,* 99.

Not everyone is a monk, but we all need discipline in this domain.

There are two bases for governing our speech so that we can control our tongue and use our words for the Lord. First is recollection. Only then will we be able, in the midst of various impressions and desires, to think about truth and goodness, and also discern which words are fitting. Furthermore, if we taste the beauty of high values and, especially, the presence of God, we will appreciate silence and have no impulsive need to speak.

The other base, which is the ultimate reference for talking as for all action, lies in the double commandment of charity. We must seek, through our words, to love God above all things and our neighbor as ourselves for love of Him. We are to be quiet or speak in order to serve Our Lord. We use words to seek to advance toward Him and lead those around us, with ourselves, to Him. If we do thus exercise charity in our words, if we seek to do His will through our speech, we will be able to remain in contact with Our Lord and maintain an interior silence.

Three virtues of conversation

We teach when we speak, but we also support others and seek communion with them. We can here consider three virtues for a good conversation brought out by Aristotle, that, in fact, for us Christians, are aspects of charity. Conversation should be truthful, friendly, and playful.[6] These qualities will assist our silence.

---

6 See Aristotle's *Nicomachean Ethics*, IV, ch. 6.

Aristotle contrasts *truthfulness* with boasting on one hand and with false humility, disparagement of self, on the other. To be in conversation with others, we must be ourselves. Our interlocutor needs to be in contact with a real person. Part of this is to speak in accord with our thoughts. We need to guard against subtle, half-conscious duplicity. We do not have the right to use words merely to win an argument rather than to look for truth. Nor may we talk to show off, to fool people into thinking we are knowledgeable or whatever. That is noise.

Truthfulness would also mean that we are attentive to our words, to their meanings and how to use them to convey the truth we want to get across. What we call the *trivium* consists in the arts needed for that: logic studies how to think, grammar considers the organization of a language, and rhetoric is the art of helping the other see the truth.

Friendliness is essential to conversation. We want the good of our interlocutor. We want communion with him in the true, the good, and the beautiful. We want to rise with him to God, but we know that all good and true paths lead there in such a way that we do not have to always take on the preacher's mantle.

Aristotle opposes friendliness, on one hand, to the flatterer, to the fake friend who is, in fact, striving to get ahead in some way, and on the other hand, to the grouchy and contradicting type. Both the obsequious and the quarrelsome persons are, most of all, concerned with themselves. They are closed up in their own little worries and preoccupations, in interior noise. The friendly person, on the contrary, is silent enough to be sincerely attentive to the other person.

He has a receptive heart, is ready to listen. He is genial and affable, approachable, warmhearted, and supportive. Forgetting himself, he has a capacity to feel with the other, to share in the other's joy or pain. He is tactful and courteous in considering his interlocutor. St. John Henry Newman wrote: "[The gentleman's great concern is] to make every one at their ease and at home. He has his eyes on all his company; he is tender toward the bashful, gentle toward the distant, and merciful toward the absurd; he can recollect to whom he is speaking."[7]

We should not always be dragging those around us into our preferred subject but rather enter gladly into what pleases them. We will need patience in dealing with people, at times, putting up with a conversation that is not as agreeable to us. We must respect all men, remembering that they are made in the image of God, and be ready to learn from them. We have to know how to remain in the background when fitting, letting the other have his moment, as well as how to lead and animate the conversation when useful.

The third major disposition Aristotle mentions is *playfulness.* He contrasts the playful person with the stern, disapproving, intolerant type who does not show joy, who is burdensome to others, who hinders their enjoyment. St. Thomas tells us that "to sin by defect in game is to never joke, give a bad look to those who joke, and rebuke their moderate playfulness."[8] Aristotle and St. Thomas, however, also tell us to avoid the other extreme, that of the buffoon

---

7 Quoted in *Adventures in English Literature,* ed. Francis Connelly (New York: Harcourt, Brace and World, 1961), 463.

8 *Summa Theologiae*, II–II, q.168, a.4.

who aims at raising a laugh even if circumstances of place and time are not fitting, including through jokes that are discourteous or shameful.

It is easy to understand that one needs our words to be true as well as good to the other, and that this can be done without losing recollection. The note of playfulness might seem more difficult to integrate into a culture of silence. Yet, humor is very much a part of human conversation. Things, situations, and people are indeed often funny as they do not always measure up to what we think would be ideal, or their logic does not correspond to reality. Wit and drawing out paradoxes are thus sometimes ways of helping to see the truth. Humor can strike a facet of the truth in a way that a straightforward sentence could not. Playful conversation also relaxes people, keeps us attentive, and hits a hidden common note, stimulating sympathy between souls. Amiable and supple good humor is like salt, which brings out lighthearted spontaneity and individual riches.

"A sad saint is a sorry saint," said St. Francis de Sales. With the habit of God's presence, we can maintain a gaze on Our Lord and seek truth and good while being lighthearted with our neighbor. Saints were recollected but knew how to be agreeable. Some of them, such as Miguel Pro, Padre Pio, and Philip Neri, were pranksters. Charles de Foucauld, that austere hermit in the Sahara, said: "I laugh all the time with people. It lightens the atmosphere." Thomas More was a master of enlivening, fun-loving conversation. Before his execution, he several times encouraged loved ones by saying that they all would "make merry" together in heaven someday. Once, someone I knew asked a Missionary of Charity how the sisters could be so gay with all the suffering around them. The sister replied: "Life is tough enough for these people without us adding to it."

For a proper playfulness, permit me to quote one of my monastic brothers who died of cancer while still relatively young. Father François de Feydeau, of whom I will speak later, wrote in a letter about visitors at his deathbed: "I am happy to see my brothers joyful, and to help them be so, but I must learn to do that in such way that I do not harm their union with God but lead them to God without them noticing it."

We have now envisioned a first step in our pilgrimage, basically, that of quieting down our interior life and fostering receptivity and attention. I said that, to come together harmoniously, our faculties need something higher to which they can be ordered. Adherence to high values is, in any case, the goal of the mortification of the sensibility, of the ordering of our spiritual faculties, and of the custody of our lips. Ultimately, silence in all our being can only be accomplished by ordering all things to God, our end, the end of all things.

Next, then, with Our Lady, we need to fill that interior stillness by pondering God's mystery in our heart. That will be the object of the second phase of our journey. With a certain discipline over our lips, custody of our exterior senses, some control over machines and gadgets, with the passions and imagination calm and fairly well disposed, with a focused intelligence and will, we are ready to hone in on beautiful mysteries that lead toward God.

C | S
P | B

Part II

Finding the Path: Looking toward God

"Mary's example enables the Church better to appreciate the value of silence. Mary's silence is not only moderation in speech, but it is especially a wise capacity for remembering and embracing in a single gaze of faith the mystery of the Word made man and the events of his earthly life. It is this silence as acceptance of the Word, this ability to meditate on the mystery of Christ, that Mary passes on to us. In a noisy world filled with messages of all kinds, her witness enables us to appreciate a spiritually rich silence and fosters a contemplative spirit."

—St. John Paul II[1]

We are silent in order to listen to God and to be led by Him to His transcendent silence. To advance in the direction of the great mystery of God, we need to meditate first on more accessible mysteries. These various mysteries are like the radiance of His but tempered so that we can approach Him without being blinded. They teach us to gaze beyond or through limited beings toward He Who Is. We are able to obtain some grasp of these mysteries, but our knowledge

[1] General Audience, November 22, 1995.

nevertheless ends up rather in silence as we look past what we clearly know. After such meditations, our silence is richer, as we have improved our aim and obtained a better sense of what we do not see. Our pilgrimage begins to find the path to the Sanctuary of Silence.

We could meditate on particular mysteries, such as the Incarnation or the Annunciation, but I have chosen to work with three major divine attributes that are present in all the mysteries and are also rather direct approaches to God's silence.

First, we will direct our attention to God's transcendence, on how much He is of another order than creatures, and thus especially on His silence. Then, we will consider His beauty, which is an especially fascinating and attracting aspect of His transcendent mystery. Lastly, we will reflect on God's love, where God's transcendence stoops down in order to lift us up. All three of these attributes can be attained in a measure already in the natural order but in a superior way through revelation.

Let us go forward, trying to enter somewhat into the obscure pillar of fire that will lead us to our goal. Maybe we will already perceive from afar the Sanctuary of Silence glittering in the sunlight. Perhaps we will begin to feel its warmth.

Chapter Four

God's Transcendence

"One of the outstanding favors God grants briefly in this life is an understanding and experience of Himself so lucid and lofty as to make one know clearly that He cannot be completely understood or experienced. Those who understand God more, understand also more distinctly the infinitude which remains to be understood."

—St. John of the Cross[1]

The term "transcendent" indicates an order superior to that with which we usually deal. Something transcendent would not simply be of a higher degree, like a yellow more beautiful than others, but beyond degrees. For example, monkeys are more or less clever, you might say, but one passes into another order with man's intellect.

God does not fit into any creature category. Everything created is subject to limits and determinations, whereas God is infinite, has no determinations strictly speaking. He is unique and incomparable. "No one is good but God alone," Jesus said (Lk 18:19). We must use a different scale when thinking about God, or rather, there is no scale at all in His case. He is beyond any measure. We can merely designate

1 *The Spiritual Canticle,* stanza seven, no. 9.

the proper direction to look toward Him. Good things we know point toward His transcendent goodness, beauties toward His beauty.

It is easy enough to recognize the truth of these formulas, but in order to acquire a better sense of God's greatness, we will here especially meditate on some Old Testament passages. The people of Israel made an experience of God that we all are to relive. Israel was in the midst of peoples who worshiped personified natural forces—spring, winter, lightning, the stars, the sun—and used what often seem to us silly stories about gods imagined along the lines of superhumans. On the other hand, Greek philosophers were then groping intellectually toward some principle of this universe. Yet Israel received, as a gift, the experience and knowledge of a God closer to us than the mythical gods, yet further surpassing the world than anything the philosophers had conceived.

The Creator

Right away, in its first words, the Bible leaves behind anything religions or philosophy had come up with: "In the beginning God created heaven and earth." For Judaism, that was the fundamental dogma: Yahweh is the one God, the Creator of all things. With time, it became clearer to the Hebrews that God created everything, including spiritual beings, from nothing. In pagan myths, the world was fabricated out of preexisting stuff, sometimes from the parts of a gigantic monster that had been killed and cut up. Pagan philosophers themselves did not rise to the idea of a creation *ex nihilo.* The First Mover of Aristotle is part of the universe and simply sets all in motion by attracting what already exists.

All the rest of Scripture builds on the fact that God is the Creator. That is the first motive for worship being due to Him alone. The Creator carries it away without possible contest over all earthly and heavenly powers honored elsewhere as divinities. Isaiah intimates how God is incomparable:

> Behold, the nations are like a drop from a bucket, and are accounted as the dust on the scales . . . as less than nothing and emptiness. . . . [They] are like grasshoppers. . . . To whom then will you compare me, that I should be like him, says the Holy One. Lift up your eyes on high and see: who created these? He who brings out their host by number, calling them all by name; by the greatness of his might, and because he is strong in power, not one is missing. . . . The LORD is the everlasting God, the creator of the ends of the earth. . . . Before me no god was formed, nor shall there be any after me. (Is 40:15, 17, 22, 25s, 28; 43:10)

There are immediate consequences of the fact that God is the Creator. He is eternal, almighty, omnipresent, omniscient; He is Lord.

God is *eternal.* The Hebrews intuited that since God was already there when the world began, He is above things which begin and end. He transcends time. As the psalmist proclaims: "Before the mountains were brought forth, or ever you had formed the earth and the world, from everlasting to everlasting you are God" (Ps 90:2–4). Another psalm contrasts how the Creator remains while everything else passes. "Of old you laid the foundation of the earth, and the heavens are the work of your hands. They will perish, but you endure; they will all wear out like a garment. You change them like clothing and they pass away; but you are the same, and your years have no end" (Ps 102:25–27).

God is *almighty*. To create, He simply spoke, as the psalmist tells us: "By the word of the LORD the heavens were made" (Ps 33:6)—that is, all was created by an effortless act of His will, in absolute sovereignty. His action does not presuppose any condition. When we make something, we need material to work with—wood to build a house, stone to sculpt a statue, cloth to fabricate a garment. We only transform that material. God alone can directly cause existence, make something from nothing. He thus can do anything. He is of infinite, inconceivable force. Think of the power of the atom bomb, of the unimaginable energy the sun pours out daily and over centuries on the entire solar system, of the power of all the billions of billions of suns in the universe. Yet, all that is as nothing compared to God. He is the source of all that power. His power is of another order.

God is *omnipresent*. He transcends space. Whereas pagans localized their gods who were present only in a sanctuary or perhaps in the region of a tribe, the Hebrews proclaimed a God who is present to the extremities of the earth. The psalmist confesses to God: "Where shall I go from your presence? If I ascend to Heaven, you are there! If I make my bed in Sheol, you are there. If I take wings of the morning and dwell in the uttermost parts of the sea, even there your right hand shall lead me, and your right hand shall hold me" (Ps 139:7–9).

He is everywhere because He is the Creator. Paul will say: "In him, we live and move and have our being" (Acts 17:28). God does not merely launch things into existence; He supports them in their being and activity at each instant. When a man and a woman have a child, that child can eventually go on living without his father and mother. But if God stopped causing our existence, we would instantly disappear, like a ray of light in the atmosphere does when the sun goes down. The universe is thus penetrated in its most intimate fibers with God's presence, saving it continually from nothingness. And His presence is at the deepest point in everything, for existence is the first act, as is said in philosophy, the very foundation of all things. Whatever a thing might be, it first has to exist.

God is *omniscient*. He is not present as a mere force. He sees all things, as He told Jeremiah: "Can a man hide himself in secret places so that I cannot see him? says the LORD. Do I not fill heaven and earth?" (Jer 23:24). Jesus assured us that all our hairs are counted and spoke of the Father seeing us in secret, knowing our hearts. The epistle to the Hebrews taught: "Before him no creature is hidden, but all are open and laid bare to His eyes" (Heb 4:13). Psalm 139 wonderfully meditates on God's knowledge of all things:

> O LORD, you have searched me and known me! You know when I sit down and when I rise up; you discern my thought from afar. . . . Even before a word was on my tongue, O LORD, you know it all together. . . . If

> I say, "Let only darkness cover me and the light about me be my night," even the darkness is not dark to you. . . . Your eyes beheld my unformed substance; in your book were written, every one of them, the days that were formed for me, when as yet there was none of them. (vv. 1–2, 4, 11–12, 16)

God conceives the entire universe with all its indefinite laws, from all the intricate particles of the atom to the dozens and dozens of billions of galaxies, passing by the amazing complexities of living beings. Albert Einstein said that the laws of the universe reveal "an intelligence of such superiority that, compared with it, all the systematic thinking and acting of human beings is an utterly insignificant reflection."[2] Furthermore, the Creator does not know His creatures from the outside. He knows them like the artist knows his work, from the inside. Also, our attention concentrates on one place, one thing at a time, but God, so to speak, concentrates on everything everywhere at once.

And He is *Lord*. This is an aspect of God's omnipotence. Because He made it, the world belongs to Him, as the psalm tells us: "The earth is the LORD's and the fullness thereof, the world and those who dwell therein; for he has founded it upon the seas, and established it upon the rivers" (Ps 24:1–2). He governs His possessions; He is actively present in His creation. He interweaves all in harmony.

When Paul proclaims that God is "above all and through all and in all" (Eph 4:6), the "through all" means that He

---

[2] Quoted by Pope Benedict XVI in the General Audience of November 14, 2012.

acts through His creatures, that everything is under His sway. He is so powerful that He can give creatures to act, but since He provides the very foundations of reality, all their actions unfold in His hand. Divine and created causality are not opposed to each other because they are not on the same level; the causality of creatures operates in radical dependence on divine causality. This Lord is so transcendent, so powerful, that He can govern even human acts without violating our freedom, in a sort of enveloping causality.

Evil itself does not escape God's government. He does not cause evil but is vigorous enough to bring good from it. One can think of Joseph being sold into Egypt. His brothers really, freely sinned, yet God was the master. He, among other things, was preparing the family's escape to Egypt during the famine. Likewise, Judas freely committed a crime in betraying Our Lord; he freely chose to do evil; yet God used that crime as the opportunity for the greatest action of all time, Christ's offering of Himself. God achieves His purposes even through crooked lines, as they say.

We need now to meditate on a scene which bears a revelation even more fundamental, in a way, than that of God as Creator. God is Creator, eternal, almighty, omnipresent, and omniscient because He IS, absolutely.

He Who Is

Chapter three of Exodus presents Moses's calling, an important step toward God establishing the Covenant with the House of Israel. One day, Moses was shepherding his father-in-law's flock. He spotted a bush on fire, but the flame somehow did not consume the plant. He left his flock to investigate. As he approached, God spoke from the bush, telling him to take off his shoes because he was on holy ground. It was holy because God was present there, manifesting Himself.

The Hebrew word "holy" has the etymological meaning of separate. It marks that the Creator is of another order than what He makes. Psalm 99 evokes God's redoubtable majesty and then sums it up by the fact that He is holy: "The LORD reigns, let the peoples tremble. He sits enthroned upon the cherubim, let the earth quake! The LORD is great in Zion; he is exalted over all the peoples. Let them praise your great and awesome name! Holy is he!" (vv. 1–3).

Those to whom it is given to experience this holy presence realize that they are confronted with a power of a redoubtable, unspeakable intensity. Moses, in the scene we are considering, hid his face because he was afraid to look on God. We find such a reaction to God's presence often in the Old Testament. Isaiah saw the Lord seated on a throne, in the midst of smoke and light, like a king of terrifying majesty, of blinding purity, and overwhelming splendor. He perceived angels in adoration, veiled so as not to look at God and calling out "Holy, holy, holy." This encounter was almost too much for him. "Woe is me," he said, "for my eyes have seen the king, the LORD of hosts" (see Is 6:1–8). For Isaiah, "the Holy One of Israel" is God's special title.

After God spoke to him from the bush, Moses asked for His name. The common name for the deity, Elohim, was used for all gods; Moses sought the God of the burning bush's proper name, His personal name, His secret, as it were. Then came the mysterious response: "I am He Who Is."

This name includes a revelation, a teaching about God which Israel will understand more deeply as time goes on. First, it declares that the other spirits are not gods, as God said in the book of Deuteronomy, referring to the Name: "I, even I, am He, and there is no god beside me" (Dt 32:39).

The Name also expresses something about God's being. It explains God's holiness as well as why He is able to create. The Hebrews did not have to accomplish speculative metaphysics to realize that everything depends on the Creator. Only the Creator is wholly self-sufficient; everything else exists by Him. Of themselves, therefore, His creatures are not. His existence is of a different quality and intensity from that of His creatures. He has incomparable vitality. Any other existence fades away in His presence, like stars when the sun comes up.[3]

The Fathers of the Church, bringing in philosophy to understand creation and the divine Name, understood that God is absolute being. For example, St. Gregory of Nazianzus explained notably God's eternity and infinitude by the Name: "God always was and always is, and always will be; or rather, God always Is. For 'was' and 'will be' are divisions of our time and of changeable nature. But He is

---

[3] This name was recognized as so holy, so intimate to God, that by the third century BC, Jews no longer dared pronounce it, or even write it. One used Adonai, Lord, in its place. The Name was only pronounced on the great Day of Atonement, when it was whispered by the high priest in the Holy of Holies while priests outside were singing loudly so that no one could hear it. RSV uses LORD in capital letters to translate Yahweh, respecting this rule not to use the holy Name.

Eternal Being; and this is the Name He gives Himself when giving the Oracles to Moses in the Mount. For in Himself He sums up and contains all Being . . . like some great Sea of Being, limitless and unbounded, transcending all conception of time and nature."[4]

The Church holds this revelation of the Name to be central for knowing God in some philosophical depth. The *Catechism* writes: "The revelation of the ineffable name 'I am who am' contains then the truth that God alone IS. . . . God is the fullness of Being and of every perfection, without origin and without end. All creatures receive all that they are and have from Him; but he alone is his very being."[5] St. John Paul II presents "He Who Is" as God's fundamental name, the secret of His nature: "The Sacred Scriptures give different names of God. . . . But the name which Moses heard from the midst of the burning bush is as it were the root of all the others. *He Who Is* expresses the very essence of God."[6]

Theologians and spiritual writers have meditated on this Name. St. Thomas calls God *Esse purum,* the pure Act to Be, to express how He even transcends being—that is, things that exist. Things, beings, only participate in the act of being. Fr. Hyacinth Paissac tries to help us better realize what it means to possess all the riches of being at once: "God is infinitely more beautiful than the Greek temple, more accomplished than the best quartet, greater than a life terminated by the most heroic death, for He is the act that all these things and

---

[4] *In Nicene and Post Nicene Fathers* VII, ed. Philip Schaff, trans. Charles Brown (Grand Rapids, Michigan: Eerdmans nd), Oratio 45, no. 3.

[5] No. 213.

[6] General audience of July 13, 1985.

all these persons attempt to imitate from a distance. God is, to the point of surpassing all determination, all limit, all end. He is like an artist who would realize at once all his possibilities, like a saint who would live at one time all possible forms of heroism, like an act that would be all acts."[7]

All perfections are in God according to a surpassing mode, a mode above all modes, something like how all colors are in white light. We cannot conceive such perfection. The Siracide tells us that one cannot say enough good about God: "Where to find the strength to glorify him? because he is great, above all his works the redoubtable and sovereign great Lord, whose power is marvelous. May your praise exalt the Lord, according to your power, for he surpasses you. Who has seen him and can explain him? Who can glorify him as he deserves?" (Sir 43:28–31). This leads us to reflect on how this God, who transcends our being, also exceeds our knowledge.

God surpasses our clear knowledge

God is not a type of being, like a tree or a rock is. He is absolute being, without limits. He IS, simply and absolutely, infinite. Moses explained the interdiction to make any graven images of God in this way: "Since you saw no form on the day the LORD spoke to you at Horeb out of the midst of the fire, beware lest you act corruptly by making a graven image for yourself in the form of any figure" (Dt 4:15–16). He has no colors, no shape, no determinations,

---

[7] *Theological Library* II, ed. A. M. Henri, trans. Charles Miltner (Chicago: Fides, 1955), 67.

because having them would imply limits. With Him, we have nothing to grasp directly or clearly.

In our Exodus scene and at Mt. Sinai, God manifested Himself in a fire. Later, He made known His presence similarly through a bright cloud, sometimes also called a pillar of fire. These mark God's powerful presence while also veiling His dazzling majesty. Scripture speaks of God's glory coming in the cloud, this glory which is a refulgent manifestation of God's beauty and holiness. When Moses entered the thick cloud, he bathed in His radiant presence—so much so that when he came out, the people could not even look at him because God's glory was reflected on his face (see Ex 34:35).

One day, Moses asked God to show him His glory. God replied: "You cannot see my face; for man shall not see me and live." But "while my glory passes by . . . I will cover you with my hand until I have passed by; then I will take away my hand and you shall see my back; but my face shall not be seen" (Ex 33:18, 22–23). Moses had an experience of God but was denied a direct perception of His inner secret. Man can only support seeing God's "back," an afterglow of His glory, a trace of His presence. We cannot apprehend God because His burning existence is too bright and strong for our mortal eyes. God is not dark but too bright for our mind. God's unknowability derives not from a lack on His part, but from what is for us an excess of intelligibility. He is unbearable to our gaze because of the superabundance of His vitality. He is holy.

The Fathers again put in more abstract, philosophical terms this recognition that God surpasses our comprehension, that we cannot encompass Him by our thought. St.

Hilary wrote: "This is a true statement of the mystery of that unfathomable nature which is expressed by the name 'Father': God invisible, ineffable, infinite. Let us confess by our silence that words cannot describe Him; let sense admit that it is foiled in the attempt to apprehend, and reason in the effort to define."[8] All the adjectives he used are negative, simply denying God's visibility and limits as well as our ability to know and express Him. Our ideas are limited, and we grasp realities by their limits. The mind faints away in its quest because it does not find any hold.

God is like the vanishing point in a painting: All points to Him, all is organized around Him, He gives meaning to everything, but He is outside the painting. He is not seen. St. John of the Cross tells us that creatures speak of God rather like little babbling children who do not really know what they are talking about:

> [They] tell me a thousand graceful things of you;
> all wound me more
> and leave me dying
> of, ah, I-don't-know–what behind
> their stammering.[9]

They point in God's direction but cannot express Him adequately. Mark Van Doren begins a poem by praising stars:

> Praise Orion and the Great Bear
> Praise icy Sirius so burning blue

---

[8] St. Hilary, *De Trinitate*, trans. E. W. Watson and L. Pullan (Peabody, Massachusetts: Hendrickson, 2004), II, no. 6.

[9] St. John of the Cross, *The Spiritual Canticle*, stanza seven.

He continues calling us to praise other creatures, then concludes that all these simply witness to God. He is really the one to praise because He alone absolutely is, so much so that we cannot comprehend Him:

> Praise [the Father] because he is, because he has
> His being where no eye, no ear can follow,
> No mind say whence or whither,
> Yet he is, and nothing else is
> Save as witness to his wonder,
> Save as hungering to praise him—
> Let all things then, great or little,
> Praise him, praise him
> Without end.[10]

Scripture, the Fathers, tradition, and Church teaching nevertheless proclaim that we can know certain positive truths about God. We have considered His power, His presence, His omniscience, His eternity. To make such statements about God, we use qualities we find in creatures and apply them to Him because the first cause contains all created perfections.There is some relation between perfections as we encounter them in creatures and their infinite realization in God, which is to say, between effects and their cause, or between particular beings and Absolute Being. There is a certain analogy.

The analogy of creatures with God is, however, of a unique type. When we compare, for example, our visible

---

10 "Psalm 3," in Mark Van Doren, *That Shining Place* (New York: Hill and Wang, 1969), 73.

"seeing" with mental "seeing," we know both types directly, clearly, whereas when we compare a perfection as found in creatures with God, we do not apprehend how God accomplishes that perfection. Any analogy with God has one term which we know, while the other is enclosed in the clouds, so to speak. He is indeed powerful, good, true, wise, and loving, but eminently, infinitely beyond what we can conceive. God is far above our always limited ideas. We know something about goodness by our mother's goodness, but God is infinitely better. We know that He is good, but we are unable to think how good. The ecumenical Council of Lateran IV in 1215 insisted on God's transcendence even in positive knowledge about Him: "Between creature and creator one cannot designate a resemblance without there being a greater dissemblance."[11]

We have true knowledge about God, by which we aim at the divine perfection that escapes us in its supereminent mode beyond modes. All the valid ideas we accumulate about God nurture and orient our gaze toward Him. Each has its value, but none is adequate. As we go beyond one concept after another that is always insufficient, God's mystery tends to stand out, as when we cut down trees in a forest, more light enters, and we perceive better how many, many more trees there are.

Like St. John of the Cross in the text at the head of this chapter, Fr. Donald Haggerty describes how, in our growing knowledge of God's mystery, every idea about God enlightens us more on how much He transcends us: "Every truth

---

[11] *Denzinger-Hunermann*, 804.

about God, embraced after labored reflection or in a swift insight, is soon perceived to extend beyond what we have grasped in thought. A backlash of incomprehension follows every deeper insight we receive about God in prayer. . . . We discover for ourselves how quickly an infinite light overwhelms every lesser light. Every glimpse of his truth draws us into a more piercing awareness of how little we know."[12]

Our ideas on God are like arrows. They have a mission to signify God, but when they are used for Him, they sink into His bright cloud. We can think about the beauty of a horse, the goodness of our mother, but although God is beautiful and good, the determinations that give us a grasp of created perfections are not in God. Our ideas direct our thought toward God; they are more true about Him than we can conceive, but their particular light goes out in His presence, and the one true Light shines out a little more; we hear a little better the one Word. We speak, we think, in order to have nothing more to say. Our gaze is enriched as we go beyond what we know. St. John of the Cross sang:

> For I know well the spring that flows and runs,
> although it is night.
> That eternal spring is hidden,
> for I know well where it has its rise,
> although it is night.
> I do not know its origin, nor has it one,
> but I know that every origin has come from it,
> although it is night.

[12] Donald Haggerty, *Contemplative Provocations* (San Francisco: Ignatius, 2013), 37.

> I know that nothing else is so beautiful,
> and that the heavens and the earth drink there,
> although it is night.
> I know well that it is bottomless
> and no one is able to cross it,
> although it is night.
> Its clarity is never darkened,
> and I know that every light has come from it,
> although it is night.[13]

We have in this chapter mainly meditated on the Old Testament and considered how the mind rises to God from creation. The accomplishment of God's plan of salvation through the Incarnation turned the focus of the New Testament to God's love, but it is against the background of God's transcendence that the revelation of that love stands out in brilliant relief. All the authors of the New Testament were very conscious of God's majesty, even if they mainly emphasized the stupendous revelation of how this God, "who dwells in unapproachable light, whom no man has ever seen or can see" (1 Tm 6:16) loves men. It is because God is so great that His condescension and love are stunning, incomprehensible.

Furthermore, beyond all that natural knowledge can ascertain about God, beyond what the Old Testament has told us about Him, the New Testament reveals His interior life—that is, the three Divine Persons, the highest, ultimate mystery, which we could not have discovered on our own. God is more unfathomable than we could have dreamed.

---

13 "Song of the soul that rejoices in knowing God through faith," in St. John of the Cross, *Collected Works*, 59–60.

Our Lord said that "no one knows the Son except the Father, and no one knows the Father except the Son." They are in a mystery all their own, in a transcendent, hidden mutual knowledge and communion. But He added: "and anyone to whom the Son chooses to reveal him" (Mt 11:27). God has spoken to us of His most intimate mystery, which makes our interior silence even thicker. Max Picard evokes this: "The silence of God is transformed by love in the Word. The Word of God is a self-giving silence, giving itself to man. If a man like Paul 'has heard unspeakable words which is not permitted to man to utter,' then this unspeakable word falls like a heavy weight into the silence of man. It makes the silence deeper, and the word that comes from the depths in which that which is unspeakable lies, has a trace of the divinely Unspeakable in it."[14]

We continue on our meditative path to the Sanctuary by first considering how transcendent is God's beauty, then how transcendent and beautiful is His love.

[14] Picard, *The World of Silence,* 230.

Chapter Five

Beauty and God

"Late have I loved you, Beauty so old and so new, late have I loved you! Lo, you were within, but I outside, seeking there for you, and upon the shapely things you have made I rushed headlong, I misshapen."

—St. Augustine[1]

Beauty should help us progress in our pilgrimage to God and His Sacred Silence. St. John Paul II writes: "The Fathers of the Church have called the spiritual path *philokalia*, or the love of the divine beauty, which is the reflection of the divine goodness. Those who by the power of the Holy Spirit are led progressively into full configuration to Christ reflect in themselves a ray of the unapproachable light. During their earthly pilgrimage, they press on toward the inexhaustible source of light."[2] We do not yet see God's eternal and infinite beauty, but we can rise in its direction from the transient, partial beauties in this world, recognizing in them some echo of His. They lead us to a silent gaze of mind and heart toward His beauty, beyond all beauty.

---

1 *Confessions,* X, ch 27.

2 St. John Paul II, Apostolic Exhortation *Vita Consecrata*, no. 19.

The paradox of beauty

On one of those days in December when the sun renders the afternoon almost warm, but at dusk the cool sets in quickly, I saw a bald eagle high in a tree, facing the setting sun for the last half hour of the day. You would have thought that he was in awe before this splendid spectacle. In fact, he was merely soaking in the last warm rays. Only man enjoys a sunset for its beauty. He is distinguished by the fact that he makes tools, but even more in that he adorns them. He is a contemplative and takes pleasure in looking at comely things.

Fyodor Dostoevsky speaks forcefully on how necessary beauty is for a truly human life: "Without science, without bread, life is possible—only without beauty is it impossible, for there will be nothing left in the world. That's the secret at the bottom of everything, that's what history teaches!"[3] The Russian novelist has in mind Our Lord's injunction that we are not made for bread alone. We have a hunger deeper than the physical. To live humanly, we need beauty.

Yet, the experience of beauty is paradoxical and mysterious. Before becoming a Benedictine nun, Sister Elisabeth-Paule Labat, while out on a lake one day, heard some Mozart played on shore. Years later, she recalled this experience, still pondering why this music roused profound and contrasting emotions in her:

> What was the mystery this enchanting music conveyed? What secret message disclosed itself through a

[3] Fyodor Dostoevsky, *The Possessed*, trans. Constance Garnett (New York: Heritage Press, 1916), 417.

> few scattered notes cast into the air without leaving more trace than the flight of a bird? . . . Was it the echo of a lost paradise of happiness and innocence that reached me, the unspeakable language of something divine akin to my innermost being, permeating me with an obscure feeling at once of satisfaction and longing? How to account for a joy that, for being pure, was heartrending, for an emotion felt beyond the clear consciousness of self, which nonetheless seemed to reveal more of me than feelings woven on the warp of everyday experience?[4]

Music is often an especially intense experience, but any beauty can stir up such emotions. What is in this "secret message" that touches us so intimately, that gives us deep joy but also tears our soul apart? There is the question of beauty: What is it? But our experience also raises the question of man: Why does beauty provoke us so deeply? What is this correspondence with beauty "beyond the clear consciousness of self"? Why do we so long for beauty? Beauty seems to be a key to give access to man's own mystery.

Dostoevsky recognized another aspect of beauty: "The terrible thing is that beauty is not only frightening but a mystery as well. That's where God and the devil join battle and their battlefield is the heart of man."[5] We must follow

---

4 Elisabeth-Paule Labat, *The Song that I Am. On the Mystery of Music*, trans. Erik Varden (Collegeville, Minnesota: Liturgical Press, 2014), xiv.

5 Fyodor Dostoevsky, *The Brothers Karamazov*, trans. Andrew R. MacAndrew (New York: Bantam, 2003), 140.

beauty, but which? he asked. Beauty is powerful, and it can allure us in a bad direction. It can lead us up but also down.

The nature of beauty

What then is beauty? St. Thomas explained beauty as something that, when seen, pleases.[6] Thus, our pleasure in beauty as such lies in the fact of seeing it, not in some ulterior goal. I perceive a deer marvelously running and jumping. The beauty is in the experience of this object, not in some hope to shoot it and eventually eat it. I look at the stars, I admire their beauty, I rejoice in what they are. I do not plan to use them. Simone Weil wrote: "The beautiful is that which we cannot wish to change." "We want to eat all the other objects of desire. The beautiful is that which we desire without wishing to eat it. We desire that it should be."[7]

"Pleasure" is the subjective side of our experience of beauty, but what causes this pleasure? What would be more objective characteristics of beauty? Traditionally, one holds that the properties of beauty consist in integrity, proportion, and splendor. Something has *integrity* when it is complete, has all its parts, is not deprived of something it should normally have. For example, an orchestra should have strings, woodwinds, brass, and percussion. A church without an altar is not integral. *Proportion* or harmony is the fittingness of parts in their relations between themselves, to the whole, and also to the context. Thus, the violins should accomplish

---

6 *Summa Theologiae*, I, q.5, a.4, ad1.

7 Simone Weil, *Gravity and Grace,* trans. Emmas Crawford Mario von der Ruhr (New York: Routledge, 2002), 65 and 149.

their role without being too loud or out of rhythm. A face may have its integral parts but have eyes or ears that are too big. A private chapel should not be as grandiose as a cathedral. *Splendor* is both the most important and the most difficult to situate. An orchestral performance is splendid when a sort of center beams through the harmony of the whole. A handsome face shines with the human spirit manifesting itself in proportionate features and a happy countenance.

According to this perspective, the experience of beauty consists in intuiting that wholeness and proportion splendidly flow out from a fundamental unity. We enjoy music's accords and partial repetitions because we recognize a coherence in these riches, an idea, as it were, behind these relationships. We recognize in the visible harmony a gracious expression of a principle. Beauty is the radiance of perfection, like when we perceive a glorious stallion trotting across the field. The horse's beauty is the flowering of its nature. Manliness should shine through a man's physical appearance. A chapel should draw one to prayer.

The experience of beauty is not mere feeling. It is our intellect that detects this unity in diversity. Yet, man's awareness of beauty is not the ordinary way for the intellect to know, because beauty is perceived in the absence of any direct reference to ideas—Sr. Elisabeth-Paule referred to the "unspeakable language" of beauty. There is something immediate and experiential in the intellect's recognition of beauty. We can analyze how something is beautiful, identify its proportions and integrity, but awareness of beauty is in the experience itself, in the direct view of the concord of elements making up the whole. It is a glimpse in and through concrete reality of an interior secret. Consequently, the perception of beauty is not merely subjective or even less an evasion from reality. It is a complementary and, at least in some ways, a more profound perception of reality, as if dust had fallen off things. We glimpse a being's depths shining through its qualities.

We now are able to suggest some response to our question of why beauty touches us. The "pleasure" we have in the experience of beauty seems to come, at least partly, from the correspondence the soul feels with the object, from the intellect glimpsing something at its level shining through the sensible. It experiences an affinity with the order it perceives. There is a special delight in that both senses and intellect are involved in this appreciation, and the intellect is in contact not with abstractions but with reality.

The doctrine of the three properties of beauty—integrity, proportion, and splendor—was elaborated for sensible beauty, but we do recognize beauty analogously at other levels, where some unity shines through the multiple. There can be an intellectual aesthetic pleasure when, in physics or philosophy, we find a principle that brings many problems together into one simple solution and thus provides a harmonious view of diverse data. More important for our purposes is the distinction between the sensible and the moral or spiritual levels. One could witness an act that was rather clumsy physically but generous. It was a beautiful action, one fitting for a human soul, revealing depths of human goodness. We are attracted by the radiance of a pure, loving soul, devoid of egotism, even manifested through an old, wrinkled face. In moral beauty, a person is proportioned to what a human being should be. Adam and Eve were no longer beautiful when they willingly threw away their order to God. Someone who lacks moral sense is not integral; he is disproportioned. His deep humanity does not shine through.

We are obliged to keep physical beauty subordinated to moral beauty, which is the more properly human beauty. A fashion is thus indecent if it makes bodily attractiveness triumph over the moral and spiritual. More precisely, clothes should bring out the moral beauty and spiritual dignity of the person. We now can understand that beauty's ambiguity consists, to a certain extent, in the fact that there can be beauty that points to a superficial form to the detriment of deeper reality. Beauty can be a trick, as in an advertisement or a movie where a smile on a face entices ugly deeds. Since the Fall, truth, goodness, and beauty have become disjointed. It's not always true to say that beauty is truth. Beauty exerts a strong pull on us. We must be wary of its seduction.

Yet, beauty can and should lift us up. Plato said that beauty wounds you. You begin to grow wings and want to fly. Beauty wakes you up from the shadows of the cave and draws you to the good.[8] Beauty we experience is a penetration of the material by a spiritual reality and ought to lead us up to the spiritual, and so also to our deeper self, which is ordered to the spiritual. We feel called in that direction. We begin to feel there is another world, that there is a heaven. Michelangelo intimated that beauty comes from the heavens and draws us there:

> Mine eyes that are enamored of things fair
> And this my soul that for salvation cries

[8] For the growing of spiritual wings, see *Phaedrus*, 155d; for turning from shadows, *Republic*, 7.514ss.

May never heavenward rise
Unless the sight of beauty lifts them from there.
Down from the loftiest star
A splendor falls on earth,
And draws desire afar
To that which gave it birth.[9]

Edgar Allen Poe expresses this attraction as a call toward ideal beauty: "It is wonderful, this immortal instinct of the Beautiful, that makes us consider this earth and its spectacles as a glimpse of, as a correspondence to Heaven. . . . The soul glimpses the splendors situated behind the grave. And when an exquisite poem brings tears to the edges of our eyes, these tears are not the proof of an excess of enjoyment, they are rather the witness of . . . nature exiled to the imperfect."[10] This hint of a better world kindles in us a yearning and can account for the restlessness beauty can provoke in us. One has often remarked that deep beauty delights us but also makes us sad with some sort of nostalgia. Sr. Elisabeth said Mozart's music was a pure joy but also "heart-rending."

This rising through beauty must nevertheless go in the right direction. Some artists tend to make an idol out of beauty, doing what they call art for art's sake or beauty for beauty's sake. Yet, beauty is merely one aspect of being, not to be cut off from truth and goodness. Beauty is the deep idea of a thing shining out, it is the splendor of being and so is falsified, not fully itself, if the other aspects are not

---

9 *Le Rime,* quoted in *Creative Intuition in Art and Poetry* by Jacques Maritain (Princeton, NJ: Princeton University Press, 1953), 198.

10 Quoted in Maritain, *Creative Intuition in Art and Poetry*, 166.

recognized. It is the power of attraction of truth and goodness. If we follow beauty properly, it raises us toward absolute being, truth, and goodness, toward God.

God beckons to us through beauty

Natural order

Genesis tells us that after creating the world, God saw that "all was good." The term for "good" in Hebrew is very close to the word for beauty, and the ancient Greek version, called the Septuagint, translated it as "All was beautiful." Scripture praises God for the splendor of His work: "The glory of the stars is the beauty of heaven, a gleaming array in the heights of the Lord. . . . Look upon the rainbow, and praise him who made it, exceedingly beautiful in its brightness. . . . He scatters snow like birds flying down. . . . The eye marvels at the beauty of its whiteness, and the mind is amazed at its falling" (Sir 43:9, 11, 17–18).

There is, of course, the beauty of individual things—a calm blue lake, the elegance of the deer, the soaring bird that then swoops down to land gracefully on a little twig, the verdant trees. But realities also come together in harmony; their complementarities reveal hidden aspects, as music brings out riches of the individual notes not recognized in their isolation. Colors are more beautiful together. The human, moral world also has its beautiful complementarities, revealed in relationships, in the arousing of each individual's hidden riches by family life and friendships.

This handsome complementarity applies also to the rhythm of the day and seasons. The beautiful night, sparkling with the stars, gives place to the glorious morning, alive with riotous birdsong, which then mellows into the quieter, warm day; eventually, dusk gently glides in and softens all into the sweet tranquility of evening. The year has its pattern as well, when the silent whiteness of winter bursts into the song of youthful spring, and then turns to the ripe green summer, and later falls into the gold and red of autumn.

The order of the universe manifests that there must be an intelligence that caused it, but it is the beauty shining through this order that especially strikes us and attracts us. The beauty we experience shows that reality has depths, and we are drawn toward them. This eventually leads us to their Maker. Coleridge, astounded by the beauty in the sights and sounds of a valley just before sunrise, asks who made it:

> Who made you glorious as the Gates of Heaven
> Beneath the keen full moon? Who bade the sun
> Clothe you with rainbows? Who, with living flowers
> Of loveliest blue, spread garlands at your feet? . . .
> Sing ye meadow streams with gladsome voice!
> Ye pine groves, with your soft and soul-like sounds![11]

The beauty of the universe brings home that this intelligence behind the world is not a machine or a sort of computer, because this beauty is gracious, chosen. There is not simply the order as we might recognize in a forest where all the trees are in a row. The order is not merely functional. The beauty of nature is an unforeseeable, unnecessary elegance.

---

[11] "Hymn before sunrise in the Vale of Chamouni." The translation from the original French is mine.

A free person must be behind it. Dr. Watkins describes the following scene where Sherlock Holmes points out the gratuity of beauty:

> "What a lovely thing a rose is!" [said Sherlock] He walked past the couch to the open window and held up the drooping stalk of a moss-rose, looking down at the dainty blend of crimson and green. It was a new phase of his character to me, for I had never seen him show any keen interest in natural objects. "There is nothing in which deduction is so necessary as in religion," said he, leaning with his back against the shutters. "It can be built up as an exact science by the reasoner. Our highest assurance of the goodness of Providence seems to me to rest in flowers. All other things, our powers, our desires, our food, are all really necessary for our existence in the first instance. But this rose is extra. Its smell and its colour are an embellishment of life, not a condition of it. It is only good which gives extras, and so I say again that we have much to hope from the flowers."[12]

God could have made it so that bees came to plants without flowers and plants could multiply without both; birds could find their mates without their marvelous colors and cute little tunes. The flowers and the birds, the stars and the sunset certainly seem to be a gift from Someone who desires to please us, who is reaching out to us. Atheists have

[12] Quoted in Michael Augros, *Who Designed the Designer?* (San Francisco: Ignatius, 2015), 179.

expressed a melancholic sorrow in seeing a sunset or a starry sky while having no one to be grateful to for it.

The then Father Joseph Ratzinger, in a dialogue with a scientist who affirmed that the God of nature is only a geometer, replied: "The man who seeks a view of the whole will have to say: In the world we find present, without doubt, objective mathematics; but we also find equally present in the world unparalleled and unexplained wonders of beauty, or, to be more accurate, there are events which appear to the apprehending mind of man in the form of beauty, so that he is bound to say that the mathematician responsible for these events has displayed an unparalleled degree of creative imagination."[13]

Through beauty, God not only beckons to us, but He teaches us about Himself. The Creator must be even more beautiful than His creatures, the source than what flows out of it, as the book of Wisdom exclaims: "If through delight in the beauty of these things men assumed them to be gods, let them know how much better than these is their Lord, for the author of beauty created them" (Ws 13:3).

We can aim, then, toward God's beauty through the beauties He made. They point to Him. The *Catechism* tells us that "God created the world to show forth and communicate his glory. That his creatures should share in his truth, goodness, and beauty—this is the glory for which God created them." "The beauty of creation reflects the infinite beauty of the Creator."[14]

---

[13] Joseph Ratzinger, *Introduction to Christianity*, trans. J. R. Foster (San Francisco: Ignatius, 1990), 168.

[14] Nos. 319 and 341.

Created beauties help us look in the direction of the ineffable mystery of God's beauty. Yet, as we saw in the last chapter concerning perfections in general, God is not a specific, particular type of beauty, that of a tiger, or of a tree, or a diamond. He is beauty itself, absolute, pure, and infinite beauty. The Pseudo Dennis called God the "superessential beauty."[15] Any representation of beauty we might forge can only be a particular beauty. Beauty consists in a unity shining through multiple perfections. God is the transcendent beauty where all riches are present in the absolute One. When we glorify the Lord, we are attesting to the fact that His dazzling beauty is unique. He is not ten or a hundred times more beautiful than what we see. He is of another order.

Supernatural order

God makes Himself known even more in the beauty of the supernatural order. There He reveals a beauty close to His heart. We notably recognize marvelous integrity, proportion, and splendor in the plan of salvation, with the original creation being taken up onto a higher level, that of the re-creation. Man was placed in paradise, in God's friendship, but he fell. After millennia and many peripeteia, he was redeemed and restored to friendship with God. He is being

[15] *The Divine Names*, ch. 4, no. 7, I give here a literal translation. The Paulist Press edition (trans. Colm Luibheid) renders it "the beautiful beyond any individual being." Dennis says later in the paragraph that God is the "all beautiful, and the beautiful beyond all." Dennis is the pseudonym of an important but unknown author thought to have written at the end of the fifth century or the beginning of the sixth.

led back to paradise but a superior one, with the greatest possible union with God: "Then I saw a new heaven and a new earth. . . . And I saw the holy city, new Jerusalem . . . and I heard a loud voice from the throne saying, 'Behold the dwelling of God is with men. . . . Then he showed me the river of the water of life . . . [with] on either side of the river the tree of life" (Rv 21:1–3; 22:1–2). The parts fit together marvelously well. The story is a masterpiece.

The heart of that story, its key, is, of course, our Lord Jesus Christ. He is the Second Adam, in whom all is to be recapitulated, says St. Paul. He restores and lifts up creation; the new creation is reorganized around Him. We might mention especially the splendid integrity and proportion of the plan of salvation at work in the Passion. Christ wanted to fulfill all justice and order by compensating for our sins through His filial, loving obedience, by living as the Son in the midst of our miseries, carried for us, "in the likeness of sinful flesh" (Rom 8:3). Through the horrible physical ugliness of His suffering and death, Christ's interior beauty became the cause of supernatural beauty for souls, reconnecting them to the source of beauty. The hymn of the feast of the Exaltation of the Holy Cross speaks of the splendor of the cross shining out on all the world: "The royal banners forward go, The Cross shines forth in mystic glow . . . O Tree of beauty! Tree of light."

Christ is also beautiful in Himself. The principle shines out there as nowhere else. He is divine beauty incarnate, the perfect human expression of God's glory, as John declared: "We have seen His glory, the glory of the only begotten of the Father." In Christ, beauty, truth, and goodness are reunited. It is in prayer that we can best glimpse Christ's beauty, God's beauty in Him, but here we can evoke this beauty in a few points.

The very fact of a divine Person living out an authentic human life is ravishing. There is exquisite beauty in the scenes so often painted—the divine Babe in the cave at Bethlehem, the Boy helping Joseph in the shop at Nazareth, and interrogating the masters in the Temple. He was beautiful as He sat and taught the people, with His deep, simple preaching, where He spoke in such concrete, homely terms, in little stories of the great, secret mysteries of God and heaven as well as of man's deep desires and responsibilities. He transfigured and spiritualized Old Testament expressions, as well as the common elements of the life of Galilee, in such a way as to render them comprehensible for men of all ages. No one has spoken like that man, said the crowd.

His way of living was beautiful. We have mentioned how Our Lord practiced virtues in an eminent way, appreciating the value of creatures while being always completely free in their use. He walked firmly forward in His mission as witness to the Truth. He never sought His own satisfaction, His own comfort, or pleasure. He was exclusively and totally attentive to establishing the Kingdom. Nothing could make Him deviate from His mission, which was the glory of God and the bringing of souls to Him. He was very demanding and held sin in horror, yet He was gentle with souls when He recognized a spark of goodwill. Confronted by great obstacles, He was the perfect, faithful Son for the heavenly Father and the compassionate brother to us. His gift of self for us was beautiful.

Christ's beauty shines out through the rest of time. It especially and first of all beams in Our Lady. She exquisitely fits into the re-creation. She is even a founding piece. It is splendid how God thus began and achieved the story with both a man and a woman, these complementary modalities of the human species. Her beauty adds to Jesus, completes Jesus, for Jesus as man is limited. So next to the second Adam, we indeed need and find the second Eve, as the original couple is assumed into the new economy.

In the radiant events of Jesus's life, Mary has an essential role. There is no scene more gorgeous than when God proposed the Incarnation to the little maiden of Nazareth, and she responded for us all with such simplicity in the total gift of herself to her Son and to the work in view: "Behold the handmaid of the Lord." She is present again at the more hidden beauty of the cross, where she offered herself with her Son, the new Eve collaborating with the new Adam in redeeming mankind. At the cross, Christ established Mary as the "mother of the living" for the new creation, the mother of His brothers and sisters.

She, too, is beautiful in herself, a pure mirror of her Son's beauty. *Tota pulchra es*, the liturgy tells us. Mary is totally beautiful, without any stain, all the way to the very grounds of her immaculate soul. Even the greatest saints during their earthly life are like a bent rod, twisted back into shape, but which can never be as good as new. Mary is totally new and fresh, purer than light, younger than a child, in the words of Georges Bernanos. "Only the Virgin looks at us with the eyes of a child; hers is the only truly childlike gaze which has ever rested upon our misfortune and our shame . . . it's a look of tender compassion, of sorrowful surprise, of some inconceivable, indefinable feeling which makes her younger than the race to which she belongs, and although Mother . . . the youngest daughter of mankind."[16] Hers is the beauty of humility, of goodness, and of innocent simplicity.

Our Lady is the mediatrix of Christ's beauty. In Dante's *Divine Comedy,* St. Bernard describes how we need to look at her in order to be able to gaze on her Son: "Look now upon the face which is most likened unto Christ; for its brightness, and no other, hath power to fit thee to see Christ."[17] Mary transmits God's beauty in a way we can receive it. She is like the moon that sweetly reflects the sun's rays. Hopkins expresses how she transmits God's beauty:

> Mary Immaculate
> . . . who
> this one work has to do—
> let all God's glory through.
> Through her we may see him,
> made sweeter, not made dim;
> and her hands leave his light
> sifted to suit our sight.[18]

Christ's beauty shines through the Church, through the rich harmony of the Church's unity in diversity all over the globe. The Church's teaching—on God and His work of

---

16 Quoted in *Georges Bernanos,* Robert Speaight (New York: Collins 1974), 149.

17 *Paradiso,* trans. Carlyle-Wicksteed (Random House 1932), Canto 32, 85–87,

18 "The Blessed Virgin Compared to the Air We Breathe."

salvation but also on human life in the natural order, on economics, and social life, on the family especially—is the splendid light of the world. I could especially mention her so balanced doctrine on two poles of Christian life, each with its beauty: Christian marriage, as a unique friendship participating in Christ's love, this pair consecrated to work together to progress on the way to heaven with the children God gives them, and then consecrated life, this journey alone, all for Christ, this marriage with Christ. There is also the Church's exquisite liturgy and the art that has sprung up around the Church, the like of which the world has never seen.

Finally, there is the deep, uniquely beautiful goodness of saints, of their so different and vibrant personalities, from Augustine to Bernard and Francis, from Catherine to Joan and Teresa, and closer to us, John Bosco, Gemma Galgani, Teresa of Calcutta, John Paul II, and Gianna Mola. E. I. Watkin wrote concerning our exposure to God's beauty shining through saints: "The mystics contemplating God are bright with the reflected light of His countenance. It shines in their descriptions and burns in their ardours. And when we in turn contemplate this reflected glory . . . we contemplate God in His Saints and feel the awe and fascination of the Godhead which has taken possession of their souls."[19]

Behind the beauty of God's works lies the transcendent model of all beauty, both natural and supernatural, the eternal splendor of the Blessed Trinity, this surpassing

[19] Watkin, *A Philosophy of Form,* 415.

communion and friendship of the Three Persons rejoicing together in the dazzling splendor of the divinity.

We are called to come into this glorious communion. This entry will be the ultimate beauty of salvation history. The book of Revelations uses the most spectacular images of beauty to give us a feel for God's radiance in the magnificent ending of the story, in our complete fulfillment: "And I saw the holy city, new Jerusalem, coming down out of heaven from God, prepared as a bride adorned for her husband . . . having the glory of God, its radiance like a most rare jewel, like a jasper, clear as crystal. . . . The wall was made of jasper, while the city was pure gold, clear as glass. The foundations of the wall were adorned with every jewel . . . each of the gates made of a single pearl. . . . And the city has no need of sun or moon to shine upon it, for the glory of God is its light" (Rv 21:2, 11, 18–19, 21, 23).

The culture of beauty

God has promised us that, by His grace, and if we correspond to that grace, we will one day be immersed in the ocean of divine beauty that we will explore together for all eternity. Beauty is St. Augustine's special, cherished name for God. In the text at the head of this chapter, he says he compulsively ran after created beauties in such a way that he could not turn to God's beauty. He was following his senses' desires instead of corresponding to his deep spiritual inclinations. He eventually realized that he had been desiring created beauties as idols and that their beauty is only a participation in God's. He rose to the unique Beauty greater than all the beauties of this world, and he yearned with all his heart to see it: "Therefore, we are to see a certain vision, my brethren, 'which neither eye hath seen, nor ear hath heard, nor hath entered into the heart of man': a certain vision, a vision surpassing all earthly beautifulness, of gold, of silver, of groves and fields; the beautifulness of sea and air, the beautifulness of sun and moon, the beautifulness of the stars, the beautifulness of angels: surpassing all things: because from it are all things beautiful."[20]

To advance on the path of *philokalia*, of the love of beauty, is the task of our life. The psalmist sings: "One thing have I asked of the LORD, that will I seek after; that I may dwell in the house of the LORD all the days of my life, to behold the beauty of the LORD" (Ps 27:4). We need to learn how to use created beauties as stepping stones, following their upward movement to aim for His absolute Beauty. We need to taste created beauty in such a way that we aspire to taste His. All beauty should guide us toward a gaze on God's unspeakable glory, toward listening to His silence, full of His beauty.

For a few indications on how to cultivate a proper taste for created beauty, we can reflect on a line from John Ruskin. Something like Dostoyevsky, he states that admiration as a response to beauty is necessary for true human life. He explains that admiration consists in "the power of discerning and taking delight in what is beautiful in visible Form, and lovely in human Character, and necessarily striving to

---

[20] *Nicene and Post-Nicene Fathers* Vol. 7, trans. H Browne (2004), homily IV on the First Epistle of John, No. 5.

produce what is beautiful in form, and to become what is lovely in character."[21]

We need to *discern and delight* in beauty, both in form and in character. According to Plato, the fundamental education of youth essentially nurtures an appreciation for beauty.[22] For this attention, we must first cultivate interior silence and calm. Noise, especially under the modes of greed, lust, and haste, take away our wonder and our contemplative gaze. Secondly, we need to practice looking at things and souls for their beauty, discerning the spiritual shining through. We should look at Christ, read Scripture and lives of saints under the perspective of beauty. And then, we must let ourselves delight in that beauty, Ruskin tells us, rest in it a moment, let it resonate in our soul, taste it.

We need to *produce beauty,* Ruskin said. We must strive to do things in a lovely way. We should speak and write handsomely, make our bed properly. If we do fashion something—woodcraft, a garden, clothes—we want to make it attractive. A culture of beauty includes the way we dress, the way we hold ourselves, our manners, our courtesy, with a dignity befitting children of God.

This production of beauty includes putting beauty around us so that all may reflect God's beauty. We should have a general care that all be comely. Our habitat, our furniture, our utensils, our property should be clothed in beauty. A beautiful environment fosters our rising above the material

[21] Quoted in Quinn, *Iris in Exil,* 289.

[22] See, for example. *The Republic, 3.403c.*

in our mind and heart. It will liberate our daily lives from grayness; it will transfigure them.

And we are to *become lovely in character.* John Senior wrote for high school teachers that their boy pupils should be both physically and morally lovely: "A good student is good-looking. Grooming, dress, deportment, tone of voice—these must be taught. . . . Teachers . . . also make [the boys] . . . beautiful of soul, handsome, decent, manly and pleasant."[23]

Desiring to beautify all things, we indeed want, most of all, to help souls be lovely for God. We are morally handsome by our virtues—by our prudence, justice, fortitude, and temperance, but even more by our faith, hope, and charity, and by the gifts of the Holy Spirit, where we put on God's beauty. In a quotation at the beginning of this chapter, St. John Paul II spoke of us ascending the path to beauty by our conformity to Christ. We need to keep our eyes on His beauty and imitate Him. By God's grace, Christ's beauty will penetrate us little by little, as St. Paul wrote: "We all, with unveiled face, beholding the glory of the Lord, are being changed into his likeness from one degree of glory to another" (2 Cor 3:18). St. John of the Cross, in an ecstatic exclamation, prayed to enter into the communion of God's own beauty through Christ: "That I be so transformed in your beauty that we may be alike in beauty and behold ourselves in your beauty. . . . I shall see you in your beauty and you will see me in your beauty, and I shall see myself in

[23] Senior, *The Restoration of Innocence*, 14.

you in your beauty and you will see yourself in me in your beauty."[24]

The education of the wondering, delighting gaze for beauty is accomplished especially through art. Ruskin and Dostoyevsky said that we cannot live without beauty and admiration; one could almost say, without art. This role of art is worth looking into more closely.

Art, beauty, and God

What is art? In the ancient sense of the word, it is any human production as opposed to the simple workings of nature. We not only pick grapes to eat, but we also ferment wine. We fabricate tables from wood. We cultivate nature. Today, one speaks of the "fine arts" for works whose first purpose is not usefulness but significance and beauty. I want to speak about art in this sense.

As for significance, art is contrasted to more philosophical types of communication in that it cultivates our view of reality not by explanations nor by universal ideas but by conveying an experience. There is a difference between defining friendship and living it through a story. While reading *Ivanhoe*, we do not hear any definitions, but we experience and learn about chivalry. Philosophy produces an abstract universal; art presents concrete realities while underlining a message present in them.

In what concerns beauty, art's ability to draw us into an experience renders it apt for bringing out the spiritual

---

[24] St. John of the Cross, *The Spiritual Canticle,* stanza 36, no. 5.

shining through the material and thus for communicating an intuition of beauty. Art has the role of helping us perceive beauty, notably in ordinary, homely things and happenings.

Meaning and beauty take place at various levels. One can compare artistic works to the human face: the face has proportions, it expresses emotions and thoughts, and through its eyes, is a hint of an opening to the spiritual. Similarly, some art deals more with the superficial beauty of sounds, words, and images, some more with the human heart and its deeper beauty, some more with the meaning of life and the ultimate beauty.

In art, beauty should normally serve meaning, making truth and goodness more marked and attractive so that they shine out with new profundity and power. Art can speak with concrete beauty more effectively and movingly than philosophy can with its abstractions. It gives to experience these values, to recognize and love them.

Art does not, should not, artificially add beauty to truth and goodness. We said that the experience of beauty is a deeper perception of reality, that the apostles saw Christ on Mount Thabor with a glory that manifested His real self. Hopkins spoke of the "smudge and smell" covering things, but "lives the dearest freshness deep down things."[25] The role of art is to bring out the freshness—that is, the beauty of being, truth, and goodness—found in the midst of "smudge," among the shadows in human life, the miseries and ugliness in this world.

25 "God's Grandeur."

By unveiling beauty and meaning, by manifesting the mystery of being, art ushers beyond the material world. The most noble function of art is to intimate invisible beauty and reality by visible beauty and reality. In the old face of a peasant, we recognize a noble soul. Art and beauty then bring our sensibility into its proper role, as servant of the spirit. Ultimately, art should point toward the absolute beauty. This is indeed an uncovering of freshness, for the world refers beyond itself, and art can underline this reference by finding reflections of God's beauty in all the parts of creation—in the physical, the moral, and the spiritual, recognizing the universe, history, and human relationships as a network of signs of God.

The poem "Love" by George Herbert works through the analogy of a beautiful human friendship to communicate a sort of experiential knowledge of the beauty of Christ's delicate, attentive, merciful, tender love, and through Christ's of God's. I have already quoted the Jewish philosopher Simone Weil. While memorizing this poem merely as something humanly beautiful, she discovered Christ.

> Love bade me welcome. Yet my soul drew back
> Guilty of dust and sin.
> But quick-eyed Love, observing me grow slack
> From my first entrance in,
> Drew nearer to me, sweetly questioning
> if I lacked anything.
> "A guest," I answered, "worthy to be here."
> Love said, "You shall be he."
> "I, the unkind, ungrateful? Ah my dear

I cannot look upon thee."
Love took my hand and smiling did reply,
"Who made the eyes but I?"
"Truth, Lord, but I have marred them; let my shame
Go where it doth deserve."
"And know you not," says Love, "who bore the
  blame?"
"My dear, then I will serve."
"Now you must sit," says Love, "and taste my meat."
So I did sit and eat.

All art does not have to be directly religious in its subject, but it should be healthy, uplifting, and open to the supernatural. A painting of a harmonious countryside can evoke God's hidden presence. Instrumental music, by its sheer beauty, arouses the presentiment that there is more than the material order. The beautiful goodness in Charles Dickens's tales makes us realize that love and generosity really exist, that there must be a goodness behind this world.

Nevertheless, we need art with directly religious subjects. The *Catechism* presents the goal of art especially used for prayer: "Sacred art is true and beautiful when its form corresponds to its particular vocation: evoking and glorifying, in faith and adoration, the transcendent mystery of God—the surpassing invisible beauty of truth and love visible in Christ. . . . Genuine sacred art draws man to adoration, to prayer, and to the love of God."[26]

While one may prefer a particular medium or style for religious art, the various ones have their role. We must know

---

[26] No. 2502.

how to use them. Religious art can be of the icon sort, an instrument of prayer which does not try to reproduce the physical details, the better to orientate us right away to the spiritual. It can be more humanly developed but bathing in God's sweet light and quickly escorting us into the supernatural, as in paintings by Giotto and Fra Angelico, or Rembrandt and de la Tour, or in music by Palestrina, Bach, or Handel. Until the Renaissance, all art was imbued with God's presence, whether it was directly religious or not. Since then, even in art with religious themes, the attention is often on natural physical beauty. On the other hand, in the last couple of centuries, art, especially literature, often takes up natural stories and settings while seeking to translate the Christian mystery in human life. Works such as Sigrid Undset's *Kristin Lavransdatter* or Evelyn Waugh's *Brideshead Revisited* want to show the beauty of human life illuminated by the quest for God, by God's quest for man.

Art rises to the fullness of its role in sacred liturgy. The Spanish novelist Natalia Sanmartin Fenellora writes of the importance of liturgy making us realize that this world reflects God's beauty as the ultimate reality: "Liturgical prayer was the backbone of ancient spirituality and immersing oneself in this form of prayer means immersing oneself in beauty. . . . This prayer that draws from Scripture and fills our souls with beauty of the world as a reflection of God reminds us that this beauty really exists, that it is part of the world, even though before our eyes we see so many times how man and sin ruin this gift of beauty. Praying the liturgy puts the mind and heart in order and reminds us that beauty is eternal whereas evil is fleeting."[27]

In the liturgy, beauty and truth, sensibility and spirit are united as nowhere else. Different types of religious art—sacred images, music, poetry and literature, harmonious colors, and graceful gestures—collaborate through beauty to draw us into the mystery. The meaningful beauty all around us in the liturgy captures us, leading us to be enraptured by God's terrible splendor so that we realize the need to worship Him.

In the liturgical context, the entire sensible side already of itself has a pacifying, uplifting, and purifying power. It takes the soul away from profane cares and provides an atmosphere of recollection. Thus, a church building is normally already like a sacrament of peace and harmony for our heart. It should reflect divine splendor so that the work of recollection begins spontaneously when one enters. The harmony of the volumes, the play of light and darkness, the comely images and statues, the stained-glass windows, the silence, all that separates from the profane and disposes us to enter into God's presence and receive His message.

The art that is employed in the church and in the liturgy must be beautiful but with a certain simplicity, so that it does not take on an independent character. We might illustrate this with sacred music. We are not to listen to liturgical music for itself but as a support for our meditation and prayer. Sacred music should clothe the words with noble beauty so that they speak more to us, become more alive, and

---

[27] Letter of February 2023 to the author.

help our whole being enter into the reality of the mystery. The melody should both spring from the text and enlighten it. The rich, simple beauty of Gregorian chant and of similar, more ancient chants affects us sensibly and emotionally, but it is not sensual—it does not center on the sensibility or emotions. It nearly always remains serene and balanced, even when expressing jubilation or deep sorrow or anguish.

Nevertheless, although purely instrumental music naturally attracts attention to oneself, it can, in a service, create a climate favorable to prayer. Polyphony likewise tends to become autonomous, and the words are not as well served, but it can help our devotion, striking us more strongly. It can still bring out the depth of meaning of the sacred texts and make them more compelling and persuasive.

The beauty of the natural order of the world and of man's soul, both underlined by art, supernatural Revelation shining out with God's transcendent beauty in the Incarnation and Redemption, God's beauty in the Church and in His saints—all that leads us beyond what words and ideas can adequately express, into a beautiful night with our gaze toward God's Sanctuary, our heart listening to the silence.

We continue our pilgrimage, going forward with our meditations. However beautiful God might be by His omnipresence, His wisdom, and His almighty power, He is most beautiful in His love.

Chapter Six

God's Love

"We have come to believe in God's love. . . : In these words the Christian can express the fundamental decision of his or her life."

—Benedict XVI[1]

God's love is itself one of His transcendent attributes, which introduce us into the silent, luminous cloud. His love for us is part of His infinite mystery. Love springing forth from the first principle of the universe was inconceivable for the Greeks. How could the unmoved Mover care for us; how could He need us?

It is indeed astonishing that the almighty, eternal God loves us, these tiny creatures on this little speck of dust in the Milky Way. As the psalmist sings: "O LORD, our Lord, how majestic is your name in all the earth! . . . what is man that you are mindful of him, and the son of man that you care for him?" (Ps 8:1, 4).

In this chapter, we are above all going to meditate on Scripture in order to let the mystery of God's love sink into our soul, so we realize in our hearts its eminence and beauty.

---

1 *Deus Caritas Est,* no. 1.

Creation

We have reflected on how creation manifests God's transcendence and beauty. It also displays His love. Scripture declares that the very fact that He gives us to exist is because of His love: "For you love all things that exist, and you loathe none of the things which you have made, for you would not have made anything if you had hated it" (Ws 11:24). The act of creation consists in God bestowing some part of His riches.

Such a view on creation as coming from God's love is behind much of the praise in the Old Testament. The psalmist calls on our gratitude for God's love shown in creation: "O give thanks to the LORD, for he is good, for his mercy endures forever . . . to him who by understanding made the heavens, for his mercy endures forever . . . to him who spread out the earth upon the waters, for his mercy endures forever, to him who made the great lights, for his mercy endures forever, the sun to rule over the day, the moon and stars to rule over the night, for his mercy endures forever" (Ps 136:1, 5–9).

God's love for creation comes out all the more in that He had no need to create the world. The *Catechism* teaches with all tradition that "God has no other reason for creating than his love and goodness. . . . The First Vatican Council explains: 'This one, true God, of his own goodness . . . not for increasing his own beatitude nor for attaining his perfection but in order to manifest this perfection through the benefits which he bestows on creatures,'" created the world.[2]

[2] No. 293.

Only God's generosity renders Him interested in the little ants that we are.

Frank Sheed articulated well how God's love is manifested through creation:

> Why did God create the universe at all? Obviously because He knew that we should like it. It brings Him no gain, but it can bring us tremendous gain. And apparently it goes with the infinite goodness of God that our gain can be a motive for Him. . . . God could love things lesser than Himself and could act to give them pleasure. So He brought them into existence. He knew that there were possible beings capable of enjoying Him, and He made them. "The Lord has made all things for Himself" (Prv 16:4): apart from Himself there existed nothing to make them for. He made them for His own sake, for His pleasure. But it was His pleasure to bring into existence things which could take pleasure in existence. For our sakes He made us for His sake.[3]

God not only makes us and supports us at every moment. He provides us with beautiful and useful things around us, with companions and family. He watches over us and leads us to good things. Scripture professes constantly what we call Divine Providence. The psalmist celebrates how God attends to material things and animals; for example: "He covers the heavens with clouds, he prepares rain for the earth, he makes

---

3 Frank Sheed, *Theology and Sanity* (San Francisco: Ignatius, 1993), 128.

grass grow upon the hills. He gives to the beasts their food, and to the young ravens which cry" (Ps 147:8–9). God especially cares for human beings: "The LORD is my shepherd, I shall not want; he makes me lie down in green pastures; he leads me besides still waters. . . . He leads me in the paths of righteousness. Even though I walk through the valley of the shadow of death, I fear no evil for you are with me" (Ps 23:1–4).

If God loves creation and us, why is there evil and suffering? It is not overly difficult to understand evil and suffering's place in one's own life, that they are permitted to help us advance spiritually. They stimulate our generosity, our courage, and our compassion. But why so much evil, such intense suffering, and that even among the innocent? Why are some so disadvantaged from childhood on? Why do so many not even come to birth?

The *Catechism* presents three fundamental elements of response. There are opportunities for evil by the very nature of our material world and by men and angels' free will, which makes evil possible, and evil doesn't defeat God's love, since He can draw good from evil:

> God freely willed to create a world "in a state of journeying" towards its ultimate perfection. In God's plan this process of becoming involves the appearance of certain beings and the disappearance of others, the existence of the more perfect alongside the less perfect, both constructive and destructive forces of nature. . . . Angels and men, as intelligent and free creatures, have to journey toward their ultimate destinies by their free

> choice and preferential love. They can therefore go astray. . . . God is in no way, directly or indirectly, the cause of moral evil. He permits it, however, because he respects the freedom of his creatures and, mysteriously, knows how to derive good from it.[4]

Obscurity on the problem of evil remains, but it cannot wipe out the revelation and overwhelming experience of God's tender love, which supports our trust. Benedict XVI wrote: "Even in their bewilderment and failure to understand the world around them, Christians continue to believe in the 'goodness and loving kindness of God' (Ti 3:4). Immersed like everyone else in the dramatic complexity of historical events, they remain unshakably certain that God is our Father and loves us, even when his silence remains incomprehensible."[5]

We need to consider this revelation of love.

The former Covenant

I said that creation was a sharing in God's good. In fact, He shared His good all the way to calling us to enter into His intimate life. He has given us His very own good. God graciously lifted us up into communion with Himself, but we turned away from Him and fell into miseries and death. God's response to our sins was mercy. He not only persisted in offering His friendship but came after us and wooed us. This effort to win us back constitutes the history of salvation.

---

4 Nos. 311–312.

5 Benedict XVI, *Deus Caritas Est,* no. 38.

To accomplish our return to Himself, He first worked through the people of Israel. The doctrine of salvation in the Old Testament is founded on the two fundamental articles of Israel's faith. I mentioned the first article, that of the unique, transcendent, moral God, Creator of all things, the Lord of the universe and of history. The second is that He chose Israel as His people.

This choice began with the patriarchs—Abraham, Isaac, and Jacob—whom Scripture repeatedly tells us God loved. When it was time to establish the covenant with Israel, God reached out to Moses. We have noted how Moses's request for God's name was audacious, because it was like asking Him to disclose His first name, His intimate secret. God nevertheless complied. In so doing, He was beginning an alliance with Moses and the people. In the name "I am," there is, in fact, the expression of a helpful proximity: "I am" there for you—He is present to help Israel. He soon stipulated the clauses and established the Alliance at Sinai. As Yahweh told Israel: "If you will obey my voice, and keep my covenant, you shall be my own possession among all peoples" (Ex 19:5). The Law was given in order to begin teaching man how to walk toward God.

All of the Old Testament presupposes God's goodness. Yahweh continually invites the Israelites to an absolute trust in Him. He indeed took special care of His people. "For what great nation is there that has a God so near to it as the LORD our God is to us, whenever we call upon him?"(Dt 8:18). In the desert, He led them like a shepherd does his flock. Holy Scripture glorifies God's generosity in guiding the Hebrews. After several chapters praising God for His providence in regard to Israel, the book of Wisdom closes with: "For in everything, O Lord, you have exalted and glorified your people; and you have not neglected to help them at all times and in all places" (Ws 19:22). God not only watched over them. He abided in the midst of them. In the desert, He was present in the pillar of fire, then His glory settled among them in the Temple and later even followed them into exile.

God chose and established an alliance with Israel, gave the people the Law, dwelt in the Temple, and cared for Israel because He loved this people. Scripture insists on the absolute gratuity of this choice and love: "The LORD your God has chosen you to be a people of his own possession out of all the peoples that are on the face of the earth. It was not because you were more in number than any other people that the LORD set his love upon you and chose you, for you were the fewest of all peoples" (Dt 7:6–8).

This love continues when confronted with His people's revolt. The Old Testament strongly underlined God's mercy and gracious forgiveness, which showed itself time and time again. In Hosea, God exclaimed to Israel after its rebellion: "How can I give you up, O Ephraim! How can I hand you over, O Israel. . . . My heart recoils within me; my compassion grows warm and tender. I will not execute my fierce anger, I will not again destroy Ephraim. For I am God and not man, the Holy One in your midst" (Hos 11:8–9).

In all this, God was like a father to Israel, as Scripture indicated mainly by referring to Israel as His son. Moreover, He showed the tender love of a mother in regard to His people: "As one whom his mother comforts, so I will comfort you" (Is 66:13). In fact, His love is more sure even than a mother's: "Even [mothers] may forget, yet I will not forget you" (Is 49:15). He went further, expressing His love in the terms of the passionate love of a spouse, for example in Hosea where He said to Israel: "I will espouse you for ever; I will espouse you in righteousness and in justice, in steadfast love, and in mercy. I will espouse you in faithfulness; and you shall know the LORD" (Hos 2:19–20). The battle against idolatry can be taken in the perspective of this spousal type of love. God is "jealous"; His love for Israel tolerates no rival. The alliance with Israel is like a marriage bond that demands exclusive commitment.

Nevertheless, the Old Testament revelation of God's love is limited and incomplete. This love was scarcely expressed in regards of non-Israelites. There is little revealed in the Old Testament about God's plans for peoples other than Israel. Another limit was that God's love was nearly always manifested to the people of Israel as a group. Only for special individuals, such as Abraham, David, and Jeremiah, are affectionate relationships proclaimed.

The Old Testament is an initiation into the knowledge of God's love. It was "written down for our instruction" as St. Paul tells us (1 Cor 10:11). The New Testament bursts out of the limits of the Old Testament to plunge us into an even more incomprehensible love.

The New Covenant

The incarnation of love

The major event separating the two covenants is, of course, the Incarnation. Naturally, we know God only indirectly. From things that we know directly, we conclude certain truths about Him as their cause, as when we hear a symphony and then deduce certain traits about the composer. The Old Testament would be like the composer now writing a letter and sending messengers to tell us about himself and that he would like to make us happy, as God began, through the prophets, speaking to Israel about His love and showing it in many ways. The New Testament is like the composer coming among us and even inviting us into the intimacy of his family life, as God became man, fully revealed His love, and opened to us His inner life, the communion of the three Divine Persons.

God's love revealed in the Old Testament is now, as it were, incarnate in Jesus. The divine gift of self has become concrete reality in Our Lord. St. John spoke of God's grace—that is, His love—coming through Christ: "For the law was given through Moses; grace and truth came through Jesus Christ" (Jn 1:17). Benedict XVI wrote: "The real novelty of the New Testament lies not so much in new ideas as in the figure of Christ himself, who gives flesh and blood to those concepts—an unprecedent realism. . . . Divine activity now takes on dramatic form when, in Jesus Christ, it is God himself who goes in search of the 'stray sheep,' a suffering and lost humanity."[6] Jesus reveals the Father's love by His words

---

6 Benedict XVI, *Deus Caritas Est,* no. 12.

and deeds; He also reveals His own love, and all His work is consummated in the gift of the Holy Spirit.

The Father's love

Jesus revealed the secrets of God's heart. He shattered the limits of the Old Testament revelation. First, the Alliance and God's friendship are for all people. Jesus, in His public life, essentially confined His ministry to Israel, but He several times mentioned the extension of the kingdom to the Gentiles. This extension broke out after His resurrection, as we see in the book of Acts. Paul wrote that God "desires all men to be saved and come to the knowledge of the truth" (1 Tm 2:4).

Also, God's love is shown to be very much addressed to individuals. As Our Lord said: "Are not two sparrows sold for a penny? And not one of them will fall to the ground without your Father's will. But even the hairs of your head are all numbered. Fear not, therefore; you are of more value than many sparrows" (Mt 10:29–31). Jesus graphically brought home how intensely the Father seeks each of us. He goes after the stray sheep, diligently searches for the drachma, and eagerly awaits His prodigal son, yearning to forgive him everything and bring him back into the joy of the family. The New Testament will reveal God's desire for intimacy with everyone. The tender words used for Israel will apply to each person united to Christ.

The goal of creation and of the Incarnation is communion with us. God wants us to be with Him in eternity. He came down to our level in order to lead us to His. Two main aspects of our relationship with God, metaphorical in the Old Testament, become real in the New: God is our Father and our Spouse.

Christ brought God's paternal love to the forefront. It is a central emphasis in His preaching that the infinite, almighty, eternal God wants a father-son relationship with us. In the Old Testament, God's fatherhood is a metaphor to indicate God's special heed for Israel and for certain members of the people. He is not, properly speaking, their father, for He does not transmit to creatures His own nature as a father does. Jesus alone, the second Person in the Holy Trinity, is absolutely and by nature the Son of God, receiving the divine nature. Yet, the Christian's adopted sonship is more than a metaphor. Christ's apostles brought out that by the Christian's union with Jesus, he receives participation in the divine nature. Thus, God's fatherhood in the New Testament, in regard to Christ's disciples, is something very real. God regenerates them; He passes His life into them as a father does his child. He likens us to His only Son. We do not become God by nature as Jesus is, but our activity is lifted up into God's own intimate sphere so that we know and love Him as He knows and loves Himself.

The Old Testament depicted God as the bridegroom of Israel more often than as father. This expression indicated God's intense desire for Israel's good. The use of this term in the New Testament goes further by referring to a unique spiritual communion between God and us, the transcendent model of the union of spouses. This God seeks not only our good, like a father would, but also to be our good. The New

Testament teaches that He wants the closest possible union with each of us. That is the kingdom of God.

When the New Testament wants to manifest the Father's love, it points first and foremost to the Passion. Thus St. John wrote: "In this is love, not that we loved God but that he loved us and sent his Son to be the expiation for our sins" (1 Jn 4:10). Benedict XVI noted that in other religions, we see man striving to appease the gods by offering sacrifice. In Christianity alone is it God who expiates in man's place. God conquers evil for us. This is a greater love than simply pardoning our sin. The former pope concluded: "That which is wrong, the reality of evil cannot simply be ignored; it cannot be left to stand. It must be dealt with, it must be overcome. Only this counts as true mercy. And the fact that God now confronts evil himself, because men are incapable of doing so—therein lies the 'unconditional' goodness of God."[7]

Christ's passion gives us a fresh light on the problem of evil. This God, who cannot suffer in Himself, found a way to suffer with us. He wanted to be with us even there. St. John Paul II remarked: "Could God have justified Himself before human history, so full of suffering, without placing Christ's Cross at the center of that history? . . . [God] is not the Absolute that remains outside of the world, indifferent to human suffering. He is Emmanuel, God-with-us, a God who shares man's lot and participates in his destiny."[8]

---

7 Benedict XVI, *Jesus of Nazareth. Holy Week* (San Francisco: Ignatius, 2011), 132–133, 232.

8 St. John Paul II, *Crossing the Threshold of Hope*, ed. Vittorio Messori (New York: Alfred Knopf, 1994), no. 62.

Jesus reveals His love

Christ became man partly to offer us human features so we can know God more easily. It is arduous to think of and even more to love philosophy's unmoved Mover, but with Jesus, we have someone we can relate to and be attracted by. In Christ, divine perfections are reflected in human qualities. Christ notably revealed divine love through His human love, through His Sacred Heart. Christ's love is the perfect human expression of the Father's. Even this human love is so momentous that we cannot completely grasp it. St. Paul prayed that Christians would "know the love of Christ which surpasses knowledge" (Eph 3:16). Let us make a couple of remarks on the love that Christ displayed.

First of all, Jesus's love was personal. He looked on the rich young man with love, says the Gospel; He was moved by the young man's good desires. He loved Martha, Mary, and Lazarus in a special way. His tender love for His disciples was especially expressed in His farewells at the Last Supper, when He prepared them for His departure. John opened the scene by saying that Jesus loved His own unto the end. Then Jesus, like a servant, washed the disciples' feet. During the intimacy of that supper, Jesus several times told His disciples to love one another as He loved them. He confided to them God's secrets because they were His friends, He said.

Our Lord's love was merciful. He felt pity for the widow of Naim and compassion for the crowd without food and without a shepherd. He did not allow His disciples or others to turn away the sick, the inopportune, or children. He had austere demands but was full of kindness when He found someone wrestling with sin. He loved sinners as a mother does her wayward children. He came for them, He said. He was of easy access to St. Mary Magdalen, to the woman caught in adultery, to Zachaeus the publican, and to the thief on the cross. He prayed for His executioners. He taught that we should forgive seventy times seventy. He lamented over Jerusalem, saying He would have liked to have gathered the inhabitants around Him as a mother hen does her chicks. He tells all those who are burdened to come to Him to find repose.

This mercy explains why Our Lord chose the path of identification with sinners. Thus, at the very beginning of His public life, He received with the others John's baptism of repentance of sin although He of course never sinned. During the forty days in the desert, He assumed our struggles against evil. He even took on our miseries, our punishment for sin. The cross makes His love more manifest and sensible. He delivered Himself for each of us, as St. Paul said for his own case: "The life I now live in the flesh I live by faith in the Son of God, who loved me and gave himself for me" (Gal 2:20). Christ's love turned our punishment around, making it an act of love.

Our Lord even desired to consume all His humanity in His love for us. He wanted the offering complete, through the intense sufferings He accepted for us on all levels: physical with the scourging, the thorns, and the nails; moral through being forsaken by His faithful and the object of the hate shown by the authorities of His nation; and spiritual through the mystery of a seeming abandonment by the Father.

In all this, Christ is seeking us. On the cross, we have a sort of ikon of His love, as He stretches out His arms to embrace us. He said He thirsted—for our good and for our love, for communion with us. In fact, it is He whom the New Testament presents as the bridegroom of the New Israel and of each of its members. He seeks an intimate relationship with each of us. Christ indeed spoke of our communion of life with Him, describing Himself as a vine and us His branches. This corresponds to St. Paul speaking of the Church as the body of Christ, we being His members. He dwells in us, as the Lord told the disciples at the Last Supper: "In that day you will know that I am in the Father, and you in me, and I in you . . . he who loves me will be loved by my Father, and I will love him and manifest myself to him." "Abide in me and I in you." (Jn 14:20–21; 15:4). And in Him we find the Father. "If a man loves me . . . my Father will love him and we will come to him and make our home with him" (14:23). And He prayed: "Even as you, Father, are in me, and I in you, that [my disciples] also may be in us . . . I in them and thou in me" (17:21, 23).

Christ ascended to heaven, returning to the Father. He nevertheless continues His loving, active presence among us, as He said right before His ascension: "Behold, I am with you always, to the close of the age" (Mt 28:20). He is with us, especially through the gift of the Holy Spirit.

The gift of the Spirit

In the Old Testament, the Holy Spirit was presented as the great eschatological gift, the power of the new age. It is affirmed constantly in the New Testament that the Holy Spirit dwells in us: "I will ask the Father, and he will give you another Counselor, to be with you forever, even the Spirit of truth, whom the world cannot receive, because it neither sees him nor knows him; you know him, for he dwells with you, and will be in you" (Jn 14:16–17).

The Holy Spirit makes us a participant in the divine life. By Him, we are attuned to God, to the Trinity. The divine realities are made accessible to us by Him: "What no eye has seen, nor ear heard, nor the heart of man conceived, what God has prepared for those who love him, God has revealed to us through the Spirit. . . . No one comprehends the thoughts of God except the Spirit of God. Now we have received not the spirit of the world, but the Spirit which is from God, that we might understand the gifts bestowed on us by God" (1 Cor 2:9–12). Through the Spirit, God's depths are opened to us to such an extent that they become experiential. The Holy Spirit gives us a certain awareness of these depths.

The New Testament teaches that the Holy Spirit unites us to Christ, makes us in Christ a child of God. The Holy Spirit is the Spirit of Christ, of the Son. Through the Holy Spirit, we are adopted in Christ and put into a filial relationship with the Father. St. Paul wrote: "All who are led by the Spirit of God are sons of God . . . you have received the Spirit of sonship. When we cry 'Abba! Father!' it is the Spirit himself bearing witness with our spirit that we are children of God, and if children then heirs, heirs of God and fellow heirs with Christ" (Rom 8:14–17). We thus enter into the

Trinitarian relationships by the Holy Spirit. In Christ, by the Holy Spirit, we are children of the Father.

Through the ages

The Holy Spirit is the essential gift, but Christ, by His desire for our happiness, has provided complementary ones to help us live in communion with Himself and the Father.

He left us His mother. To have a mother in the spiritual order is a need of the human heart. Mary has, or seeks, a motherly relationship with each person. This woman is needed for a fuller manifestation of God's love. She helps us be united with her son. She has come to us often in spectacular apparitions during the last couple of centuries, very much a mother making a special effort with her wayward children.

Christ also left us His Church. Thanks to the Church, the inspired Word of God has come down to us through the Scriptures. And to guide our reading, the Church has authority to interpret God's teaching for us as she more fully grasps its significance over the course of centuries.

The Church also supplies us with the sacraments, these concrete, sensible means of grace, adapted to our condition in this time of faith. Through the sacraments, she follows us step by step in our life, from Baptism at our birth to the Anointing of the Sick, passing by major moments of our life with Marriage and Orders. En route, she heals our souls in confession through a personal encounter with Our Lord. She especially nourishes us with the Eucharist, by that stupendous invention of Christ's love. In Holy Mass, we can join with Christ in His passage to the Father, and in Holy Communion, He comes to each one personally to unite us intimately to Himself. And He remains in the tabernacle, waiting on us to come to Him. He is there present to us, accessible to us, drawing us.

The Church, furthermore, provides us with our needed fellowship. The communion of saints in the same truth and same life supports and encourages us. It also supplies us with prodigious witnesses of God's love. Christ gave special messages on His merciful love to St. Margaret-Mary, St. Faustina, and St. Therese. Many relate how tenderly loving He is to those who open themselves to Him. John of the Cross exultantly wrote of his experiences: "In this interior union God communicates himself to the soul with such genuine love that neither the affection of a mother, with which she so tenderly caresses her child, nor a brother's love, nor any friendship is comparable to it. The tenderness and truth of love by which the immense Father favors and exalts this humble and loving soul reaches such a degree—o wonderful thing, worthy of our awe and admiration!—that the Father himself becomes subject to her for her exaltation, as though He were her servant and she His Lord."[9] St. Teresa of Ávila transmitted to us a word from Jesus to her: "From now on you shall look to My honor not only as Creator and as King and thy God, but as My true wife. My honor is thine and thine mine."[10] He told her that if He had not created heaven, He would make it simply for her. He has related to other

[9] St. John of the Cross, *The Spiritual Canticle,* stanza 27, no. 1.

[10] Thomas Walsh, *Life of Teresa of Avila* (Milwaukee: Bruce, 1943), 406.

saints that He would have died on the cross for them alone. He made known to St. Gertrude that He would not be happy in beatitude without her: "I have so placed My love in thee, that I could not bear that we should be separated from each other."[11] He has expressed to saints how much He finds delight living in their hearts. One could even mention how St. Therese prayed that it snow for the day of her profession, September 8; and indeed it did. The lives of saints are full of little caresses from God like this.

The witness of God's love continues also with our own experience. In good Christians we know, we encounter a ray of God's love. Most of us can detect in our life, notably through our family, teachers, friends, and providential occasions, how God's love has been leading us, even and especially in difficult times. Perhaps we have felt His tenderness in our prayer. And if we are attentive, we can discern His love manifesting itself in the details of our days. God maintains us in the semi-obscurity of faith, in a regime of trust and desire, but also reminds us from time to time of His loving gaze upon us.

God is love

St. John deduced from the Father's gift to us of the Son and of the Holy Spirit that God is love. We have seen that God's love is, in fact, the reason for all His actions, both in the order of creation and that of salvation. All His actions are a self-communication. The three Divine Persons want us to

---

[11] *The Life and Revelations of St. Gertrude the Great* (Gastonia, NC: TAN Books, 2002), 133.

share in Their life. They desired other persons among them, one might say, for our joy, by gratuitous love for us, that all might rejoice together in Their beauty and love. Jesus and the Holy Spirit lead us to understand that the bosom of the Father is our true life and our home.

The Trinity's love for us is the radiance of the eternal love among the three Persons. Jesus prayed just before the Passion "that the world may know that you . . . thou hast loved [those who believe] even as you have loved me. . . . I made known to them your name, and I will make it known, that the love with which you have loved me may be in them, and I in them" (Jn 17:23, 26). This love has been given to us in the Holy Spirit, whom theology declares to be divine Love in Person, the love of the Father and the Son. St. Paul wrote: "God's love has been poured into our hearts through the Holy Spirit who has been given to us" (Rom 5:5). The Holy Spirit produces divine love in us, thus giving us to share in what He is and enter into the life of the Trinity, which is love: "By this we know that we abide in him and he in us, because he has given us of his own Spirit . . . God is love and he who abides in love abides in God and God abides in him" (1 Jn 4:13, 16).

Thus, behind communication to creatures is the total communication in the Trinitarian exchanges, as the *Catechism* teaches: "God's very being is love. By sending his only Son and the Spirit of Love in the fullness of time, God has revealed his inmost secret: God himself is an eternal exchange of love, Father, Son and Holy Spirit, and he has destined us to share in that exchange."[12] These are the two major revelations of the New Testament: God's Trinitarian interior life and our call to enter into it. At the foundation of everything, of the entire universe, of all the history of the world, and the economy of salvation, is the mystery of God's eternal love, the life of the three divine Persons in love, this perfect personal communion of the Three. This intimate, eternal love opens to us, becomes our heritage.

In this world of pain and darkness, of God's seeming absence, a word of love has been spoken through Christ. We wait in trust, praying to participate more and more in that word, that it lead us to God's Sanctuary of Silence. Our meditations, even when aroused by grace, can only take us so far in the direction of God's inconceivable beauty and love. We have begun to gently ascend by our meditations, now we have an abrupt mountain before us, far beyond our strength. We need God's. We will strive to open ourselves to God's gift by the theological virtues and prayer so that God may carry us forward.

---

[12] No. 221.

C | S
P | B

Part III

Approaching the Sanctuary: The Theological Virtues

"Thou, oh eternal Trinity, art a deep sea, into which the deeper I enter the more I find, and the more I find, the more I seek; the soul . . . continually hungers after Thee, desiring to see Thee with light in Thy light."

—St. Catherine of Siena[1]

After the first two stages on our journey—fostering interior, receptive silence and then nourishing it by meditating on beautiful mysteries that lead the gaze toward God's silence—we are ready to work on coming into contact with that silence. This is principally the work of the theological virtues, but we need humility to be receptive to God's gift. Humility is especially the response to God's transcendence; faith, hope, and charity respond to His beauty and love.

1 *The Dialogue,* trans. Algor Thorold (Rockford, IL: TAN, 1974), 331.

Chapter Seven

Humility

"Take my yoke upon you, and learn from me; for I am gentle and lowly in heart, and you will find rest for your souls."

—St. Matthew 11:29

All spiritual writers acknowledge that humility is a fundamental virtue because it frees us from the obstacle that is directly opposed to God's action in us—namely, pride. There are two main vices. We have in us a beast seeking sensual pleasure and a devil who wants to be God in any big or little way he can. Our inordinate self-esteem notably pushes us to want to be independent even from God. The humble man, on the contrary, perceives his need to be receptive to God's action. Humility walks hand in hand with the effort of this book to cultivate silence in order to receive from God.

The way down is the way up

Chapter seven of St. Benedict's Rule deals with the virtue of humility. For St. Thomas, humility is the stable inclination to occupy the place that we recognize as due to us. St. Benedict and the ancients would accept that, but they look on humility in a larger, more concrete perspective, as an essential facet of our basic attitude before God, penetrating and marking all our activity.

As always, St. Benedict presents Scripture quotations to provide the light for all he is going to say. The essential principle is from Our Lord Himself: "All those who exalt themselves will be humiliated, whereas all those who humble themselves will be exalted" (Lk 14:11). St. Benedict then quotes the psalmist as an example of someone who indeed avoided self-exaltation and gave the reason why: "If I did not think humbled but exalted my soul: like a child that is weaned from his mother, so wilt thou require my soul" (Ps 131:2).

Because we want to be independent and live on our own strength, we push away God, our life-giving source, like a silly baby would its mother. Similarly, when Adam and Eve, through the devil's instigation, wanted to become like gods on their own, they weaned themselves from God, lost His friendship and His gifts, and quickly experienced how weak and miserable they were by themselves. They learned the hard way. We, too, should know by experience that we cannot lift ourselves up very far. To pretend to be able to ascend to perfection by our own strength is fantasy, self-deception, puffing ourselves up with hot air.

Humility brings us to the simplicity and truth of what we are. We should remember St Paul: "What have you that you did not receive?" (1 Cor 4:7); and Our Lord: "Apart from me you can do nothing" (Jn 15:5). Humility is truth, the truth before God, before other men, and before ourselves. The humble man accepts things as they are, the proud is unwilling to face reality.

It is true, good, and just to remain at our place, like the psalmist, but St. Benedict certainly does not intend to stifle our generosity and desires. He teaches that humility gives access to a true elevation: "If we want to arrive at heavenly exaltation, we can only ascend by humility." We all want to grow in wisdom, in love and friendship, in joy. Man has been described as an "ardent emptiness." He is empty by himself, but made in the image of God, he possesses the privilege of being able to relate to God, who is infinitely rich. Benedict XVI wrote: "Life in its true sense is not something we have exclusively in or from ourselves: it is a relationship. And life in its totality is a relationship with him who is the source of life."[1] By his relationship with absolute truth, pure beauty, and infinite love, man can become true, beautiful, and good. Humility causes us to realize, on the one hand, that we have no strength in ourselves, and on the other, that our possibility of true greatness is founded only on the fact that we are capable of receiving God's gift. St. Paul wrote: "For when I am weak, then I am strong" by God's grace (2 Cor 12:9). St. Francis, St. Bernadette, St. Therese—they all said the same thing. Recognizing their weakness, they yielded themselves to God's action.

Thus, we are confronted with another paradox of human life, of Christian life: the way down is the way up. This seeming descent, which is in fact an ascent, corresponds to St. John of the Cross's axiom: "To arrive at being all, desire to be nothing."[2] Before John of the Cross, Our Lord not

[1] Encyclical *Spe Salvi*, no. 27.

[2] St. John of the Cross, *The Ascent of Mount Carmel*, I, ch. 13, no. 11.

only taught this paradox but also lived it. St. Paul contrasts Christ's descent and then His exaltation with Adam's pride and fall: "[Christ], though He was in the form of God . . . emptied himself, taking the form of a servant . . . he humbled himself and became obedient unto death. . . . Therefore God has highly exalted Him and bestowed on him the name which is above every name" (Phil 2:6–9).

Christ, by love for us, descended, taking on our littleness in order to compensate for our self-exaltation. In our case, however, to descend through humility is simply corresponding to truth. Our going down consists in pruning away our superficial, egotistical, false self. The humble man makes place for God. He takes down the tower of Babel so that the Lord can construct the Temple of God in him. His real self is liberated, and he can grow tall and strong by God's grace.

Foundations

Knowledge of God and of self

If we want to become humble, our first task is to regulate the gaze of our soul according to what God is and what we are in relation to Him. Knowledge of God and knowledge of self exist and grow together, as they bring about a sense of the infinite distance between God's splendor and our poor human reality. St. Catherine of Siena spoke of our need to dwell in the interior cell of knowledge of self and of God.

It is most of all by grace, by God's light, that we can be possessed by a perception of God's transcendent existence and therefore of our emptiness. Reason is able to provide glimmers of the infinite abyss between God and us, but the gifts of the Holy Spirit provide a certain experience of it. We nevertheless are to do our part to acquire knowledge of God's majesty and of our poverty. Our efforts will show our goodwill and open us to God's grace. We need to pray for this knowledge of God and of self, but also meditate on it prayerfully in His presence.

Our attention should chiefly bear on God's fullness of being rather than on ourselves. The soul intimately realizes its extreme littleness and misery in the perspective of God's infinity. It is not by self-analysis that we gain a healthy sense of our unworthiness and miseries. We like to think about ourselves quite enough as it is. The isolated consideration of self, even with moaning about our miseries, nurtures interest in self, whereas humility is, rather, forgetfulness of self, realizing our unimportance. One can think of two holy superstars of our day, St. Teresa of Calcutta and St. John Paul II. They were in continual adulation by immense crowds but had their eyes totally on Christ. They did not think about themselves because they were convinced of their insignificance. They just wanted to be Our Lord's instruments.

In chapter four, we meditated on God's greatness. We will never have too grand an idea of God. We also recognized that we are created and so are nothing in ourselves. Every good we have is a continual gift. And the bit we do have is finite, with no proportion to the infinite God. Compared to Him, we are less than a drop in the ocean or than an atom in the universe.

Thus, for the recognition of our littleness, sin is not even necessary. The Blessed Virgin Mary had no part in sin and yet had the greatest humility before God. Nevertheless, sin does enter the picture for us. We are nothing by ourselves, but one could say that we are even less than nothing if one adds our revolt against God, our Father, against truth in person, absolute goodness, and being. We are a grain of sand who is also egotistical, greedy, and rebellious.

Reverence

From the vivid awareness of our nothingness in the presence of the almighty, all-knowing, eternal God should issue the sentiment of reverence. Christ Himself was filled with religious respect, as the Epistle to the Hebrews said: "He was heard for his godly fear" (Heb 5:7). No one penetrated the depths of the abyss between creatures and the divine majesty like Jesus did.

Reverence is not fear in the sense of fright, as when one runs from a wild beast. It proceeds not exactly from danger, but from our littleness in the face of God's greatness. It is the feeling of the distance between creature and Creator. Reverence is awe and admiration for something that surpasses us. The *Catechism*'s description of the attitude of adoration corresponds to reverence: "To adore God is to acknowledge him as God, as the Creator and Savior, the Lord and Master of everything that exists, as infinite and merciful love. To adore God is to acknowledge in respect and submission, the nothingness of the creature who would not exist but for God. To adore God is to praise and exalt him and to humble oneself, as Mary did, confessing with gratitude that he has done great things and holy is his name."[3] Indeed, God's

[3] Nos. 2096 and 2097.

"infinite and merciful love" does not take away our respect and adoration; on the contrary, we should all the more be in awe and reverence before Him because He is all the greater that He deigns to stoop down to our littleness, like a mother playing on the floor with her little ones.

True reverence does not exclude the desire and love of God. Adam fled from God, but his reaction was not a positive, virtuous, fruitful fear of God. Moses and the prophets, in their experience of God, were greatly moved with reverence but did not run away. In their encounters with the Lord, they fell to the ground and lowered their eyes, but they were also attracted; they approached Him. Moses even had the audacity to ask God to show him a little bit of His divine splendor. God's presence and incomparable splendor at once shake us to our roots and also arouse in our soul a powerful yearning to perceive that infinite beauty. As it is said, God is a *mysterium tremendum et fascinans*. He is redoubtable but also fascinating. We take courage also because this great God has revealed His love to us; He has invited us to come forward to Him. And He has lifted us up by grace into His own life, into His friendship.

Exercises in humility

In his rule, St. Benedict did not expand on the greatness of God and the consequent sentiment of reverence. His teaching on humility is practical: how to submit ourselves in our heart and actions to God and to our neighbor for God. Even with a lofty view of God and reverence for His majestic presence, we have prideful habits to mortify. Pride easily mixes itself in our intentions and actions. There is something in us that wants to be God and tries to be so wherever it can. Effort and purification are required if we are going to root that out and realize in our bones what our meditations on God's greatness and our littleness entail.

St. Benedict set forth twelve degrees of humility as means to become truly, deeply humble. The degrees detail the attitudes and actions needed to correspond to our situation as creatures and children of God. They are essentially exercises in submission. These degrees are very demanding. We must pray about them and keep striving to progress in them. Here, we will briefly discuss them.

"The first degree of humility is that a man always keeps the fear of God before his eyes, avoiding all forgetfulness. Consider how you are always beheld from heaven by God, that your actions are everywhere seen by the eye of the Divine Majesty. Be ever mindful of all that God hath commanded, and that those who despise God will be consumed in hell for their sins, and ever reflect that life everlasting is prepared for them that fear Him."

St. Benedict thus awakens our faith, places us before the real and absolute framework of our life—namely, God's gaze upon us, His commands, and His rewards and punishments. The rest of the text on the first degree details how God's look pierces to our deepest thoughts and the bottom of our hearts so that we avoid evil.

A holy fear is certainly part of our life here below. In his Rule, St. Benedict continually reminds us that we will be judged for our actions. We need to keep in mind this final reckoning for the use and abuse we have made of our freedom and of the talents given us by God. When we are deciding what to do or how to do it, we must remember that we are responsible before God for it and will answer for our fidelity. In Scripture and tradition, the God-fearing man is the just servant of God, the religious man who carefully makes every effort to put God's word into practice.

The second degree flows immediately from the first. If we remember God's presence and want to avoid punishment and attain heaven, we will strive to do His will. If we begin our journey to God without trying to do His will, we are building on sand. This quest for God's will liberates us from the tyranny of our self-will.

The third degree reminds us that this seeking of God's will includes obeying human authorities—that is, those who represent Him. Without this submission to human superiors, our supposed desire to do God's will could easily follow our preferences, calling them God's. The divine will is made concrete and clear through the orders of these human beings. Obedience is a source of security, peace, and efficiency because we are then in God's hands.

The fourth degree warns us that we must be patient in our obedience to human beings. There may be misunderstandings, harsh words, and a lack of consideration. One could also demand of us very difficult actions. St. Benedict exhorts us not to complain in the midst of trials in our obedience, not to dwell on difficulties and pains, but to trust in the Lord to go forward frankly. We peacefully serve the Lord.

St. Benedict here adds recommendations of generosity in our service, presenting as reference Our Lord's exhortation that when someone takes away our coat, we give him also our cloak, or when someone asks us to go one mile, we go two. This magnanimity, going beyond the call of duty, releases us from our absorption in ourselves. We do not simply obey; we do not try to do the least in our service, but the most, the best.

The fifth degree exhorts us to unveil our conscience to our spiritual director or confessor. We must be aware of our deficiencies and faults, but it does not suffice to think of them. We need to admit them to others before God. It is humbling to reveal our defects, and so we tend to hide them. This disclosure to another, besides of course permitting our director to know us so he can help, keeps us from concealed duplicity, in which we often engage in an interior casuistry that closes off a section of our heart from God and His light. This concrete avowal very much helps us be sincere in our conscience, simple and silent.

In the sixth degree, St. Benedict urges us to be content with what is ordinary, with even the worst and lowest. As for tools and comfort, we are not important people who should have more or better than our neighbor. As for little esteemed jobs one might entrust to us, we should simply want to serve, and it is up to our superiors to choose our role for the common good. We must not be envious of those who seem to have more talent or hold a more highly reputed office. We ought, on the contrary, to be glad that someone else is able to carry out the work well. We should recognize that it is spiritually beneficial for us to have more hidden and modest tasks because they give us less food for vanity. Who had what task will not matter in heaven, but only the love we put into the work assigned to us.

In this sixth degree, St. Benedict calls upon us to recognize that we are imperfect workers. If we do succeed in a measure, we must thank God and also recognize that we are nevertheless still far from the ideal and that many others could have done the job better. We also know that any permanent fruit could only come from the Lord. We are simply His instruments. We generously do our duty and leave the results to Him. St. John Bosco and St. Teresa of Calcutta labored vigorously and diligently, but they well realized that they did not cause the tremendous good they saw around them; it was the Lord's work. They were little workers in His vineyard. We should joyfully do everything as well as we can for our heavenly Father, without complacency in our accomplishments, looking only to His good pleasure, like a wife and mother who forgets herself in serving her loved ones.

To be happy with the ordinary and to recognize that one is a poor worker does not mean that the humble man is afraid of being enterprising. Saints are audacious precisely because they do not rely on themselves but on the Lord. We accept the place and role Providence has reserved for us, but this place could be the first. We could be commanded to lead the attack in a battle. Christian humility does not lead to pusillanimity, to failing to accomplish the good for fear of difficulties. It does not destroy our desire to do great things, to aim for perfection, but now this desire is not animated by egotism. We are working for the Lord and by His strength. Nevertheless, knowing our own weakness, we are not surprised by failures and faults. We do not get discouraged when they happen. We bear with our limits as we do with those of others. If we fall, or do poorly, we get up and go forward without moaning and wallowing in our misery. We accept our humiliations and our limits, trying to do better, and trusting in the Lord. We do not get discouraged.

The seventh degree exhorts us to consider ourselves the last of all men, as St. Paul writes: "In humility, count others better than yourselves" (Phil 2:3). Amazingly, saints really think like this. Their assiduous consideration of God's holiness and purity makes them better perceive their weakness. Their experiential knowledge of their littleness before God leads them to seek the last place, to prefer others to themselves. We need to direct our gaze on the other as the image of God, as a certain presence of God, and for that reason, to honor him, render services to him. As God's child, as the image of God, our neighbor is our superior.

The eighth degree enjoins us not to seek out flashy, singular actions that draw attention to ourselves. It is hard on our pride and vainglory to be merely one of the group, not to stand out. One can say that pride is to think you are somebody and vainglory to desire that at least others think you are somebody. Even if we know some of our weaknesses, we still like to have people consider us important and excellent. Yet, we should not glory in this shadow that consists in what men think of us. We must not create a façade to fool others into esteeming us. It is what God thinks of us, and so what we are in truth, that matters, as St. Paul wrote: "For it is not the man who commends himself that is accepted, but the man whom the Lord commends" (2 Cor 10:18). To combat our tendencies to vainglory, we should prefer little acts of virtue that no one notices, and where there is less danger of complacency in ourselves and our productions.

Yet, once again, this avoidance of doing something different or outstanding does not mean that we should seek mediocrity. Her sisters in religion said of St. Bernadette that she did not do things other than what the other nuns did, she just did them better. The good to be accomplished has primacy over our desire to hide. When it is time to take on outstanding works for God's glory and the good of souls, we do not hesitate. St. Therese of the Child Jesus did not want to seek the extraordinary for fear of stepping out of the providential plan and of God's grace. She was nevertheless ready when she knew an action was God's will, whatever it was. Even if we have thoughts of self-complacency and desires of vainglory, we must accomplish the good, while still, of course, working to diminish those vices.

Degrees nine through eleven come back to silence of the lips already mentioned. The humble man knows how to keep his tongue, using it for love of God and neighbor, not to put himself forward.

Lastly, the twelfth degree concerns the modesty of our posture before God. The proper physical attitude is mainly a consequence of humility, and St. Benedict is certainly not inviting us to focus on our exterior, to want to appear humble. Nevertheless, bearing ourselves in an unpretentious fashion because we are in God's presence is true and good, and can influence us in a positive way. Actions of worship of God, notably, are an important part of cultivating a sense of our littleness. Signs of reverence for God—genuflection and bowing—signify and help realize a subjection of mind and heart to Him. We also should take the proper physical attitudes in regard to those around us. We ought to stand when an elder enters the room.

Spiritual childhood

At the end of his chapter on humility, St. Benedict tells us: "Having, therefore, ascended all these degrees of humility, the monk will presently arrive at that love of God . . . whereby he shall begin to keep . . . all those precepts which he had hitherto observed not without fear, no longer through dread of hell, but for the love of Christ." St. Benedict considered the degrees of humility as a path to the love of God. The submission exercised in the degrees empties us of ourselves and delivers us to the action of God's grace. We become attuned to God. We had to force ourselves to be attentive to God's presence and do His will, now we rejoice in it. Humility, as St. Thomas tells us, resides in the will. It is essentially a decision to accept that God is God and we are His creatures. We need first to know that He is great and we are little, but then we are to willingly accept this truth, even like it. We have considered how it is good for us to become humble. St. Benedict here tells us that another major motivation comes into play, the love of God. These are the two major aspects of our relationship to God: Reverence developing into humility must be completed by a trusting love. He is our infinite Creator, our tremendous Lord and Judge, yet also our Father and Savior. We address Him as "our Father," but then "who art in heaven," and we pray that "hallowed be thy name." My master of novices, bringing to their core our efforts to go to God, told me as a young monk to "be as little as you can and as loving as you can." We must recognize our infinite distance from God and our total dependency, that all the good we have comes from our Father; and then, with trusting desire, return to Him as best we can, by His grace abandoning ourselves to His merciful love that wants only our good, which is to be with Him.

Humility, reverence, and trusting love come together and blossom in spiritual childhood, in filial piety. Our reverence is not tension under the frown of a severe, exacting master but rather admiration for a firm, tender father who wants our good. We are to be like little children who, with loving veneration, like to be near their father. Like a child, we should be poor in spirit and trusting, looking to the Father for everything, living by His light and strength. Hope and charity make one take delight in being needy in order to remain in the Father's strong hands. To the contrary of pride, which wants to be independent, we want the Father's presence. We love His transcendence, His greatness. If we do something wrong, like a child in trouble, we flee to, not from, the Father.

Growth in the spiritual life is growth in dependence; it is becoming littler by love. The way down is the way up, we said. We want to grow in humility and dependency all the way to letting Christ's Spirit both love and act through us. As St. Paul wrote: "All who are led by the Spirit of God are sons of God" (Rom 8:14). "It is no longer I but Christ who lives in me" (Gal 2:20).

An excellent way to become little is to practice being Mary's child. The first abbot of Fontgombault, Dom Edouard Roux, served as an officer in World War I for four years, was wounded several times, and once even led an attack across a river under fire! This very manly man nevertheless said he wanted the novitiate of Fontgombault, and even the whole monastery, to be "a child's nursery of Our Lady." He highly encouraged his monks to make the consecration to Our Lady according to St. Louis Marie Grignon de Montfort. Learning to be children of Mary will teach us to live as children of God.

Dom Roux also made St. Therese of the Child Jesus patroness of the novitiate. He constantly put her forward as a model for spiritual childhood. Like St. Francis of Assisi, Therese relished the Father's greatness and her dependency. She was aware of her constant need and cherished giving pleasure to the Father by providing Him opportunity for His bounty.

This dependence does not mean passivity in a bad sense, or, even less, childishness. Therese was valiant in her action, never missing an opportunity for a sacrifice to show her love. She compared our activity to the little child always lifting his foot to climb the stairs even though the step was too big for him; he knows the Father will come to his aid. She also said that we are the little bird who cannot fly but tries and tries until the eagle comes to pick it up. We must be convinced of our weakness in relation to the results of the action envisioned, but strive to please Our Lord in all things. We indeed see in her life how vigorous were her actions; she never missed an opportunity for a loving sacrifice.

St. Benedict's degrees of humility are a school of spiritual childhood. Therese's doctrine is like a commentary on them. She practiced them deeply, with love as the goal. She brings to the surface what they are most deeply about. St. Benedict makes sure that our littleness becomes solidly rooted in our heart. He exercises us concretely in a gaze of faith, in respect and submission, in trust and love. In our days of casualness, familiarity, and irreverence, we especially need St. Benedict's training in humility. It struck me from my first experience of monks that, while they did not take themselves seriously, they took God and His service very seriously. Therese and Benedict make a good synthesis.

Now that we know and love our littleness, our needs, and our dependency, we turn to the theological virtues, where we are lifted up into God's own operation so that we can enter into communion with the living God. We receive His knowledge in faith, we rely on His strength in hope, we receive His love in charity and enter into friendship with Him. We are children reaching out to our Father by these three virtues.

Chapter Eight

Faith

"[I went out of my house] with no other light or guide
than the one that burned in my heart.
This guided me
more surely than the light of noon
to where [the beloved] was awaiting me . . .
O guiding night!
O night more lovely than the dawn!"

—St. John of the Cross[1]

St. John the Evangelist wrote: "This is our victory that overcomes the world, our faith" (1 Jn 5:4). By our faith, we rise above the rat race, above the circle of events, for we now know that this world is not all, that we are made for more than this world.

Our effective participation here below in God's life consists in the activity of the theological virtues, which unite us directly to God. Since knowledge precedes love, faith is first. The virtue of faith is the foundation of our spiritual life. By our faith, God begins to take hold of us. We obtain a contact with Him as intelligible, as first Truth, with His life as divine knowledge. Faith enables us to hear what God tells us about

1 "The Dark Night," parts of stanzas three to five.

Himself and His plans for us. Through our faith, He starts acquainting us with His secrets and teaching us how to share His intimate life.

Jesus did not have faith, properly speaking, which is adhesion to God's word without seeing Him, for He saw God. He is nevertheless the transcendent ideal for our faith because He lived in the possession of the consummation to which faith is ordered—namely, the vision of God. He is also our model in that His interior gaze was always toward the Father.

The Blessed Virgin, on the contrary, did live in faith. She was, in fact, the first one to believe in Jesus. She was the first Christian. She lived a pure, deep faith in the midst of what, exteriorly, were ordinary little duties of a wife and mother. St. John Paul II writes: "During the years of Jesus's hidden life in the home of Nazareth, *Mary's life too is 'hidden with Christ in God' through faith.* For faith is contact with the mystery of God. Every day Mary is in constant contact with the ineffable mystery of God made man. . . . [She] is in contact with the truth about her Son only in faith and though faith!"[2]

Faith is like a muscle that must be exercised if it is to grow, to become vigorous and prompt. We will especially indicate here how living our faith leads to silence, to what is beyond ideas.

Elements of the act of faith

In general, on the human level, faith is accepting as true what a person says because of confidence in that person. In

---

[2] Encyclical Letter *Redemptoris Mater,* no. 17.

supernatural faith, one likewise believes because of the person who speaks, in this case, the Divine Person. The *Catechism* defines the act of supernatural faith as "both a gift of God and a human act by which the believer gives personal adherence to God who invites his response, and freely assents to the whole truth that God has revealed."[3] Faith comes from a God-given power to adhere to God and so to believe what He tells us. The reception of this power is a personal and free response to His invitation. We see that the act of faith is not only assenting to truth. It is a yes to this God who reveals Himself to us.

The *Catechism*, quoting St. Thomas, elsewhere specifies the intrinsic components of this act in calling faith "an act of intelligence relying on a movement of the will which is moved by the grace of God."[4] The act of faith involves the intellect, the will, and grace. Let us go over their roles.

Faith is an *act of the intelligence.* It normally presupposes an antecedent work of the intelligence, which recognizes reasons to believe. These reasons are part of God's way of letting us know that He is speaking. But essentially, faith is an act of the intelligence because it assents to a truth. To believe what God has revealed is to enter into intelligible communication with Him.

By faith, our intellectual operation is lifted up to God's level in that the very object of His knowledge specifies our act of faith. As physical light is the formal, immediate object of sight and sound that of hearing, likewise, God in Himself, the

---

3 Glossary.

4 No. 155. The quotation of St. Thomas is from *The Summa Theologiae*, II–II, q.2, a.9.

Blessed Trinity, is the formal object of faith. Our faith does not see God, but it is ordered to knowing Him in His intimacy.

In a previous chapter, we considered how much this object surpasses our capacity. God's message, nevertheless, speaks to our intelligence. The words and ideas that God uses express Him in ways understandable and accessible to us. We can think them and apply them analogically to God. When we affirm that He is good, almighty, three Persons, we attribute to God the notions of goodness, power, and personality that we know through creatures. We can work with these ideas, unfold and purify their meaning in order to apply them to God, even though we will never fathom the depths of how good or powerful He is, nor all the reality of the three Divine Persons.

This act of the intellect "*relies on the movement of the will.*" The intellect, of itself, does not suffice to produce the act of faith, because the object of faith is high and obscure, and the reasons to believe do not necessarily conclude to it. Consequently, the will's intervention is needed to determine the intellect's assent.

The action of the will is all the more needed given that the divine message is a call to engagement; it lays claim to all our life, to our whole being. We are deeply and totally concerned with all that follows the assent of faith. There are sacrifices and efforts demanded if we accept the truths God teaches us. Bad desires can smother God's call if we judge that it is not good for us to believe. As Our Lord said: "The light has come into the world, and men loved darkness rather than light, because their deeds were evil. For every one who does evil hates the light, and does not come to the light, lest his deeds should be exposed" (Jn 3:19–21). Living in accordance with the appeals of our conscience is a normal antecedent to accepting God's signs and believing in Him.

The will in its turn "*is moved by the grace of God.*" Thus, the book of Acts presents the apostles preaching while affirming that it is the Holy Spirit working interiorly who brings listeners to the faith. Since the object of faith is not only not seen by the intelligence but is also of a supernatural order, it requires a corresponding affection if we are to be drawn to it. Theologians explain that grace intervenes in the interior of our free desire for happiness, giving us to perceive that we are being touched in our destiny by the Gospel message, to intuit that the secret expectation of our soul is coming to us. We intuit that we have a duty to respond favorably to this message. Signs, arguments, and experiences do not cause the faith, but they invite us and can dispose the will to receive the supernatural impulse, so as to let God produce faith in us. God alone can stir up our heart so that it recognizes His voice.[5]

Light for the intelligence

The *Catechism* speaks also of the intellect being given supernatural assistance in knowing the object of faith. A first assistance enables us to discern that it is God who is speaking: "[The Holy Spirit] opens the eyes of the mind and makes it easy to accept and believe the truth."[6] Our Lord told us that

---

5 A baptized child will one day have to personalize his faith. By the faith infused in him by Baptism, he has an inclination to an act of faith when he attains the age of reason. Hopefully, he will benefit from a Christian culture that will facilitate that act.

6 No. 153.

His sheep follow Him because they know His voice (see Jn 10:16, 27).

Some other *Catechism* texts mention a supernatural assistance that does not simply help us accept the Gospel but also understand it. "The grace of faith opens the eyes of our hearts to a *lively* understanding of the contents of Revelation."[7] Grace transforms the heart in such a way that the articles of faith come alive for us. We sense how real these truths are, how much depth there is to them. We feel God's presence in them.

"Faith makes us taste in advance the light of the Beatific Vision."[8] To "taste a light" is an odd expression, used here to signify that we do not see the object of faith but experience it in a way and perceive its sweetness. One has said that the notions used in our faith become like pearls put out into the sun, receiving a new splendor by faith. We have a sense of how they point to God's inner life. Thus, revelation tells us that God is good and almighty. These ideas, in the light of faith, emerge above natural knowledge into God's world, with a presentiment of the goodness and power of His Trinitarian life and His redeeming love.

In other words, the light of faith proportions us to God. We are in the Son and so at home in the communion between Father, Son, and Holy Spirit. We know the articles of the creed as things of our Father, in a way that only members of the family know them. We perceive what is revealed from God's perspective, from the interior, like something we are familiar with. The natural man, in regard to truths

---

7 No. 158.

8 No. 163.

of the faith, is like the non-musician who hears a symphony materially, whereas the man of faith is like the musician who appreciates the harmony, who attains the soul of the music. He has the ear for it. By the faith, we are connoisseurs of the things of God. The more we grow in the spiritual life, the more we will be attuned to God in His hidden mysteries: "The Holy Spirit constantly perfects faith by his gifts, so that Revelation may be more and more profoundly understood."[9] The gifts of the Holy Spirit provide us with knowledge by connaturality. We acquire the certitude that we are entering into the knowledge of someone. A presence fills the affirmations of dogma.

Thus, there are two dimensions of our knowledge in faith; one works through ideas, the other through an affinity with the object—that is, with God. By the intermediary of ideas and formulas, we have some definite knowledge of God's reality, some content of faith, but the light of faith stretches beyond the ideas toward the reality it is ordered to.

We find this distinction in the history of the development of dogma. The first Christians were aware of Christ's divinity long before the clear enunciation of the Council of Nicaea in 325 on the Son as consubstantial to the Father, true God from true God. Their sense of the object of faith often went further than the formulas they were using. St. Paul tells us that God gives us an interior illumination so that we may recognize Christ's divinity: "[God] has shone in our hearts to give the light of knowledge of the glory of God in the face of Christ" (2 Cor 4:6).

---

[9] No. 158.

The cases of two famous modern French converts are instructive concerning this light situated on a deeper level than ideas. At half a century of distance, they had similar experiences: each happened to enter a church one evening and unexpectedly received a sort of illumination. Paul Claudel was an atheist, convinced that scientific mechanism explained the universe. After the event in the church, he believed in Christ, but his system of thought remained the same. He had by grace a connatural perception of things of the faith, but his ideas still argued for a meaningless universe. It took him two years, he said, to reform his ideas, during which time he nevertheless vigorously cleaved to the Christian creed by the light of faith.

After his own experience, André Frossard went to be instructed in the faith by the local priest. As they went through the catechism, unknown to him before, he would continually cry out as he heard the formulas: "Yes! That's exactly it!" He had a deep sense of the truths of faith before he knew the formulas. That is something like the Church during the first centuries: As her theologians struggled for the right expression, she would judge the various efforts of formulation. Yes, she would say, that formula properly expresses the faith; or, no, that formula does not.

The two aspects of the faith go together, need one another. Blessed Marie-Eugène explains that when the experience of love triumphs, "the soul's loving gaze penetrates so deep . . . that it serves to confirm the precision of the formula . . . [but] the knowledge proceeding from connaturality of love needs the dogmatic formula in order to make itself explicit."[10]

---

[10] Blessed Marie-Eugène, *I Am a Daughter of the Church*, 552.

We need the representative aspect, but in our prayer life, we can at times leave the abstract clarity and rise to a sort of pure reference to God Himself. We must know how to jump, as it were, from the solid basis of doctrine to the reality and hide ourselves in the secret of God's face. We should hunger for Christ's Person, seek to advance into God's intimacy, into contact with the silent night of His presence. As we grow in connaturality with God, we are drawn to enter into faith's proper object, Himself. Eventually, we prefer this obscurity because it brings us the presence of the reality. The deeper and purer the faith, the more it feels the inadequacy of anything human in relation to God's mystery, and the more it aspires toward this silent night for contact with God, to open to the true light in the night of any other light which then would only distract from the presence.

John of the Cross, in his *Spiritual Canticle*, compared the life of faith to a fountain. He related the fountain's glittering surface to the articles of the faith, which at once veil and point to the unseen depths of the fountain. But it is those depths John wanted to see—that is, the reality, the Lord Himself, His eyes which John says he bears already in his heart:

> O spring like crystal!
> If only on your silver-over faces,
> you would suddenly form
> the eyes I have desired,
> that I bear sketched deep within my heart.[11]

---

[11] Stanza 11.

Practical advice

St. John of the Cross often insists on the fact that, since all we naturally know is finite, faith alone, having God as the object, is the proportionate and proximate means of coming to God.[12] He therefore exhorts to follow faith even though it is like a night for our natural intellect, since it is without a clear grasp of its object. In the text at the head of this chapter, he celebrates this obscurity as the light for our journey to God. Faith is our bright cloud for the great pilgrimage in the desert of this life. We enter into the dark and the silence, but God is present, attracting and helping us. On our side, we must cultivate our faith. We need to build up the habit of an active faith. The epistle to the Hebrews celebrates its heroes as people who lived as if they saw the invisible. There is no blossomed spiritual life without solid convictions.

First, we must pray. Faith is a gift; it is supernatural. We ask for its increase. Prayer itself is an exercise of faith, as we place ourselves face to face with the invisible and must learn to find God in an obscure and silent presence.

Second, we should have well in hand basic reasons to believe in God, in Christ, and in the Church. The *Catechism* mentions several motives for believing: miracles of Christ and saints, the Church's growth, her holiness, fruitfulness, and stability.[13] We can add the indications given in our chapter six as tokens of His love. Israel had a unique experience and knowledge of God, and the Old Testament points toward Christ in ways both obvious and discreet. Christ is

---

[12] See *Ascent,* II ch. 9, no. 1.

[13] See no. 156.

also His own witness, with the beauty of His soul and of His transcendent but simple teaching. There is the testimony of the apostles, notably on Christ's resurrection. Their teaching, too, is unique. It opened new paths for human conduct. Furthermore, we can recognize that the Church has always been the light of the world. Saints testify to their experience of Christ and His grace, as well as to their own goodness. Christ and Mary have visited us many times. Finally, we have our own personal experiences of God, Christ, and Mary.

It is good, once in a while, to read a conversion story to renew the freshness of these facts for us, or perhaps something of the apologetic type to help us think again some of the motives of credibility. We might study the case of a sure miracle, one recognized at Lourdes, for example, or one scrutinized for the canonization of a saint; we might look into a Eucharistic miracle. We could also investigate one of the major apparitions of Our Lady. The evidence for the miraculous nature of the tilma at Our Lady of Guadalupe is overwhelming.

Third, we must nourish our faith by spiritual reading and meditation. We need to reflect on the truths of faith and strive to understand them better so that they become real and present to us, interesting to us. That prayerful reflection will keep our mind lifted toward spiritual realities and foster the habit of seeing the spiritual dimension of events. This attention should also help maintain our amazement before the articles of the faith—that this eternal, almighty God loves us, that He is Three Persons, that the Second Person really became man and is present in the Blessed Sacrament, that we are called to live forever with God, to see Him!

Fourth, in our daily activity, we should be very aware of the great structure of our life: We are journeying to heaven through our acts; we live in our heavenly Father's presence; the three Divine Persons are in the depths of our soul, seeking to help us. We should habitually be aware of Jesus's and Mary's nearness to us, sometimes attentive to our guardian angel's presence. Then, faith should be the basis, the first light, for all our views and actions. We are to look on people and events from the point of view of faith, from God's perspective. We should perceive all things as in God's hands. We need to strive to recognize signs of God's activity in little things of our daily life—for example, in this person who comes for a visit when we are busy, in this little unexpected task that disrupts my schedule, in the kindness of a friend. When we go into a church, we must immediately remember who is present in the tabernacle near to the little red light. We should attentively use holy water, make the sign of the cross, and genuflect, aware of why we do these things. We are especially to awaken our faith when we use the sacraments—perceiving in the priest in confession a representative of Christ, looking toward the invisible event taking place on the altar at Holy Mass.

Last but not least, we must be faithful, act according to our faith. Often, or usually, a weak faith rises from the fact that we do not totally live according to God's revelation, that we do not want to dive in. We more or less consciously desire to reserve some place for actions, thoughts, and desires outside the faith. This erodes our faith, as we treat its objects as not really real, as less imposing. It is when we really seek

God in all things that our faith grows strong. If we seek Him halfway, we will only believe halfway.

Trial of obscurity

We have to accept passing beyond all ideas, all our reasonings, all that we understand, and entering into the darkness of faith in order to attain the realities aimed at by the faith. The pure life of faith consists in gazing toward faith's only adequate object, but which we cannot see in this life. Ideas can point us in the right direction, but our intellect is uneasy because it does not see the reality to which it assents. The obscurity inherent in the faith is especially difficult for us moderns. We like clarity and are used to dominating our objects, especially by our experimental and mathematical sciences. We habitually focus on the limits of things, not on their silent mystery.

God will intervene to strengthen our faith, to purify, deepen, and spiritualize it. All of a sudden, He might seem to pull back from us in such a way that we no longer have a sensible or emotional correspondence to the realities of faith. Maybe my little story can illustrate this.

For several months after my baptism and reception into the Catholic Church as a young man, faith was easy. In prayer, I sensed God's presence, I felt Our Lord, Our Lady, and the saints. Going on two years after my entry into the Church, I went to stay as a guest at the Abbey of Fontgombault for the winter. The experience was blissful at first. I regularly rose to what seemed to me high considerations on the beauty of Christian mysteries. However, quite suddenly one evening, it was as if the foundation upon which I was building all my "sublime" thoughts had fallen out. The feelings were gone. How did I absolutely know the Christian religion was all true?

I rather panicked and made feverish attempts to find God again. I read what had so moved me, St. Augustine's *Confessions*. But now I thought to myself: How could he be so sure? I read St. John's Gospel on my knees. Thoughts in prayer were rather a torture, and my prayer mainly consisted in silently being with Jesus at Gethsemane, trying to participate in His adhesion to the Father in the mysterious darkness He experienced. It was hard for this neophyte to be alone with God in the silence, confronted with the invisible all day long.

At the same time, although I knew it was not logical, I had total trust in Mary. I felt her presence when I turned toward her. A venerable ancient statue of her in the abbey seemed to me more bright and beautiful than ever. She was my hope, my light, and my warmth. They say that it is typical that Mary is especially present in these darknesses.

I was told that everyone goes through this sort of thing, that I would understand someday. I read a couple of authors about the dark nights. But I still had to travel through my experience of a tunnel. Gradually, I began to rely mostly on the deep, calm strength that God gave me to believe. The darkness that I experienced on a superficial level compelled me to turn to a more interior and spiritual presence.

My little episode was merely a purification from a fluffy, sensible life of faith to a more spiritual one. It was not what the authors call the night of the senses—let alone that of the spirit!—but the various nights are analogous on their different planes, like rising spirals. Such spiritual darkness proceeds from God's deeper action in us. He is working at a depth we are not used to. In my case, He had been in front of me, as it were, as I felt His presence, then He went behind me to fortify me, to lift up my actions. We have to learn to be patient in the dark until we become aware of the deeper, more silent level where God is at work. Such trials force us to learn to repose in God's obscure and silent mystery and to rely on His grace.

Only when it flows out into love does faith acquire ultimate meaning. We cannot attain to these regions of contact with God that we have evoked without love attuning us to Him. So now we need to consider hope and charity.

Chapter Nine

Hope

"There is no fire in me desiring to be fed; but there is within me a water that liveth and speaketh, saying to me inwardly, Come to the Father."

—St. Ignatius of Antioch[1]

The theological virtue of hope is not given enough attention. It is very much needed in our days, as man is despondent and therefore turning to various escapes. Only God can fulfill us, and hope provides us with the energy we need to seek and attain Him.

Our supernatural hope soars beyond all other hopes, which aim for limited objects. That means that this theological virtue leads us to silence and that any deliberate halting of its momentum brings noise into our soul. St. John of the Cross linked silence especially with hope: We must silence all these cries of creatures striving to hold us back from our pilgrimage. Hope leads us to a silent expectation of God's gift and opens us to a contact with His transcendent silence. We rely on God's strength to bring us to Himself, from silence to Silence.

---

1 *Epistle to the Romans,* in *The Ante-Nicene Fathers*, vol. 1 (Alexander Roberts ed), ch. 7.

Hope and the other two theological virtues

The nature of supernatural hope

Hope, on the natural level as well as on the supernatural level, is a confident desire of acquiring a good that is difficult to attain. One expects to overcome the obstacles either through one's own vigorous effort or through help from someone else. Hope is thus a fundamental human attitude that presides over much of our activity. Man lives by hope. Without it, he would not undertake important works but would slip into sadness and languor. Hope gives us joy, courage, even audacity. We can bear with most anything if we have a goal that is worth the effort. The quality of our existence is measured by our hope, what we are working toward. In Christ, God has opened us up to a hope for something beyond our wildest dreams.

The *Catechism* defines theological, supernatural hope as "the theological virtue by which we desire and expect from God both eternal life and the grace we need to attain it."[2] We desire eternal life—that is, living with the Blessed Trinity in heaven—and we trust God to grant us the means to attain it. We already possess divine life by grace, but it remains obscure and fragile here below. We hope for its assured possession and blossoming for all eternity.

Theologians hold that Jesus saw God and therefore already possessed the essential goal of hope. Nevertheless, He did practice hope in the sense that He desired and expected, by God's power, the glorification of His body and the salvation

---

2 Glossary.

of the world. He can be our model in that He had a very pure and ardent desire linked to an absolute trust in the Father.

Mary, once again, is the closer model for us. She hoped for her fulfillment in God and in Jesus. As a girl before the Annunciation, she hoped for the redemption of Israel, she awaited the Messiah. Then she hoped and worked for the success of Jesus's mission and His glorification. After her Son's departure, she hoped for the growth of the Church and, one day at last, to see her Son perfectly. She lived a silence of pure hope in her heart.

Hope and faith

Supernatural hope flows from faith. Faith teaches us about an unheard-of beatitude. If we believe God, then we believe His promises to make us happy. Nevertheless, if this hope is to be more than a whim, if we are to really desire and expect that accomplishment of His promises, we need another virtue, one that makes our activity tend to our fulfillment in Christ. We need a virtue that spurs us to truly thirst for this happiness and have the energy to undertake the effort of the journey to God. The theological virtue of hope impresses on the will an aspiration toward the felicity of being with God and gives us the intention and momentum to arrive there. A natural hope would not suffice to put our momentum on a divine level. A supernatural virtue is required to adapt our will because we are not proportioned to this object. Hope projects us toward God's intimacy as to our true life and our home, as to our proper end. It launches us on the conquest of the possession of God as our supreme happiness, as the unique ultimate goal of life.

Since attaining this good is above our strength, we must rely on God's power. We go to God by God. Hope is made at once of a conquering ardor and a trusting expectation. It inspires effort but also an attitude of cooperation. We act, but we especially launch a filial appeal to God, from whom we await all. The virtue of hope also infuses in us this trust in our Father.

Hope and charity

Thus, hope adds to faith the tendency to our beatitude and a filial trust in God. Understanding the relationship between hope and charity is more delicate. By hope, I love God, but not independently of what He does for me, of a reference to my fulfillment. Hope is the love of God as beatifying, whereas charity loves God for Himself. Some people, therefore, scorn hope, thinking that it implies egoism. The condemned Quietist teaching states that hope is just for beginners, that charity eventually replaces it because with perfect love, you no longer want something for yourself.

Yet Scripture is full of exhortations based on hope. Jesus Himself constantly appealed to our desire for happiness: "Blessed are the poor, for theirs is the kingdom of heaven" (Mt 5:3). We are to store up riches not for this life but for the next.

All tradition, all religious orders have always stimulated our hope in order to attract us to Christ and provide vigor for the undertaking. Monastic life, notably, is built on hope. All the monk's activities, all day long, are carried by hope. Monastic life has no sense outside of eternal life, as the monk abandons the normal human life of a family and a career. He enters the monastery to be happy because he knows that God alone can fulfill him. St. Benedict regularly put before his monks the goal of heaven, adding the promise of being happy here below as well. For example, in his Prologue, he encourages us to begin the effort: "Do not fly in dismay from the way of salvation, whose beginning cannot but be strait. As we go forward, we shall with hearts enlarged and unspeakable sweetness run in the way of God's commandments."

There is no opposition between this quest for satisfaction in God and then loving God for Himself. A desire of being happy does not contradict the love for another; that is, this desire is not necessarily selfish, making self the end and center of preoccupations. For example, it is not a subtle egoism for a woman to hope to be fulfilled in serving her husband and their children, provided she does not focus on her needs and desires, does not seek her own satisfactions at her family's expense. A mother relishes being with her children but knows that her love means that she will let them lead their own lives when the time comes for them to leave home. In fact, she sacrifices for them day in and day out. St. Paul ardently desired to be with Christ, his only good, yet he gave himself over to saving souls for God and was even ready to go to hell for that!

Thus, an ordered love of self, a quest for happiness, is not contrary to charity, the love of God above all things, including self. To refuse our happiness in Him, to want to love Him somehow without receiving joy from being near to Him, this would not be to treat Him as our Father and our Friend. Charity is of the order of friendship, where we give and receive, where we communicate together in truth, goodness, beauty, and joy. We want God's joy, our joy, and the joy of all rational creatures through a communion in God's beauty and beatitude, just as God Himself indeed desires.

If, here below, our love of God attains its perfect state in a pure gift of self, this will not destroy our hope for beatitude. This God whom we love remains the only One who can perfectly consummate our innate desire for happiness. Whatever be our love of God and forgetfulness of self, our life is not accomplished without union with Him. All the saints greatly desired to possess God. St. John of the Cross affirms the presence of hope in someone who has achieved a pure love of God for His own sake:

> It is true that in this high state the soul is conformed to the will of God and satisfied because it is transformed in love; it wants nothing for itself, nor dares ask for anything, but everything is for its Beloved. Nonetheless its sigh is great because of what it still lacks, i.e. the perfect possession of God; for it still lives in hope, in which one cannot fail to feel emptiness. However intimate may be a person's union with God, there will never be satisfaction and rest until God's glory appears, and he experiences the sweetness of that glory.[3]

---

3 St. John of the Cross, *Living Flame of Love,* first stanza, no. 27.

Until we have the beatifying possession of God, as long as we continue to tend toward Him, hope constitutes an essential part of the spiritual life, but it does need charity to be perfect and complete. Hope alone does not suffice to entirely rectify us. We could indeed hope for beatitude through Christ and still center our attention on our own happiness. We might even prefer our happiness to His will, to His happiness. We could sin while still hoping. Thus, egotism can dominate. Charity puts hope in order, purifies and perfects it, so that God is first. We need to love God as our good, but, most of all, as our Father and Friend.

Advancing in the spiritual life thus includes growth in the primacy of charity. A boy, for example, likes to be near his father, to sit on his knee, and receive candy from him. He loves him as he can, but as he grows older, he will care more and more for the father himself, will want to make him happy. If he does not, his desire and love, which were normal for a boy, now become immature and egotistical. Charity lifts hope above a focus on our own happiness.

Thus, hope continues to aim at our fulfillment but ought to be caught up more and more in the love of God for Himself, and of everything, including ourselves, for God. We are avid to be with Him as with our Father, but our attention is on Him, not on ourselves. We desire to go to heaven for our perfect life with Him, where our love and friendship will perfectly blossom. Therese of the Child Jesus wanted to be with Our Lord to make Him happy. She even said once that if, by impossible chance, she was not pleased with heaven, she would hide it from Him so as not to hurt His feelings!

Hope needs charity, but it also serves charity. First, it introduces us into charity. The boy discovers how kind-hearted his father is by the candy and in that way, comes to love his father for himself. Likewise, as we experience how good God is to us, we learn to love Him. We recognize that we cannot stop with an inclination toward our own little good. We rejoice in His perfection, His beauty, and His joy.

Secondly, charity, in its activity here below, needs hope. Hope is a virtue of the pilgrim. It gives us the courage and energy to work for perfect friendship with Christ. As Blessed Marie-Eugène of the Child Jesus writes: "Hope lies in tending toward the object known by faith and not yet possessed in the full measure of charity's desire. Hope is the virtue of progress in the spiritual life; it's the motor that keeps it moving, the wings that lift it up. A soul that no longer hopes . . . has lost its dynamism and advances no more."[4]

In prayer and action

Since supernatural hope is a gift, we must, first of all, pray that this virtue develops in us. Prayer itself is, in fact, a prime activity of hope. In prayer, we rely on God to bring us the good we seek. This does not exclude or diminish our exertion, but we pray that He help us and use it efficiently. By a tenacious hope, we must also persevere in our prayer when Our Lord does not seem to hear us. We have to keep knocking, as He Himself taught us. Finally, we recognize better as we pray what we should desire, what are worthy intentions. We pray for peace and good weather, for the elections, and

4 Blessed Marie-Eugène, *I Am a Daughter of the Church*, 379–380.

so forth, but most of all that His name be hallowed, that His kingdom come, that we enter into His intimacy. We hope for the Father Himself.

Next, we need to acquire the habit of thinking, desiring, and acting in the perspective of heaven. Jesus taught us not to amass treasures on earth, where moths devour, but place them in eternity, not to broadcast our almsgiving but distribute them in the sight of our heavenly Father alone, who will indeed reward us. In general, in dealing with things around us, we should aim, through them, toward the infinite good. If we cook a meal for our family or plant a garden, these activities have an immediate end, but we need to order them to eternity—that is, to accomplish them for God and for souls' ultimate happiness in Him. We must not let ourselves be overwhelmed or absorbed by horizontal, earthly ambitions but look toward the world to come. Thus, we redeem time, as St. Paul exhorted, drawing eternal worth out of each moment (see Eph 4:5). We will be for all eternity what God's grace has made of us during our life, with our cooperation. Life is short, eternity is long, said Cardinal Newman.

St. Benedict tells us to have our death daily before our eyes. Thinking of the terrible finality of death stimulates us to take advantage of the time we have. This life is the period of forming what we will be for all eternity. We need to remember that as we go about our day and so live according to life's ultimate meaning. Thinking of our death makes us see things in their eternal and true light.

The *Catechism* definition quoted above said we desire and expect from God eternal life and grace.

Desire

Hope gives us a desire for God as something supremely attractive to our yearning for happiness. To grow in hope, we need to cultivate our desire for the preeminent happiness in God. We indeed should have great desires. They expand our hearts and so make room for God's gifts; they give us energy for the journey.

This cultivation of our desire does not mean artificially exciting our feelings but consideration of the good we are launched toward. As we learn to gaze beyond the immediate toward the invisible, we undergo God's attraction. St. Gregory the Great remarks that when sensible things are absent, we desire them, but when we taste them, we soon tire of them, and even, at a certain point, get disgusted with them; whereas, when spiritual things are absent, we have no attraction to them, but when we taste them, they attract and we want them more and more. With St. John of the Cross, one can attain to a presentiment of how much this Beauty surpasses the beauties of this world: "Not for all the sweetness of the world will I ever lose myself, but for an I-don't-know-what which is so gladly found."[5]

To desire God, we need to know Him. If we are tepid in our desire and do not make the effort to advance, it is because we do not truly realize in our heart that God is *the* good, my good. It is important to strive by our prayer and meditation to gain with God's grace a sense of His transcendent beauty and love, as we have tried to do. Then, as

---

5 "A gloss (with a spiritual meaning)," *Collected Works*, 71.

we grow in our experience of God and Christ, we will desire to be with them.

We also need to think often of the Lord's promises about the joys we will have in the kingdom of God, which is like a wedding feast, He said, that most joyful of occasions. We could provide here a few thoughts on heaven.

Heaven is where one is indeed perfectly happy by a total, luminous communion with God in His life and joy, with all the saints. The *Catechism* tells us that heaven "is the ultimate end and fulfillment of the deepest human longings, the state of supreme, definitive happiness."[6] We will enter fully into God's life of knowledge and love, by which He Himself is infinitely happy.

We will see God, as the *Catechism* says: "God opens up his mystery to man's immediate contemplation."[7] "Seeing" does not mean with our physical eyes, but with the intellect. The use of that verb evokes the immediacy: We will not have an idea of God, a mere representation, but the intellect will be directly united to His reality. Thus, this knowledge will not be abstract. The Beatific Vision will be an unspeakable experience, echoing in all our being. All in us will thrill in unison with the divine life. We will be completely consummated in God as supreme goodness and beauty.

Also, the vision will place us in perfect possession of the infinitely tender Beloved. Heaven will be where the most intimate presence of mutual belonging with Our Lord will exist, like a gaze between two deeply loving friends, in a

[6] No. 1024.

[7] No. 1028.

perfect friendship made of a total reciprocal gift. Yet, at the same time, because we are creatures and adopted children, our love will also adore and be full of praise and thanksgiving.

Our first essential beatitude is to be with God, but God wants our human friendships also to be lifted up into divine life. Heaven will be the accomplishment of human community. Our human relations will flow from a shared participation through Christ in the communion between the three Divine Persons. They will well up from our vision of God. God will be all in all. We will be like one big family. We will be in perfect communion with other souls and, in a simple look, perceive the spiritual beauty which shines out from them. We will be with our loved ones. We will get to know the great souls of Paul, Augustine, Francis, Teresa, John Bosco, and so many others. We will also meet many beautiful souls that we never knew. There will be no envy in heaven. We will be proud of others, happy for them.

With the resurrection of the body at the end of time, we will have the fullness of our nature, with all our normal human activity lifted up. The resurrected body will be completely in accord with the spirit. God's presence will be transparent to the sensible world. An author writing a story about a little boy who goes to heaven evokes this, referring to what the book of Revelation says about the blessed not needing the sun or moon because God will be their light, and the Lamb their lamp:

> The entire landscape was bathed in a dazzling but gentle light. What a strange light! In fact, this was perhaps the uncreated light itself, a light Jamie sensed as being

> alive. Turning, he looked back toward the Lord and saw that this light emanated from Him. Clothed in white garments, Jesus alone was the source of all light in Heaven; all things were visible by virtue of Him. And it seemed as though it were by this light radiating from Him that Jesus reached out, touched and poured into each creature His life, His beauty, His joy. Jamie noticed that the unity of the creation and the glory due to the Creator could be read everywhere. All was God's; all gave itself to God. Creatures everywhere were nestled and pressed about the Trinity, in the shadow of His infinite tenderness.[8]

That total joy is what we are heading for, by God's grace, "in trembling hope," as the poet said.[9] Our only regret in heaven would be not to have done better here below. Yet we will be as happy as we can be, and having totally left self behind, we will be content that God's mercy was able to manifest itself through us. Each will have his perfect, personal joy, as Cardinal Ratzinger explained: "Heaven is individual for each and every one. Everyone sees God in his proper way. Everyone receives the love offered in the manner suggested by his own irreplaceable uniqueness. . . . God gives each person his fulfillment in a way peculiar to that individual and in this way each receives to the uttermost."[10]

---

8 Dom L. Roberts, *Jamie in Paradise,* mss, 7.

9 Thomas Gray, "Elegy in a Country Graveyard."

10 Cardinal Ratzinger, *Eschatology,* trans. Michael Waldstein (Washington: Catholic University of America, 2007), 235–236.

Detachment

St. John wrote: "Beloved, we are God's children now; it does not yet appear what we shall be, but we know that when he appears we shall be like him, for we shall see him as he is. And everyone who thus hopes in him purifies himself as he is pure" (1 Jn 3:2–3). In so doing, we dispose ourselves for the object of hope; we liberate our supernatural desires.

A multitude of too human and too noisy hopes, founded on goods that perish, smothers our supernatural desires. We easily try to fill ourselves with creatures. We become glued to things, attached in the sense of tending to put something ahead of God's will and friendship. We do not see God, whereas these things are sensibly present and pull us toward themselves.

We must tear ourselves away from disordered attachments. We prune the tree in order to channel its vigor into the upward movement. We quiet created voices in order to hear and await the Father. We have to let go of things, not hold onto anything in ourselves, allow emptiness in us so that we hunger for God.

To motivate the effort of detachment, it is beneficial to reflect not only on the positive, on God and heaven, but also on how we are not made for this imperfect world, that we cannot be ultimately happy with it alone. Creatures are good but limited and so cannot fill our soul. In any case, all will quickly evaporate—fame, pleasure, riches, even friendship.

Thinking of our death also helps our detachment because we realize we are going to leave behind all these things we are attached to. St. Thomas More, in prison and waiting for his execution, wrote an allegory where he compared this life to men in prison, all condemned to death by the king. All will be executed in a few days, some earlier, some later. Yet, he says, while they wait, they argue over who will have the best spots on the filthy bench, quarrel over who will have the best of their miserable food, grab other people's raggy garments, try to be seen as someone important. We see how silly this is. The thought of death indeed moderates all ambitions in this life. It turns us away from this diversity of desires, from transitory modalities of life, toward its essence. It obliges us to go beyond circumstances and all perishable goods, for they will not profit us on our deathbed.

Our journey to the Sanctuary of Silence necessarily passes through some goods, but it must do so without making them our end. We are to profit from them to go to God, use them as if not using them, as St. Paul exhorted us (see 1 Cor 7:31). We are to be thankful for God's gifts and attend to them in God's presence, for and according to Him. Proper detachment is to go beyond all while nevertheless appreciating God's gifts in their place. Things can lead us toward Him if we follow their pointing. We scorn not God's creatures themselves but our tendency to seek contentment in them.

Acts of mortification are necessary to consolidate this detachment. We can think all we want about spiritual things, but our lower man does not really care as long as he procures his pleasure. We must discipline him like a child, even like an animal sometimes, notably by tempering tendencies to immediate gratification. We can secure an interior distance from creatures by the habit of stopping short in our use of them. We can ordinarily take a little less than we might desire in both quantity and quality of things in order to favor our freedom as well as our hunger for God. The reward is worth the toil. As St. Paul wrote: "This slight momentary affliction is preparing us for an eternal weight of glory beyond all comparison, because we look not to the things that are seen but to things that are unseen; for the things that are seen are transient, but the things that are unseen are eternal" (2 Cor 4:17–18).

Trust

The *Catechism*'s definition of hope also said that we expect from God eternal life and the means to attain it. This expectation boils down to trusting in God. We have to learn to abandon ourselves to His power in expectation of what He alone can do. When we put our trust in the Father, we throw from the stormy sea of this world an anchor onto the solid shore of heaven. It is painful to keep striving for a good we cannot clearly conceive. We need God's strength to patiently remain empty, expecting fulfillment, waiting on God.

Knowing we have infinite resources at our disposal, we can aim high, at great things, especially holiness. My Father Master used to tell us novices that we should have the audacity to become a saint, knowing that God will support us in our élan. As a child, St. Therese said in confession that she wanted to love Jesus more than Teresa of Ávila did. Her confessor reproached her for that, fearing that this came from pride, but she was right since she was relying on God to bring her to that point.

We count on God to lead us to heaven, but we also trust Him in our undertakings in His service. I have mentioned that the saints had audacity in such projects as well as in their spiritual life. We also commit to God our earthly needs. We have human hopes—that our family be happy, that I pass my test, that my friend finds a job, that my son recovers from his illness. Theological hope does not suppress or even devaluate other hopes but assimilates them into the perspective of our final end. It orders them to our true happiness, employs them to help us and others go to God. If these hopes do not come out as we planned, these failures are only relative, and we know that Our Lord can use them to bring us nearer to Himself.

To practice this trust, let us be attentive to the fact that our Father is presenting all the situations we encounter during the day to lead us to happiness. Even if what we are called to do does not seem to advance us toward Him, we have confidence in God and His Providence. Someday we will learn how God used the circumstances for our good.

An important practice for hope consists in cultivating joy. We can maintain a serene, steady joy, whatever our difficulties. The revelation of God's goodness and promises gives us the counterweight of a sure, absolute happiness to come. Joy will give us motivation and energy for our spiritual life.

One of the monks at Fontgombault, Father Jean-Marie Barais, was a marvelous storyteller. We just thought he was jolly by nature and enjoyed telling funny yarns. After his death, we found in his personal notes the following, which shows that behind his contagious good humor was an engagement for joy built on abandonment to God's providence:

> I engage myself to be joyful in all circumstances, because everything that happens to me comes by the very Father who gazes upon me with love, in spite of my defects or perhaps because of them. That means accepting the here and now. I promise joy in the measure that it depends on me, that is, I will manifest no sadness, I will cultivate supernatural ideas that will found my joy, I will manifest that joy whatever happens. I will exercise myself at joy. This engagement for joy founded supernaturally has great advantages. It's a very practical way of mortification in all things because I must renounce my pleasure, to find my joy in what comes from God, whatever it be. That keeps one from weighing on others. All that renders one strong and permits to give of self in a better way.

Trials

God comes to our aid in this detachment and trust, notably by permitting some suffering in order to enable our heart to recognize the limits and imperfections of creatures, of this life, of everything outside Himself. He forces us, so to speak, into detachment and trust.

We could mention here two main types of trials that especially touch on purification of hope. Like Job, we could be struck in exterior or physical goods: an illness paralyzes our activity that was going so well, a loved one dies suddenly, we lose our job, our children don't speak to us anymore. Or, as described in Ecclesiastes, a trial might be interior: we lose our taste for life, our interest in the activities that we used to enjoy. In either case, our earthly hopes have been dashed. There may be a temptation to revolt or toward lassitude and acedia. We might lose courage and want to give up. We may no longer perceive how we could be happy anymore.

First, this helps our detachment. Trials, suffering, and evil in general help us realize that this world is not our home. We learn by experience how much all is fragile, that everything passes. Suffering enters into our life to express, in palpable language, that no other happiness than union with God should be sought as fulfilling, so that we do not settle in here below as if we were no longer on pilgrimage.

And we learn that our only hope is to trust in God. The revolt and lassitude can be defeated only by abandoning ourselves, by trusting God, and giving the direction of our life over to Him. We may not feel much desire for God, but in the bottom of our heart still lives the little flame of hope. Through these trials, in which we lose our created joys and attachments, God is cornering us in order to propel us to rise to higher regions—the only way out of this pain. He is allowing this suffering as the opportunity for us to engage ourselves more purely and deeply for Him. This is a way for Him to teach us or even force us, as it were, to rely on Him and truly seek Him instead of earthly consolations. We learn that He alone can be our joy. There are tunnels in our life where we must trust, waiting for the light from the other side. We know that Someone is there in the dark silence. God leads us along His paths, not by our plans. We know that God is good, powerful, and wise, and will lead us to great good if we continue to devote ourselves to His service and persevere in prayer.

I have mentioned my first weeks at the monastery, when in the silence and solitude the bases of my spiritual life seemed to disappear. I went home for a while before entering. It was painful to say goodbye to everyone, seeing my friends getting married and moving on in life. For the first time, I no longer felt a great desire to be a monk. Yet, I knew that God would not let me down, that I would be happier in heaven for having spent a monastic life seeking Him alone. I knew I would be happy someday, even here below.

As St. Peter said when many disciples left Jesus and the Lord asked him if he would depart as well: "Lord, to whom shall we go? You alone have the words of eternal life" (Jn 6:68). There is no ultimate hope anywhere else. We cling to Our Lord, and we go beyond our human, natural, and limited hopes. Our act of hope consists largely in a patient, silent expectation of God's gift. As the book of Lamentations tells us: "'The LORD is my portion,' says my soul, 'Therefore I will hope in him.' The LORD is good to those who wait for him, to the soul that seeks him. It is good that one should wait quietly for the salvation of the LORD" (Lam 3:21–28). "And Benedict XVI wrote: "It is not by sidestepping suffering that we are healed but rather by our capacity of accepting it, maturing through it, and finding meaning through union with Christ." We must find in suffering "a path of purification and growth, a journey of hope."[11]

---

[11] Benedict XVI, *Spe Salvi,* No. 37.

One day, from the midst of our lonely, silent desert, a spring will gush up. God will have brought us to a deep peace and joy where we thought we could not find them. We will enter into an intimacy with Him that compensates for everything else. It is a great experience to recognize, years later, that God was with us, leading us during a dark time when we only felt His absence.

Saints have experienced God's love even in the midst of extreme afflictions, deepening their hope. Benedict XVI, in his encyclical on hope, mentioned two models. St. Josephine Bakhita was a slave who emerged from her hopeless life when she discovered Christ: "Now she had 'hope,'" the pope wrote, "no longer the modest hope of finding masters who would be less cruel, but the great hope: 'I am definitively loved and whatever happens to me—I am awaited by this Love. So my life is good.'" The pope also cited a letter from prison by a nineteenth-century Vietnamese martyr, Paul Le-Ras-tinh: "In the midst of these torments, which usually terrify others, I am, by the grace of God, full of joy and gladness, because I am not alone—Christ is with me."[12]

I have mentioned Fr. François de Feydeau, who, in 2009, died at the age of fifty-six from a brain tumor. This vigorous, very active man was abruptly struck down with brain cancer. Six months before his death, he became crippled, was soon in a wheelchair, and dwindled physically and mentally week by week until his death. He was, nevertheless, the entire time full of joy and even good humor. A letter during this period expresses a beautiful, supernatural hope in Our Lord: "Now

[12] Benedict XVI, *Spe Salvi*, Nos. 3 and 37.

begins a new phase which is, like the preceding, in the hands of God and the Blessed Virgin. . . . Good cheer will help a lot. Pray that I have the strength and humility needed to let God act freely, so it be clear that the good that I hope for comes from Him by the hands of His Son and the Blessed Virgin. They are putting gold in my hands. . . . I experience my little problem as a gift, one of the most beautiful that the Lord has given me."

For such abandon, we need love of God. It is time to turn to the third theological virtue: charity.

Chapter Ten

Charity

"When by much joy or suffering one perceives the troubling desire to see God at last, when the most beautiful country-sides on earth, the most refined art, the most perfect literature one after the other has been exhausted, when the gift of self to the most noble cause or the most marvelous friendship has dug the desire of God without ever filling it, one can no longer be satisfied by anything, one expects almost nothing from things or men, or even from God in men, one awaits God Himself."

—Fr. Hyacinthe Paissac, OP[1]

We all are called to holiness—that is, to the perfection of love of God and of neighbor for God. Faith and hope are needed here below for divine charity, but in themselves, they are imperfect: we do not yet see what we believe, nor do we possess what we hope for. As St. Paul has told us, faith and hope are linked to our time of pilgrimage; they will cease when it does, since we will then see and possess God. But charity will not be evacuated by the Beatific Vision; it will find its complete development, its full activity. It is by

[1] Hyacinthe Paissac, *Le Dieu de Sartre* (Paris: Arthaud, 1950), 146–147.

charity that we decisively approach God and enter into His intimacy. It is by charity that we most resemble Him and share in His life.

Consequently, charity should be the fundamental motor of our life and the first reference for all our actions. Other virtues treat of a particular good; it is up to charity to orient all to our final end. The other virtues are like charity's concrete presence in the world for this or that type of activity, as I am temperate and strong for love of God. It is only in charity that all activities and faculties unite in such a way that our soul is no longer torn by divergent desires but becomes ordered, peaceful, and silent. The reign of charity thus brings about what I called subjective silence. It also ushers us into objective silence and points toward that silence, because it has for its object truths that surpass what we can know clearly. In the silence of hope, we desire our fulfillment beyond anything this world can give. Now we will consider how charity guides us into a solitude where we seek friendship with the Unique and must rise above all other friendships.

Christ totally lived by and for the Father's love. For Him, God was all; everything was considered only in relation to Him. His Person is a pure filial relation to the Father. He said that the Father's will was His food, that He always did what pleases the Father. He referred everything to Him, desired to turn all eyes toward Him.

The *Catechism* reiterates the classical definition of supernatural charity: "to love God above all things and for himself, and one's neighbor as self for God."[2] We will here consider our direct love of God, then our love of God through our neighbor. First, however, it would be useful to reflect on how man is made to love.

Man and love

I have mentioned how man is able to appreciate objective values for themselves. Nevertheless, he is ordered to other persons, to communion with them rather than abstractions. The person is not simply a pile of qualities. I could esteem someone's talents without loving that person. Likewise, we sometimes love someone who has poor qualities. When I love a person, his qualities are part of a whole, aspects of this unique individual.

Man is a social animal, made to live with other human beings. Our entire life is interwoven with that of other people. We require others for everything—for food, clothing, shelter, and education. Nevertheless, human beings come together not only for such aid but also for personal relationships. When a person does something for us, the witness of their affection often means more to us than the help itself. Our good is not something isolated; it is woven into relationships. We desire to be happy, but to be so, we have to be in communion with other persons. We enjoy observing the stars, but we need someone to admire them with us.

I like my puppy dog, but there is no subject there that responds to mine. Scripture tells us that it was not good for Adam to be alone. He had everything in plenty—a beautiful

---

[2] Glossary.

garden, wonderful animals—but he was lonely because none of that was on his level. He had no one on earth to speak with, no one he could share himself with. So God made Eve to be a friend for him, someone with a depth that answered to his.

Thus, man seeks, needs personal relationships. He can unite to others spiritually; that is, he can identify himself intentionally with them. He can make their pains and joys his own; he can want their good and rejoice in their happiness. Man expands his life in this way, enriches his existence. When we enter into communion with someone, deeper parts of ourselves come alive. A man cannot be himself fully unless he goes beyond himself, comes into relationships with others. The ability and the desire of entering into relationships is part of the mystery of the person.

The Persons par excellence, the transcendent, absolute Persons, are the Three Divine Persons, who are pure relations one to the other. St. John Paul II taught that man's ability and desire to enter into personal relationships is part of what makes him an image of God, makes him resemble the Blessed Trinity: "Man became the 'image and likeness' of God not only through his own humanity, but also through the communion of persons. . . . He is not only an image in which the solitude of a person who rules the world is reflected, but also, and essentially, an image of an inscrutable divine communion of persons."[3]

---

[3] St. John Paul II, *The Theology of the Body* (Boston: Pauline Press, 1997), 46.

Persons are made to form relationships; we must love. The work of this life is to love properly, to put order in our love. Hope responds to our desire for happiness, charity, to our need for love and friendship.

Love of God

We are to love God with all our heart, soul, mind, and strength, so we are to be totally focused on that goal. The love for God is to be deeply rooted in our soul and penetrate all our being and activity. We must truly seek to be His friend and His child, tend to the most intimate union with Him, and live for His glory.

Principles

There are two principles of any love: the perfection of the beloved and our communion with him. As for the first, God is not simply the best but the absolute. Any perfection we know is only a finite imitation of His infinite riches and beauty. St. Thomas taught that even in the natural order, we should love God above all things and more than ourselves, since we are simply a participation in His perfection.[4]

In our communion with God, we know by revelation that God is not only a spectacle of perfection for us. He has revealed His love for us—and what love! His love is an absolute as well. He came down to our level to lift us up to His, to enter into personal communion with us as our friend. He has brought us into His life, into His truth, goodness, and beauty, into His Trinitarian joy. We can be close to God as

---

4 See, for example, I, q.60, a.1.

to no other because with Him alone can we have contact in the bottom of our soul. As St. John Paul II wrote: "In the countenance of Jesus, we glimpse the depths of an eternal and infinite love which is at the very roots of our being."[5] God is present in us where no one else can be. A unique communion is possible here.

In view of that communion, God requests our reciprocity. He desires that we freely respond to His love. Our first response, as Benedict XVI told us, is to believe in God's love, trust it. We should be grateful and full of reverence for God's loving initiative toward us, but it also requires and stimulates us to render love for love. God, giving His heart, asks that we give ours as well. "In this is love, not that we loved God but that he loved us," writes St. John (1 Jn 4:10), but His love should arouse ours, as St. Paul wrote: "Christ's love urges us on" (2 Cor 5:14).

Our response of love is itself a gift from God because to rise to a level of familiarity with the eternal, infinite God, to enter into a communion of life with Him, can only be by grace. God infuses divine love in us. He opens our hearts for His intimacy, offering Himself in the charm of His love and beauty to our need for love. Our response is a cooperation with grace.

Saints tell us that they even attain a level where they experience that their charity participates in His. St. John of the Cross speaks several times of this: "[The soul] will love God as she is loved by him. . . . Her love will be God's love. . . . The two wills are so united that there is only one will and

---

[5] St. John Paul II, Apostolic Exhortation *Vita Consecrata*, no. 17.

love, which is God's. Thus the soul loves God with the will and strength of God himself." "The soul here loves God not through itself but through Him. . . . The soul loves through the Holy Spirit, as the Father and the Son love each other."[6]

If we love God, we want His good and also communion with Him, the two elements of love I mentioned. As for His good, what can we give to the infinite, eternal God? We can add nothing to His perfection or His happiness. We can, however, rejoice that He is infinitely great and blessed. He also wants something. We can work that His will be done, His plan accomplished. We want the good of His creatures, of His children, as He does.

In what concerns communion with God, we rejoice to be with Him, and He to be with us! It is a mutual complacency. God's plan of Redemption will one day be totally accomplished, and there will no longer be any good we can do for God or our neighbor. This mutual loving regard between Him and us, however, will remain. It is how we will love and glorify God forever. In fact, that is what the three Divine Persons do among themselves in all eternity. We are to join Them in that by God's grace, in heaven, of course, but already in a measure here below. That is, in fact, God's plan, His goal, which is the good we want for Him and for all people: that all hearts come to Him, that we all exult together in His beauty.

---

6 St. John of the Cross, *The Spiritual Canticle,* stanza 38, no. 3 and *The Living Flame of Love,* stanza 3, no. 82.

Growth in the love of God

Since charity, divine love, is God's work in us, we must pray to grow in it. We need also to open ourselves to the gift. We prepare for it in much the same way as I put forward for hope in the preceding chapter: by fostering desire for God and by detachment. As I said, to cultivate desire, we must work at knowing God. We need prayerfully to reflect on His beauty and His love for us so as to be attracted to Him. We should look for His love in creation and in revelation, in the life of Christ, in His actions in saints, and in events of our own lives.

As for detachment, we are to take away obstacles that block God's action in us. We have to discern in ourselves and work to eliminate what is not in agreement with the love of Christ, what in us does not flow from the life of divine love, and then work to rectify that deviated tendency in order to assume it as much as possible into our love of God.

All day long, there will be opportunities to give ourselves and to overcome resistances. Any authentic love calls for sacrifices, as Benedict XVI explained:

> Truth and justice must stand above my comfort and physical well-being, or else my life itself becomes a lie. In the end, even the yes to love is a source of suffering, because love always requires expropriations of my "I", in which I allow myself to be pruned and wounded. Love simply cannot exist without this painful renunciation of myself, for otherwise it becomes selfishness. [We need] . . . to suffer for the sake of truth and

> justice, to suffer out of love and in order to become a person who truly loves.[7]

This renunciation is all the more obligatory and universal for divine love because to make alliance with God is to sacrifice all the rest—that is, to prefer Him to all things.

We have also to correspond to the gift of charity, live it in our actions. Love of God is the absolute; all should be accomplished in reference to it. Not our feelings but fidelity is the solid touchstone for the reality of our love. Our Lord told us that those who love Him keep His commandments. Charity cannot exist without obedience to God's will. My first abbot, Dom Jean Roy, told us more than once to place our joy in God's will being accomplished. In all things, we need to reflect on what we should do as sons of God, as His servants and friends, how to open this domain of our life to His presence.

The trials I mentioned concerning faith and hope apply here as well. The experience of the absence of God is especially pertinent to the desire for Him. One has called the spiritual life a game of hide and seek. The Lord disappears in order to add intensity and constancy to our quest. The trials concerning the fragility of creatures with Job and loss of the ability to enjoy them with Solomon help also to focus on loving God.

It is by fidelity when the going is tough, without consolation, that our love begins to rise above feelings. By hope, I trust God will make me happy through this tough time; by charity, through it I want to be God's friend, show myself

---

7 Bendict XVI, *Spe Salvi*, no. 39.

His loving child. Saints tell us that eventually all the rest, even suffering, even earthly happiness, does not matter all that much and become only secondary considerations. They speak of the pure joy of belonging to God alone, that one finds at the foot of the cross. They have learned to love God for Himself, because He is God and our Father. They seek God, do His will, serve Him, love Him, not to spare themselves suffering or even directly to seek their happiness, but only for Him, for the pleasure of their Father.

In his great trial, as he lay crippled psychologically and physically, as well as dying, Fr. de Feydeau expressed his pure supernatural joy, which consisted in being with God and being able to give to Him in a way: "There is still no sadness. As God wills. I can say that these four weeks have been the happiest of my life, a ripe happiness. . . . I am happy simply because the Lord gives me what I have desired since my childhood: to be near to Him and able to give what He wants at my expense. He gives me much more and I am making a good deal. I desire only to make Him smile and persevere to the end. I continue to have the eyes easily wet, not by affliction but by gratitude."

Love of neighbor for God

Principles

Since we are to love God with all our heart, soul, mind, and strength, it might seem that we could love nothing else. Our Lord, however, commanded us to love one another. This love of neighbor is even one of the two great, essential commandments, like to the first. Christ made it plain that He does not consider us to really love Him unless we also love our neighbor: "By this all men will know that you are my disciples, if you have love for one another" (Jn 13:35).

It follows, nevertheless, that love for our neighbor should not deflect us from the love of God or even take away any energy from it but, on the contrary, serve it, strengthen it. Benedict XVI explains how: "Love of neighbor takes place on the basis of an intimate encounter with God; I learn to look on this other person not simply with my eyes and feelings, but from the perspective of Jesus Christ. His friend is my friend. I can see in him the image of God."[8]

The former pope here brings out two aspects of how our fraternal charity flows from the love of God. First, we love our neighbor because "[God's] friend is my friend." My neighbor belongs to God. God loves this person; He created him and redeemed him with His blood. This person is called to be a son of God. God wants his good, and so must we. Secondly, we see in our neighbor "the image of God." He resembles God because he participates in some degree in God's goodness, truth, and beauty. I love this reflection of God.

Through both of these aspects, we exercise our love of God by loving our neighbor. We need our neighbor to learn to love God. Our neighbor is like a sacrament of God's presence. The reality and authenticity of our love for God are manifested in this way. By my devotion to my neighbor, I prove that my love of God is not an egotistical dream.

---

8 Benedict XVI, *Deus Caritas Est*, no. 18.

The commandment of charity provides us with the reason of our love—namely, God—but also the measure of our love: *as self*. That is, we want our neighbor's good and happiness absolutely, as we do our own. Supernaturally loving our neighbor, we essentially want him to be a better friend of God and resemble Him more. We want him to participate in God as much as possible. We want his fulfillment in God. We also want human, earthly good for our neighbor—that is, what contributes on the human level to prepare for divine goods, but also to normal human happiness, for otherwise, our love might tend to dissipate into unreality. Saints have always ministered to their neighbor's human and physical needs. We are called to exercise the spiritual but also the corporal works of mercy. We know that in this indirect way, we are also helping them turn to the Lord. Our love will attract them to its source, as we see notably with St. Teresa of Calcutta and her daughters.

There are immediate consequences of this love of neighbor as self for God. We are to love *everyone*, for all resemble God, and He wants all to be His friends. Jesus died for all. Consequently, loving our neighbor for God permits us to love our neighbor *unconditionally*. We want the good of someone, even if he has injured us, for he is still in God's image and called to His life.

Loving all men unconditionally for God does not signify, however, that my love is to be anonymous, treating others as abstractions in a general type of love, or that I use my neighbor as a means to an end, simply to love God as it were. I do not love my neighbor as myself if I do not love him as a particular person. And God indeed loves our neighbor for himself. Each person is created by an act of love by God; he was chosen. Each is a unique mystery, a particular flower, an irreplaceable way of reflecting God's beauty. God has a special plan for every person; each has an unrepeatable vocation and a particular story. God wants a special friendship with each. He loves everyone in a unique way.

Loving someone as a friend of God and as resembling Him implies that there is a certain order in our charity. We love someone by charity in the measure that he resembles God, according to the proportion of his participation in God, according to the degree, then, that he is loved by God, is a friend of God. I want more good for who is better, closer to God. A person's perfection is what we can call the objective principle of our love.

St. Thomas furnishes another principle of the order of charity that we can call subjective: I love more intensely someone closer to me. It is normal, willed by God, that we more ardently want the good of those with whom Providence has linked us, for whom we are more in a position to accomplish some good. According to the objective principle, I want a saint to have a greater glory than my brother because he deserves it, but according to the subjective principle, I more intensely want my brother to grow in the Lord.

The subjective principle shows us that charity assumes human affection, as in general, grace heals and elevates the natural order. Indeed, supernatural communion does not eliminate our correspondences and communion at other levels. It should, rather penetrate and purify them, putting them in order to God. For St. Thomas, so much the better if you have healthy natural reasons for affection toward someone, because that way you can love him supernaturally with all the more vigor.

Saints had particular, real, friendships in which human tenderness had its place. St. Paul had a passionate love for his faithful. He suffered when the Corinthians did not respond to his love. St. Teresa of Ávila is also a remarkable example of someone who loved God with the greatest purity and yet had strong and pure human affections. Here's how Fr. Marie-Eugène presents the so moving scene of her death. Blessed Ana of San Bartolomé, her secretary and inseparable companion, was watching at Teresa's deathbed. A priest finally told Ana to get a bite to eat. Father quotes a witness: "Teresa, not knowing where she had gone, kept looking around for her and did not rest till she saw her returning. Then by a sign she called her near her, took her hands, and rested her head on the shoulder of her dear nurse." The next evening, she died in Ana's arms. Father concludes: "The love that carried away the soul of Teresa to God kept to the last moment an attitude and expression delicately human. While resting on the heart of Ana de San Bartolomé, she was preparing for her eternal rest in the bosom of God!"[9]

We have special relationships—our families, our friendships, our parishes, our neighborhoods, communities of various sorts. These relationships are a great and necessary good. God created us dependent precisely so that we would complement one another and so form these communities. In them, we learn to love. We acquire patience, the ability

---

9 Blessed Marie-Eugène, *I Want to See God*, trans. Verda Clare (Allen, TX: Christian Classics, 1982), 271–272.

to forgive, and we are instructed in respect and fidelity. We receive lessons in forgetting our little preferences in view of the common good and the good of others. They thus constitute a good basis for our supernatural love, and our charity should assume them.

In fact, our friendships, relationships, and communities are part of God's glory. The world was made to glorify God by manifesting in a finite way His infinite beauty. Each of us presents a unique feature of the divine riches, but so do our relationships. As I said, these are notably a special pointing toward God's interior life, the communion of the three Persons. The supreme created reflection of the divine beauty, the culmination of creation, is the communion of saints, this community of Christian friends with all their relations, the whole network of all our friendships assumed in Christ's mystical body.

Growth in fraternal charity

St. Therese wrote, commenting on Christ's commandment that we love our neighbors as He loves them: "[This commandment] assures me that it is Your will to love in me all those whom You command me to love. When I act and think with charity, I feel it is Jesus works within me."[10] Therese also said that the more she loved Our Lord, the more spontaneously she loved her neighbor. She nevertheless fought tenaciously to grow in fraternal charity, as we see in her writings.

---

[10] St. Therese of the Child Jesus, *The Story of a Soul*, trans. John Beevers (Garden City, NY: Image, 1957), 123.

Since our supernatural love for neighbor is a share in God's love, we again must pray for an increase of this gift, take away obstacles to it, and let His love shine through us. Taking away obstacles means, most of all, fighting our selfishness, where we seek our happiness in ourselves and look on others as something to use for ourselves.

As for letting His love shine through us, we should want to be God's instrument for our neighbor's good. We then approach all people with the basic intention of helping them progress toward God. For that, we try to look on our neighbor as God sees him. We must not stop with our neighbor's superficial aspects, which might be pleasing or not, but rather aim at the depths of his heart where we find the mystery of his relation to the true, the good, and the beautiful, to God. We look for manifestations of his deeper soul, made for God. One should discern our neighbor's good desires—for God, for friendship, for love, for truth and beauty—and cultivate them, recognize the marvelous possibilities in this person and discreetly try to help them blossom. It helps to look with Mary's eyes and heart as well, let her love her children and work through us for their good. With her, we want to help Christ grow in our neighbor.

With this gaze, with all men we have some communion. Father Paissac wrote:

> Man bears in himself the beginning of salvation, that mysterious relationship that links him to God his creator in a concrete link of person to person. That is the link also between men, the brotherly communion that permits us to go beyond ourselves. . . . The gaze

> of God on all of us assures men the privilege of being brothers and equal. . . . This man exists by God like I do. I become aware and consent to God's gaze on both of us. . . . Thus love can be established, founded on this communion of each with God. . . . Friendship consists in seeing in our friend this self that God gazes upon and gives to exist. To love is to will the one we love as he is in God's gaze.[11]

In addition to this communion that we have with all men, we especially have one with all Christians. We need to keep our attention on that Christian communion. St. Paul, urging Christians to work for unity and peace, spelled out the fundamental elements of that unity: "There is one body and one Spirit, just as you were called to the one hope that belongs to your call, one Lord, one faith, one baptism, one God and Father of us all" (Eph 4:4–6). We live one life, are called to the same beatitude. Next to that, our differences are secondary. And they are often complementary, as St. Paul mentions in what follows this quotation, when he says that each has his gifts.

Besides these deep human and Christian communions, we should strive to foster other ones, find other ones, such as common tastes and healthy activities. That will provide bases for our Christian friendships.

It is good to be aware of two modern factors omnipresent in our culture which hurt these relationships so that we can counteract them and work, rather, to build community. First, with modern technology, we do not need each other

---

[11] Dieu de Sartre, 141–143.

as much since machines replace human collaboration, and our electronic gadgets lead us, rather, to isolated activity. Having fun is often no longer enjoying people and spending time with loved ones, but isolated, individualistic activity, as we play computer games and watch videos. And even when family members, friends, or colleagues are together, they are often distracted by their phones instead of engaging in conversation. So, it is crucial to discipline these devices from this point of view as well. The other factor, modern individualist ideology, corrodes communal bonds by prioritizing individual autonomy. The focus is on individual rights rather than friendships and gift of self. We end up depending more on the government than on each other and on our smaller communities.

So, we foster family life, of course, friendships, and community life, but in all this, we must keep our true end in mind. We gratefully and with reverence accept the relationships that God entrusts to us, as His stewards. No relationship should be a diversion from or hindrance to our love for God. We attach ourselves to our neighbor as He wants. We must not make an idol out of a friend. We must be even more careful not to want to be an idol for him. We are always to accept that God has the first claim on our love and on that of others. We need to respect the sanctuary where God abides in our friend, and his relationship to God. We are simply a discreet instrument for God's work in that soul. We want to make of our friendships and communities something beautiful for God. At least on our side, all should take place in His light and warmth, like planets turning around the sun.

We might contrast two types of relationships, according to the two major vocations. The priest and the religious love their neighbor, but not in a possessive way. Their only possession is God. They are father or mother, brother or sister to all. The husband and wife, to the contrary, in a measure, possess each other by their mutual gift. Their love is exclusive. The family links naturally carry them to generosity, but they need to be attentive and assume them into the supernatural. A husband could look upon his wife as Our Lady, and he should try to be St. Joseph for her. The wife should want to shine like Mary in the home and honor her husband as Our Lady did Joseph. St. John Paul II wrote: "The family has the mission to guard, reveal and communicate love, and so become a living reflection of and a sharing in God's love."[12] The two vocations are complementary. The religious reminds the husband and wife of the supernatural end; husband and wife inspire the religious by their dedicated, sacrificial love.

The best relationship is centered around our participation together in the divine life and aims primarily at increasing that life. St. Gregory of Nazianzen described how, in his wonderful friendship with St. Basil the Great, the two were united most of all by their desire for God: "We had all things in common, and a single soul, as it were, bound together our two distinct bodies. Above all it was God, of course, and a mutual desire for higher things, that drew us to each other. As a result we reached such a pitch of mutual trust

[12] St. John Paul II, Apostolic Exhortation *Familiaris Consortio*, no 17.

that we revealed the depths of our hearts, becoming ever more united in yearning for God."[13]

For more concrete application of fraternal charity, I can refer to what I said earlier. In chapter two, I spoke of rejecting envy, which is an ugly tendency of purely selfish love and injures us, not the person we envy. In chapter three, I spoke of being truthful, friendly, and playful, all of which cultivate communion. Friendliness, in particular, means that we are kind and affable. We should manifest our joy to be with our neighbor, stimulating his trust. We adapt ourselves to various sensitivities and temperaments and find ways to make them happy. And in chapter seven, on humility, I spoke of honoring others and serving them. We might here just consider for a moment the more difficult cases, in which we try not to judge the bottom of hearts, we work at being patient and strive to forgive.

As for judging others, we need to realize that it is impossible to judge absolutely another's responsibility. We do not know everything about the case and its context, about a person's background. The facts we do know may be superficial. Most of all, we cannot see the other's heart. Only the Lord can ultimately judge His servants. So, we must get out of the habit of accusing people right and left with precipitation. The more we are intent on our relation to the Lord, then the less we will be preoccupied with condemning others.

There are objectively bad acts, even some that a person does habitually. We should find excuses as we reasonably can, at least that our neighbor did not know what he was

[13] *The Nicene and Post-Nicene Fathers, VII, de Vita Sua*, 190.

doing, or had some momentary forgetfulness, and that every soul has its ups and downs. We could recall the person's other aspects and actions that show his goodness. At times, we need to remind ourselves of Our Lord's words: "With the judgment you pronounce you will be judged" (Mt 7:2).

We need, then, to bear patiently with people. St. Paul, when speaking of fraternal charity, never missed mentioning patience; for example, in the epistle to the Ephesians: "Walk in a manner worthy of the calling to which you have been called, with all lowliness and meekness, with patience, forbearing one another in love" (Eph 4:2). Given what we are, there is no separation between consenting to love and consenting to be indulgent. We have to be large-hearted so that we do not let little things bother us. Often, we are only dealing with what simply rubs our sensitivity the wrong way. We should welcome differences of temperament, of perspective, of sensibility. We are not here to force everything and everyone into our modes. We must realistically and charitably adapt to what is.

We have to accept the limits of our neighbor, recognizing that we have our own. If he has real defects, we need to realize that they are not corrected in a day. We tend to concentrate on another's defects, whereas we should look mainly at his good sides. It helps to bear in mind that in heaven, this person will not have those defects, so they are not part of his real person. Rather than being harsh and demanding, we should be compassionate, showing understanding for his difficulties. Charity knows how to sympathize with another's trials, even little ones, how to put ourselves in another's shoes, attentive to how he suffers.

Next, forgiving. If our neighbor truly harms us, perhaps even deliberately, we should try to be objective in our considerations, as if the action had been against someone else. We must not nurture vengeful or resentful emotions but let them die down. We must notably refrain from imagining motivations behind our neighbor's actions. Often, we are angry at an imaginary person we have created, someone who does not really exist. We cannot command our emotions, but in any situation, we can say to ourselves: "God loves this person, wants his good, and wants me to will his good as well." We pray for him. We need to consider that God has permitted this harm for our good so that we rise above our egoism and act more purely by love. We also must remember what we pray in the Our Father: "Forgive us our offences as we forgive those who have offended us." Forgiving means that I give back to someone what he owes me. It does not mean that I necessarily let him into my intimacy. I might forgive someone who cusses a lot, but I am not going to allow him to be around my children.

Once again, we come to silence. Creatures harmoniously accompany and are part of our journey to God, but we go beyond them. We ascend to God through creatures, from beauties to absolute Beauty, through friends to the Friend for whom we are made. Our heart is to rise above all to God's beauty and love.

Now let us turn to prayer, which at its summit is a gaze in the night of faith, a listening in the silence of hope, a contact in the solitude of love with God Himself.

C S
P B

Part IV

On the Threshold: Prayer

"God in me, I in Him, let that be our motto. Oh! How good is this presence of God within us, in the inner sanctuary of our souls. There we always find Him even though we may have no sensible feeling of His presence. But He is there all the same. It is there that I love to seek Him. Let us try never to leave Him alone. Let our lives be a continual prayer."

—St. Elizabeth of the Trinity[1]

The theological virtues carry us to the threshold of the Sanctuary of Silence. Their highest activity lies in prayer. All our considerations up to now—the culture of an interior silence so that we can receive from God, meditations on God's transcendent Beauty and Love so that we better know the path to Him, and then our study of theological virtues by which we take up contact with God and His Silence—all culminate here with prayer, with our active and intimate relationship to God.

Christ, in His innermost self, is a relation to the Father and expresses this especially by His prayer. Cardinal Ratzinger wrote: "[Christ's] words and deeds flowed from his most

---

1 Quoted in Philipon, *Sister Elizabeth of the Trinity, Spiritual Writings*, 33.

intimate communion with the Father. The essential events of Jesus activity proceeded from the core of his personality and this core was his dialogue with the Father." "Prayer was the central act of the person of Jesus. . . . His whole human existence was directed to the Father and that was expressed in prayer."[2] To pray as children of God, we must participate in Christ's prayer. St. John Paul II wrote: "[The Church] finds in Christ's personal dialogue with the Father the source, the inspiration and the power of her own prayer."[3] Our activity should flow from that intimate communion with Our Lord.

---

2 Cardinal Ratzinger, *The Pierced One*, trans. Graham Harrison (San Francisco: Ignatius, 1986), 17 and 26.

3 St. John Paul II, General audience, July 22, 1987.

Chapter Eleven

Fundamentals of Prayer

"Prayer is a pouring of the word into silence. In prayer the word rises from silence, just as every real word rises from silence, but it comes out of it only to travel straight to God. . . . In prayer the region of the lower, human silence comes into relation with the higher silence of God. . . . Elsewhere, outside prayer, the silence of man is fulfilled and receives its meaning in speech. But in prayer it receives its meaning and fulfillment in the meeting with the silence of God. . . . [In prayer] the word leads the human silence to the silence of God."

—Max Picard[1]

This text corresponds to what we considered in our chapter three: our words actuate our silence, bringing out content so that our mind and heart can advance toward God. In prayer, they even lead us toward a contact with the transcendent, rich silence of God. We go from silence toward Silence through these words. In this chapter, we will lay out some foundations for prayer. First, we will define prayer, then consider where to find God in order to pray to Him, and lastly, we will reflect on four steps into prayer.

---

1 *The World of Silence*, 230–231.

What is prayer?

We can make some remarks on three definitions of prayer provided by the *Catechism*.[2]

St. Teresa of Ávila famously described prayer as "a close sharing between friends, taking time frequently to be alone with Him who we know loves us." We approach God because we believe in His love. He is our friend, and we want to learn to be His by His grace. We desire to be alone with Him—with the eternal, invisible, almighty, all-knowing God!—for intimate communications.

A sharing is normally effectuated through words, for that is how two people enter into and strengthen a relationship. Yet, St. Therese of the Child Jesus, in her description of prayer, scarcely alludes to words: "Prayer is a surge of the heart; it is a simple look turned toward Heaven; it is a cry of recognition and love, embracing both trial and joy." Therese does not have a conversation in mind; she does not envision a period set apart for prayer, but simply a loving movement of the soul toward God at any moment.

Similarly to Therese, St. John Damascene, a seventh-century Father of the Church, tells us that "prayer is the raising of one's mind and heart to God." He speaks of "raising" ourselves to God, but in fact, only God's grace can lift us up to a supernatural contact with Him. Only the Holy Spirit can enable us to say that "Jesus is the Lord" and cry out to God: "Abba, Father." Our baptism, uniting us to the Son of God, makes us capable of being raised by our Father to Himself. Prayer is the normal filial movement of grace, but God is the

---

[2] See Nos. 2559 and 2709.

active factor in our prayer and man is a cooperator. In prayer, we strive to dispose ourselves for being lifted up.

The presence of God

It would be beneficial to consider how God is present to us, where to find Him for our prayer. We also need to realize that prayer is very much an entering into that presence.

In the natural order

In chapter four, we recognized that God is naturally present at the core of everything that exists, since He supports all things in being. St. Paul told the pagans in Athens that God "is not far from each one of us, for in Him we live and move and have our being" (Acts 17:28). God is all around us, is at our source, and also penetrates us. He is in all, and all is in Him.

Living in God's presence, therefore, is simply awareness of the full reality, of the most important reality, the foundation of the rest. Remember Jacob fleeing his brother Esau. God appeared to him in a dream to reassure him. When Jacob woke up, he cried out: "The Lord is in this place and I did not know it. . . . How awesome is this place! This is none other than the house of God, and this is the gate of Heaven" (Gn 28:16–17). We are like Jacob; we do not practically realize that God is present everywhere. God, although hidden to our eyes, is more present you could say, more real, than the rivers, the fields, everything around us. He is immediately behind these things, as it were, giving them their reality.

All is in God, He is everywhere, but we can find Him best in the depths of our being, where He gives us existence. He is like the soul of our soul, the being of our being. As St. Augustine wrote, speaking to God: "You were more intimately present to me than my innermost being."[3] He is more intimate to us than we are to ourselves. However profoundly I descend in myself, He is always deeper. He is also at the root of our intellect and our will, launching them toward truth and goodness, toward Himself. He is at the foundation of our moral conscience, granting us the sense of good and evil. As the *Catechism* tells us, quoting *Gaudium et Spes*: "His conscience is man's most secret core and his sanctuary. There he is alone with God whose voice echoes in his depths."[4] God is there, where we make our deepest decisions and resolutions.

In the supernatural order

In the natural order, we directly know creatures, the effects of God's action, and can only reason to the existence of the first cause and to some ideas about Him. Thanks to Christian revelation, we know the interior life of this cause. And by grace, our spiritual faculties are specifically ordered to Him. God has revealed His secrets and also lifted us up to their level. He is now the formal object of the intellect and will, elevated by grace in the theological virtues of faith, hope, and charity. We do not see Him, but we are attuned to Him. One speaks in this case of an *objective presence*. In the

3 St. Augustine, *Confessions* III, ch. 6.
4 No. 1776.

natural order, He touches us by causing us to exist; by grace, He enables us to touch Him, as it were. "It" has become "Thou." We can have a mysterious, but direct, personal, and intimate relationship with Him.

I said that we naturally find God best at the bottom of our being. We encounter Him supernaturally, especially where He gives us grace, as Blessed Marie-Eugène explains: "Where could we find [God] more intimately, to establish our supernatural relations with Him, than in those inner depths where He communicates His divine life, making of us personally His child? God who is present and acting in me is truly my Father, for He engenders me ceaselessly by the diffusion of His life; I can embrace Him myself with a filial embrace, there where He is giving Himself."[5]

St. Teresa of Ávila began her decisive conversion when she experienced God's presence in her soul. She compared the spiritual life to a progressive awakening to that presence, in a journey deeper and deeper into the soul, where one is more and more influenced by Christ, more and more present to God hidden in one's depths.

Commentators on the spiritual life tell us that at the higher levels, one has first an experiential awareness of God's supernatural influence on the intellect and will. Teresa of Ávila describes this state:

> The soul clearly understands, by certain secret aspirations, that it is endowed with life by God. Very often these aspirations are so vehement that what they teach cannot possibly be doubted: though they cannot be

---

[5] Blessed Marie-Eugène, *I Want to See God*, 210.

> described, the soul experiences them very forcibly. . . . For just as a great stream of water could never fall on us without having an origin somewhere, as I have said, just so it becomes evident that there is someone in the interior of the soul who sends forth these arrows and thus gives life to this life, and that there is a sun whence this great light proceeds, which is transmitted to the faculties in the interior part of the soul.[6]

At a later stage, one receives what they call "substantial touches" from God. One experiences momentarily and from time to time a contact with what is deepest in the soul. One speaks of a divine "touch" because God does not present Himself as an object that you can perceive; you rather experience an action. They say that one can eventually attain a habitual awareness of His intimate presence, of a contact established with God. One realizes that one's entire being bathes in God. Watkin describes this: "Here the soul is habitually conscious of God as in full possession and penetration of her central substance, the root or apex of the soul and the ground of her functions."[7]

This growing and deepening awareness is not a special charism. It is normal, if not ordinary; it is a consequence of our growth in the spiritual life. St. John of the Cross tells us that we reach that presence in the measure that we know and love God: "The soul's center is God. When it has reached God with all the capacity of its being and the strength of its

---

6 St. Teresa of Ávila, *The Interior Castle*, trans. Allison Peers (London: Sheed and Ward, 1974), 136.

7 Watkin, *A Philosophy of Form,* 411–412:

operation and inclination, it will have attained its final and deepest center in God, it will know, love, and enjoy God with all its might."[8]

We know that this God we are in contact with is, in fact, Three Persons. New Testament texts show that we can distinctly experience Them. St. Thomas teaches that the baptized are all admitted to a participation in Trinitarian life through our acts of faith, hope, charity, and we can come to perceive the Persons as we grow more in harmony with Them, in connaturality with them through wisdom and love.[9] Saints testify to experiences of the Persons. They write of knowing the Word. St. John of the Cross tells us of his union with the Holy Spirit in divine love: "By his divine breath-like spiration, the Holy Spirit elevates the soul sublimely and informs her and makes her capable of breathing in God the same spiration of love that the Father breathes in the Son and the Son in the Father. This spiration of love is the Holy Spirit himself who in the Father and the Son breathes out to her."[10]

Some refer to a habitual presence of the Three, to which they can turn at will. Thus, St. Mary of the Incarnation wrote:

> One day, at prayer in the evening, a sudden attraction seized hold of my soul. The three Persons of the blessed Trinity showed themselves once again to my soul. . . . And the most blessed Trinity, in its unity, took hold of

---

[8] St. John of the Cross, *The Living Flame of Love,* first stanza, no. 12.

[9] See I, q.43, aa.3 and 5.

[10] St. John of the Cross, *The Spiritual Canticle,* stanza 39, no. 3.

> my soul like a thing that belonged to it and that it had made capable of receiving its divine impression and the effects of its divine interchange. . . . From that time onwards, the effects took root and, as the three divine Persons possessed me, so did I possess them as well.[11]

A burning presence

Our life of prayer is a deepening penetration into the divine presence. One needs courage for that because God does not come into our soul unless He rules. We have to sacrifice more and more, leave all behind. The Gospel tells us of a rich young man who asked Jesus how to be perfect. Jesus fixed a look of love on him, St. Mark tells us, and invited him to abandon all to follow Him. The boy fled when confronted with such a requirement.

We are also easily like Adam, fleeing in shame from God's face. It hurts to look toward God because of the contrast between His infinite purity and our misery. Secret duplicities and compromises, hidden even from ourselves, painfully and shamefully come to light. When Jesus looked at Peter after he had denied Him in the praetorium of Pilate, Peter wept bitterly.

In his long poem *The Dream of Gerontius*, St. John Henry Newman tells of a soul who, after his death, goes to his Maker. The soul's judgment consists in catching sight of Christ's face. Newman writes in the person of Gerontius's guardian angel speaking to the soul as he bears him toward

---

[11] Quoted in Yves Congar, *I Believe in the Holy Spirit,* trans. David Smith (New York: Crossroad, 1981), vol. 2, 82.

the Lord: "Thou wilt feel that thou hast sinn'd, as never thou didst feel; and wilt desire to slink away, and hide thee from His sight; and yet wilt have a long aye to dwell within the beauty of His countenance. And these two pains, so counter and so keen—the longing for him when thou seest him not; the shame of thyself at the thought of seeing him—will be thy veriest, sharpest purgatory." Thus, the memory of Jesus's eyes will be Gerontius's purification at once by the shame they stir up but also by his hope of seeing them again.

Peter had fled, but he eventually turned back to Our Lord. Like Peter, we must keep returning to Christ's look upon us. If we do, Christ's eyes will purify us as they did Gerontius, because the noise of the little calculations of our egoism cannot long coexist with a continual, determined regard on God's absolute purity and beauty, on His love. Benedict XVI wrote of our future judgment by Christ: "In the pain of this encounter, when the impurity and sickness of our lives become evident to us, there lies salvation. His gaze, the touch of his heart heals us through an undeniably painful transformation 'as through fire.' But it is a blessed pain, in which the holy power of his love sears through us like a flame, enabling us to become totally ourselves and thus totally of God."[12] We are made for God, so this purification renders us to ourselves.

One could say that hell is resisting God's presence, whereas purgatory consists in opening up to it; heaven is bathing in it. We must face up to God's presence and gaze, continue to look toward Him and listen to Him, not letting ourselves

---

12 Benedict XVI, *Spe Salvi,* no. 47.

stray off to horizontal goals and noise. All impurities, everything that contradicts or even hinders God's love will have to be consumed one day, either here below or in purgatory. We might as well accept the burning now for God's glory, the good of souls, and our own joy. God is not outdone in generosity. There is no risk. Monks leave the world and go to the desert precisely to direct our mind and heart constantly toward that Presence. As Blake said in his beautiful little poem: "We are put on earth a little space that we may learn to bear the beams of love."[13] We open to that presence and learn to bear those beams mainly, or especially, by prayer.

Steps into prayer

I am not dealing here with the levels of prayer that St. Teresa notably analyzed, but with steps that lead, rather, to what she called prayer of recollection, or perhaps of quiet. Tradition lines up four steps in a progressive prayerful activity: *lectio, meditatio, oratio,* and *contemplatio.* We read, we think about what we read, we pray that Our Lord allows us to enter into the mystery evoked by the text, and then, by God's gift, we lovingly taste that mystery. These activities concretely overlap. They nevertheless are basic and normal stages in our turning to God through prayer.

Lectio

Most of us need regular reading that nourishes us spiritually, keeps our mind on high things, and challenges us to rise above mediocre views and activity. Frequenting the spiritual

13 "The Little Black Boy."

classics, we begin to think and desire more like the saints do. We learn to look on ourselves, others, and events in God's light. I recommend that, if one has not done so, one read an overall view of the spiritual life—for example, *Introduction to the Devout Life* by St. Francis de Sales, *The Three Ages of the Spiritual Life* by Fr. Reginald Garrigou-Lagrange, *Christ the Life of the Soul* by Blessed Columba Marmion, *The Spiritual Life and Prayer* by Mother Cécile Bruyère.

Spiritual reading is not merely a quest for information. It seeks a knowledge that involves one's whole life. We want to get to know Christ and the paths to Him. We consider what God is teaching us, what He is asking of us or inviting us to, and what He is promising. *Lectio divina*—divine reading—is a slow, prayerful, thoughtful reading, in contrast with "study," which is a more detached and objective activity. At its most intense, we read as if the Lord were speaking to us through the text in hand, calling upon us to yield our mind and heart to Him. We receive the words as a personal message addressed to us, as a living word, from His heart to ours.

Such attentive listening and reception presuppose basically two dispositions. First, interior silence is important so that we can focus on what the author—and God through that author—has to say to us. This silence implies that we are calm. Haste rises, rather, from curiosity. We must counteract the habit of skimming a text in order to pick out a few formulas we can use or to grab a little information. Second, we need commitment and docility, readiness for a cordial and practical assent to the teaching. We must respond with our intellect, heart, and acts. We read with faith, hope, and charity.

Scripture is primary material for spiritual reading since it sets forth our Father's message, leading us back to Himself. We can and should study Scripture with commentaries and biblical theology, using cross-references perhaps, but the essential is a more directly prayerful reading, listening to God here and now. The word of God is charged with creative power, as St. Paul says: "[The Gospel] is the power of God for salvation to everyone who has faith" (Rom 1:16). Scripture is a sacramental, acting on us according to our attentiveness, faith, trust, desire, and love. There is, as it were, a mysterious and active presence in the words of the Bible, where we can personally encounter Christ. When God speaks, He communicates Himself.

Other books can be used, spiritual writings that bring out the light of Christ found in Scripture, while illuminating the way to the Father in Christ by theology and experiential knowledge acquired by the Church. Such writings are indeed also places where we can listen to God speaking to us. Some are more ascetical, concerning our effort of discipline, others more spiritual on how to open to God's action. Some are more didactic, others more experiential, drawing us into the author's encounter with God.

It is beneficial to read the lives of saints, where Christ's life shows itself in action. We see them overcome difficulties; they show us the joy that the spiritual life brings. They help us understand Gospel teaching and spiritual doctrine by their acts. We learn how to apply the Gospel concretely.

They inspire and encourage us with their humility, faith, hope, and charity.

Meditatio

There is meditation, of course, already in reading, as we try to understand, as we think over and assimilate what we read, as we enjoy its beauty. Meditation, as distinct from *lectio,* would be to stop reading in order to examine a point more thoroughly, to plumb its depths and uncover the mystery. For example, taking up the first Beatitude, we reflect on poverty of spirit as detachment from things, as knowing our littleness and emptiness, as relying on God. Then we consider the kingdom of God, as a sharing in His own happiness, as intimacy with the Father. We next ask why poverty of spirit leads there. One could read a text and then stop to ponder on a phrase from time to time. One could also consider a line from reading done at another time. One can, of course, reflect directly on some theme without directly following a text.

The *Catechism* explains that we meditate "in order to deepen our convictions of faith, prompt the conversion of heart, and strengthen our will to follow Christ."[14] We want to *deepen our convictions.* We do not sensibly perceive the invisible; consequently, we must think about it. By this reflection, we sharpen our spiritual perception of the unseen, making it more present to us, more real and familiar. We strive to intensify our understanding of a mystery and of Christ's words. We want to impress them in our soul.

---

[14] No. 2078.

To *prompt the conversion of heart*. Better perceiving Christ's beauty through our reflection, we feel moved to respond to Him. The goal in meditation is not working out concepts or solving an intellectual problem but love. Its essential task is to seek Christ's face and commence a friendship with Him. It is kindling our desires so that we hunger for God.

Lastly, we *strengthen our will*. We personalize the teaching. As they are better appreciated, the mysteries will be more influential in our lives, but we also need to reflect in detail on how they apply to us and how our conduct measures up to them. We turn to our inmost conscience and consider the state of our soul. "In order to adhere and respond to what the Lord is asking, we make it our own by confronting it with ourselves," the *Catechism* says.[15] We resolve to live more by these mysteries.

Besides Scripture and other spiritual reading mentioned above, one could take for meditation something from the liturgy—the hymns or the antiphons, litanies, chants, and prayers of the Mass. Whether using a particular text or not, it is normal that we keep abreast of the liturgical year, prayerfully pondering the Incarnation and Christ's infancy around Christmas, then His baptism, and at the beginning of Lent, His time in the desert, meditating on His passion in Holy Week, and His resurrection around Easter. We also normally live with the various feasts that come up one after the other in the time after Pentecost.

One could also meditate on the themes we have considered: God's transcendence, His beauty, and His love. We

[15] No. 2076.

must always be thinking about aspects of Christ's and Mary's mysteries. We should often consider the Last Things—death, judgment, hell, purgatory, and heaven.

It is important not to superficially jump from one idea to another, not to wander carelessly in our thoughts. St. Francis de Sales says that we should comport ourselves like a bee that never leaves a flower as long as there is something there to make honey from. We need to acquire a certain discipline so that the mind learns to be attentive and think deeply. It is better to meditate in depth than to flit from one subject to another.

There are manuals that provide ready-made meditations, which one could use in the beginning to get started. St. Francis de Sales gives a few examples in his *Introduction to the Devout Life*. Nevertheless, our reflection should advance to something free and personal, leaving room for the Holy Spirit to lead us where He wills.

Oratio

In *oratio*, we do not merely read or think about Christ but enter into a vis-à-vis with Him. Reading and meditation should already be prayerful, mixed with prayer, as we mull over a mystery in conversation with God. St. Augustine's *Confessions* is a prime example of meditation accomplished in dialogue with God. *Oratio,* as distinct from meditation, comes in when the reading and meditation move us to turn more directly to Our Lord. The word of God has touched us; prayer is responding to that word. We have considered some aspect of Christ's mystery, and so we now desire to approach

Him and speak to Him. In the example given for meditation, we now pray to taste the beauty of spiritual poverty and the kingdom of God. We ask for God's strength and light to better know and live the mystery we have glimpsed. We also speak with Our Lord outside of reading and meditation, even outside of quiet time. We pray with the liturgy; we have our prayer books. Thus, we recite prayers composed by others, trying to enter into the views and sentiments expressed there, but we also should have free conversations with Our Lord. We should speak to Him during the course of the day, invoking Him for our various activities, lifting up our hearts. St. Therese of the Child Jesus explains in the beginning of her autobiographical manuscripts that she would therein address Our Lord rather than the reader, since she was used to conversing with Him all day long.

In our conversation with the Lord, we should put before Him our joys, our hopes, our aspirations, our temptations, our difficulties, our pains. We express our requests and our repentance, and also our praise, our thanksgiving, and our love. We share with Him, as St. Teresa told us. We need to communicate with the Lord in simplicity and sincerity of heart, hiding nothing, for He sees all. God, in fact, does not need our words, but we do. They actualize our thoughts and arouse our desires.

Contemplatio

Contemplation is a simple gaze toward the Lord, in contrast to meditation, which analyzes, links ideas, and concludes with new ones. Ideas are refractions of truth that we laboriously arrange. One compares reasoning to touching. As the hand of a blind man checks out little by little aspects of a table, so reasoning connects reasons, trying to find continuity. Vision, like contemplation, uncovers the object in one gaze. It looks at the whole table without a special consideration of the parts.

Our prayer or meditation simplifies as our view becomes more comprehensive. In meditation, we begin by getting hold of a facet of Christ's mystery. Then we recognize how this aspect fits in with others. As the blind man eventually discovers the table, reasons in meditation should come together in a simpler view of a whole, in a more contemplative view. Thus, when we have thought much about what it means for God to be Father, we can put a full content into the notion of father, without multiple, separate considerations. The riches we have perceived are present to us in that one word. Also, we delight in that view; we admire it, taste it, and open ourselves to its light. Calling God Father becomes a vibrant, loving regard of a son toward his father.

The more comprehensive view easily leads us to the reality itself. In holy reading and meditation, we should be aware of God's underlying presence. *Oratio* is accomplished in direct attention to the One we are addressing. *Contemplatio* gives itself over to that presence. We then tend to look simply toward Him rather than analyzing attributes. We want contact with this reality, not with abstractions, with the Person, not with this or that quality.

In spite of the term "contemplation," which means to look upon, we do not truly see what we are attentive to. Christian contemplation is an act of faith, faith pushed to such a point that it reposes in an invisible, even inconceivable object.

This act is directed by ideas but looks into the night, stretching to reach its proper object beyond ideas, which are straws in comparison to the divine reality, as St. Thomas famously proclaimed.

St. Thomas tells us that in contemplation, we are moved to look *propter amorem rei visae,* "for love of the object."[16] Contemplation is an act of faith but urged, fixed, by love. It's like a mother's gaze locked upon the baby in her arms. The intellect could be fascinated by a divine attribute, by eternity for example, but our hearts are seized only by a person. God's eternity, for example, here is considered as a passage to God Himself. To love is to let ourselves be attracted by someone. Our reading, meditation, and prayer ushered us into this attraction to God in Himself.

Since we do not yet perfectly possess God, this loving gaze in His direction is one of desire. Contemplative prayer is part of our quest for God. We contemplate, says St. Thomas in the same article, "insofar as by love of God we burn to look upon His beauty," *inquantum aliquis ex dilectione Dei inardescit ad eius pulchritudinem conspiciendum.* Like Moses, we want to behold God's splendor. This prayer is our desire in act. We long to enter more profoundly into God's presence and life.

Thus, although contemplation reposes in the sense that it does not pass from one object to another, it is not static. St. Elizabeth of the Trinity prayed for an immobility that still comes more and more into the mystery: "May I be immovably fixed in Thee, as changeless and calm as though my soul

16 II–II, q.180, a.1.

were already in eternity. . . . May I at every moment penetrate more deeply into the depths of Thy mystery."[17] Like when we regard an engaging painting, we do not necessarily make successive acts, but our look gains insight.

Since we cannot attain God by our own efforts but trust Him to bring us to this fulfillment, the theological virtue of hope enters into this act of contemplation. We have to abandon ourselves to the Father's power. The act of contemplation is an unspoken petition which asks that the divine presence be realized more and more intimately in our heart.

In contemplation, faith reposes in the invisible object, hope desires and trusts to possess the object more and more, and we love the Person. This simple and rich silent communion with God is thus an intense activity of the three theological virtues, but it can leave us without awareness of any short-term effect. Nevertheless, it secretly transforms us as we open to the communication of God's light and love, as we become more and more attuned to Christ. St. Therese felt only dryness in her prayer, yet her mind and heart were charged with God because her prayer was a pure contact with Him. God silently taught her deep truths and conveyed to her the strength to believe in Him, hope in Him, and love Him. Her dry prayer produced a saint and doctor of the Church at a very young age. St. John of the Cross speaks often of this secret knowledge: "In contemplation God teaches the soul very quietly and secretly, without its knowing how, without the sound of words."[18]

---

[17] Quoted in Philipon, *The Spiritual Doctrine of Sister Elizabeth of the Trinity*, 45.

[18] St. John of the Cross, *The Spiritual Canticle*, stanza 39, no. 12.

In this interior night, silence, and solitude, we expose ourselves to God's fiery presence and offer ourselves to His vivifying action. Our hunger for God is purified as we realize more deeply that creatures cannot suffice for our soul. We acquire a better sense of God's transcendent power, wisdom, beauty, and love. We can think again of St. Paul's already-quoted lines: "We all, with unveiled face, beholding the glory of the Lord, are being changed into his likeness from one degree of glory to another" (2 Cor 3:18).

CHAPTER 12

The Practice of Prayer

"Prayer will be perfect when the soul, transformed by love, has all its energies strong and supple, altogether attuned to the delicate touches of the Spirit of God."

—Blessed Marie-Eugène of the Child Jesus[1]

WHEN I STARTED visiting Catholic churches, it was the first time I witnessed people applied at personal prayer. I experienced this especially when these people were in thanksgiving for Holy Communion, but also simply at various times of day. They were calm, all about their business. Often, they were looking at the tabernacle.

We have set forth the bases for prayer—how God is present to us and what some exercises are to turn toward that presence. Here we want to consider how to apply those principles in such a way that they lead us toward God's silence.

Times of prayer

Anyone who is embarking on the adventure of a prayerful life should set up definite times for prayer. If we plan on

1 Blessed Marie-Eugène, *I Want to See God,* 63.

praying only when we have a free moment, we usually will not get around to it. A busy homeschooling mother with several small children wrote to me:

> The largest impediment to finding time for prayer is the fact that we don't practically believe prayer is important enough to do instead of other things; so when push comes to shove, we drop the prayer. Until we are convinced that prayer is the best use of our time, we will have trouble finding time for prayer. We must believe in the power and efficacy of prayer and shape our day around it. It happens that when we start spending more time on other things we fall away from prayer, and the more we fall away, the less we think it is necessary and justify our negligence with worldly prudence. We need a "firm resolution," a commitment in the will; otherwise it is wishful thinking about an ideal that we don't really believe is possible, at least not for us.[2]

The schedule of the monks could be helpful as a reference. It is well-balanced between private prayer and common prayer, between study, prayerful work, and recreation.

On an ordinary day, we rise at 4:50 a.m. I immediately kneel, thank the Lord for the night's sleep, offer my day, and invoke Our Lady, St. Joseph, my guardian angel, and my patron saints. After washing up, we go individually to the church, where we have a little time for prayer to Our Lord in the Blessed Sacrament and then before a statue of Our

---

2 Lisa Korbe, letter to the author, nd.

Lady. At that time, I usually foresee and entrust to Our Lord the various events of the day. Two or three minutes before the Divine Office, we go to our places in the choir and begin recollecting.

At 5:15, the community celebrates the Divine Offices of Matins and then Lauds, made up of psalms with a few hymns and some short readings from Scripture or the Fathers. Low Mass follows. At least fifteen minutes are spent after Mass in thanksgiving for Holy Communion. This thanksgiving, and any mental prayer later in the day, are always followed by another little visit to Our Lady. There is then a short period when monks clean their cell and maybe read for a moment. The next office, that of Prime, is at 8; then the monks go to the chapter room to read part of the Rule, pray for the dead, and commemorate the saints of the next day. A small, quick breakfast—taken standing—follows. The monks then return to their cell for well over an hour of personal Scripture study.

The next Office, Terce, is at 10 a.m., followed by what we call High Mass, which is the sung Mass, celebrated by one priest while the other priests are in choir with the rest of the monks. After High Mass, we say an official prayer together for the day's work. The monks still in formation then have study and classes, while the older monks go about their assigned tasks. The next office, Sext, is at 12:50 p.m., followed by lunch and recreation. At meals, we do not talk but listen to a reading. None is at 2:35, and then more work follows. The monks in formation stop work at 4:15, while the older ones continue until a little after 5. Most monks do their mental prayer at 5:25.

The Office of Vespers at 6 closes the active day. That office is followed by some spiritually enriching study until dinner at 7:30. After dinner, the monks individually pray the Rosary. There is a short spiritual reading in common at 8:25, followed by the Office of Compline. After Compline, the monks pray individually before the Blessed Sacrament and visit Our Lady's statue. Often, then, one prays to one or two of the saints at their various altars. Lights out at 9:45. Before I lie down, I pray for the Church and my country, for all those I dealt with that day, for those I should especially pray for; I sometimes pray for a particular project I am working on. I pray to sleep well so that I may do better tomorrow, and that if I die that night, the Lord take me to Himself. I invoke Our Lady, St. Joseph, my patron saints, my guardian angel, a couple of loved ones who have left this world, and those who especially formed me at Fontgombault.

There are also little instances of prayer during the course of the day when monks pray individually before and after study, together before and after classes, before and after work, before and after meals. We pray the Angelus together three times a day.

For the faithful, here are a few indications for possible times and opportunities of prayer. On rising, pray a moment beside the bed and entrust your day to Our Lord. Lauds or Prime, or some sort of morning prayer, could be prayed then if one has time. It is fruitful to attend daily Mass at least sometimes during the week and receive Holy Communion, followed by a period of thanksgiving.

Everyone should arrange a daily quiet time alone with the Lord for at least fifteen minutes, preferably more like a half-hour. Home-schooling mothers with little children can scarcely find a period for that except by getting up before the others, although there might be a time in the afternoon when the children are napping or busy. One could perhaps do mental prayer of an evening when they are in bed. There may be an adoration chapel with exposition of the Blessed Sacrament where one can sign up for a regular time. It is also profitable to stop for a moment in a church now and then when one is out, to be especially with Our Lord for a moment. One can also pray during a walk in a peaceful place. A little Hour of the Divine Office sometimes fits in during the day. The day should be punctuated by a few prayers together—thanksgiving at meals, the Angelus, perhaps the Divine Mercy chaplet. It is a very good thing to say a prayer together in the morning to consecrate work and studies of the day. Some families read a little at the beginning of a meal, which provides material for enriching and fun conversations.

Mothers sometimes are able to listen to a tape or podcast while they work. If the church nearby has Sunday Vespers, one should usually attend if reasonably possible. It is good to have some nourishing reading in the evening. Many families pray the Rosary together in that part of the day. The family activity should conclude with some prayers in common, such as Compline, including a brief examination of conscience. Before bed, there is a last individual prayer entrusting one's sleep to the Lord.

We monks have a week-long retreat every year when we enter into more silence and prayer. One may be generous and faithful and yet still lose a sense of the depths of the spiritual life. We need time, leisure, and silence to renew or discover deeper views and take stock of our life. It has been recommended that the faithful find one day a month for that, and a few days once a year. Perhaps one could at least go on retreat for a day three or four times a year.

Prayer amidst daily activities

St. Paul tells us that we must pray without ceasing (1 Thes 5:17). This cannot mean that we speak to God all day long, for we are not able always to occupy ourselves directly and totally with Him. We cannot do two things at once; if we try to, both will be poorly done!

To understand what St. Paul has in mind, let us follow a text of Benedict XVI: "Our relationship to God . . . should be present as the bedrock of our soul. In order for that to happen, this relation has to be constantly revived and the affairs of our everyday lives have to be constantly related back to it. . . . This orientation pervasively shaping our whole consciousness, this silent presence of God at the heart of our thinking, our meditation, and our being, is what we mean by 'prayer without ceasing.' . . . This is what prayer really is—being in silent inward communion with God."[3]

The pope speaks of our *relationship to God*—that is, basically, our believing, hoping, and loving attention to Him, our communion with Him. The goal is that this relationship becomes *the bedrock* of our life, the foundation for all our thoughts, wills, and activities. Since we are not alone, we

---

[3] Benedict XVI, *Jesus of Nazareth*, trans. Adrian Walker (New York: Doubleday, 2007), 129.

should not think, will, or act alone. We can attain an awareness of God like the awareness of self. No matter what we are doing, however absorbed we might be in an activity, we are aware of ourselves, and we can be aware of God. With the grace of God, His presence can become familiar and natural to us, and indeed shape our life.

Benedict XVI presents the two elements of what we must do to cultivate that relationship during the day, turning to that presence and referring all to it. I would add, however, that these elements presuppose two conditions. The first condition is that we have regular times of focused prayer, where we can realize that all is in Him, that His gaze is on us, that He dwells in depths of our souls. It is in this quiet prayer that we build up an awareness of God's presence and the habit of being in contact with Him. The second condition is that we have developed an interior silence, with a custody of senses and of heart, so that we do not run after the glittering noise in and around us but pay attention to the supreme reality.

The first element the pope mentions is that our relationship with God needs to be *constantly revived*. The modality of this effort depends on how absorbing our activity is. One could be working on a computer, studying, or working in the garden. Our activity could be talking with someone. In any type of work or activity, however, it is possible to recollect oneself in a free moment from time to time or at least cast a quick interior glance toward the Lord. We now are exhorted to swerve away from the computer screen every twenty minutes for the good of our eyes; surely, we could do the same for the good of our soul. We can apply our attention to Our Lord or Our Lady, or our guardian angel or a saint for a moment during a short halt. We should withdraw into our interior cell with God. A quick interior gaze is always possible. If we are outside, we can admire the beauty of the countryside or yard as part of His glory, as shining out from Him. It is good to have a crucifix or holy image nearby that we can look toward.

Little ready-made invocations during the day are useful to keep us from falling spiritually asleep; they oblige us to make an effort, warm our affections, intensify attention to the invisible, collect our intentions toward our true end. These aspirations keep alive a spirit of prayer. One can find beautiful invocations in the psalms: "To Thee I lift up my soul." "I thirst for Thee, O my God." "With my whole heart I want to seek Thee, let me not wander from Thy word." You can make up your own as well; for example: "Lord, you are the way, the truth, and the life." "Be with me, Lord, or I will fall." One can have one ready for certain circumstances. To keep myself from cussing when something unwanted would occur, I used to exclaim: "I will bless the Lord in all things."

If we are performing some simple, calm activity, such as gardening, we might take up some word from our reading or from the liturgy that we bring to mind. We could resume some thoughts we had during prayer in the morning or sweetly ponder one of Christ's mysteries and words.

The second element Pope Benedict mentioned is that everything that happens, everything we encounter, everything we do must be *constantly related back* to our relationship with God. We do not have always to turn away from our activity. We are to recognize in the most humble, familiar, and even bothersome tasks a presence and a higher meaning. Our interior consideration should support and enlighten all our occupations. It recognizes them as instruments and signs of God. We prefer reality to our little fantasies, we consent to it with gratitude for what it brings, and we respond to its calls.

We try to be attentive to God's action in little things and events of the day, in our encounters with people. We live in a tranquil watchfulness of the heart for His action and will. We look on reality and other people with Our Lord. One can thus remain in communion with God and live in the "sacrament of the present moment"; that is, we find Him in the sensible covering of the present circumstances.

If we act in faith, hope, and charity, we will look at all in God's light, trust in Him, and strive to be His friend in our activity. This means that we seek to do God's will. We offer our work as a prayer, and we rely on God so we can do our work well. If we think about Him but turn from His will, we are, in fact, running from Him. It's by the will that our contact with God is sure and solid. As John of the Cross wrote: "God communicates Himself most to that soul that has progressed farthest in love; namely, that has its will in closest conformity with the will of God."[4] Jesus said that He and the Father would come to those who do His will. Communion in their presence is a reward for fidelity and love, not for fancy thoughts. Brother Lawrence of the Resurrection wrote: "Do everything for the love of God, use every

4 St. John of the Cross, *Ascent* II, ch. 5, no. 4.

one of our duties to show that love to Him and maintain His presence in us by the communion of our hearts with Him."[5]

Then, indeed, our relationship with God *shapes our consciousness* and is *at the heart of our thinking*. Our thoughts, desires, and actions should flow from this deep communion with God. All our life becomes a culture of this presence. There is a *silent, inward communion with God* all day long. There is then no major difference in that sense with mental prayer, no big barrier between the two.

We grow into continual relationship with God not by nervous tension or by trying to feel God. If one has the intention of doing all according to God, for God, by God, and with God, if one seeks Him in that way, one will find Him. If we, day by day calmly, faithfully, and humbly strive to live in His presence, He will draw us into it. If we are really seeking God's will, doing all things as well as we should for Him, then we are attentive to Him, even if active attention to Him is not possible for long periods. We trust that even if some activities seem to take away our prayerful recollection, Our Lord is using them to bring us to Him, that they are the best for us here and now. "In everything God works for good with those who love him," wrote St. Paul (Rom 8:28).

We are now going to consider some formal prayer times, especially in their relation to contemplation and silence. A desert father said that if you pray only at those particular times, you do not pray much, but if you do not have such focused times, you will not pray at all. We see in the Gospel

---

5 Brother Lawrence of the Resurrection, *The Practice of the Presence of God*, trans. Robert J. Edmonson (Orleans, MA: Paraclete Press, 1985), 146.

that Our Lord was in deep contact with His Father at all times and often wanted, needed, to go off to pray to His Father alone.

Preparation for focused prayer

What one calls *remote* preparation for prayer consists mostly in elements we just considered: doing God's will during the day, practicing virtue, cultivating detachment and interior silence, and remembering His presence. If we have had a faithful, recollected day in the midst of our activities, we will be ready more easily to direct attention to God when we have the leisure. The coals will be warm, easy to set aflame. Even a couple of efforts of recollection during the day will be rewarded when we come to prayer. We pray according to what we are: If our heart is pure and we are really seeking God, our prayer will be real and living. On the other hand, all means for prayer will be without success if our life is on the margin of God, full of desires that divert us from Him.

There is also *immediate* preparation for prayer. We need to drop any other preoccupation as we approach prayer. We cannot expect to go directly from an absorbing or exciting activity to deep, recollected prayer. Often, we have to calm the imagination and emotions from the clutter and clamor so that our mind and heart can turn to our invisible and silent Lord. Monks have what is called the "station" before Holy Mass and Vespers, where each takes his place in the cloister for two or three minutes to let go of our other concerns so we can be attentive to God.

Sometimes, it is good, as we approach prayer, to call to mind its importance and remind ourselves that we need to abandon this time for God. We entrust our other activities to His hands and ask for help so that we will be able to apply ourselves totally to Him in this time of prayer.

Positively, we begin orienting our faculties toward the Lord. We awaken our faith in this God who is more intimate to us than we are to ourselves and yet inhabits an inaccessible light. We remember that He sees our hidden thoughts and desires. We strive, therefore, to put away our masks and be our true and deep self before Him. We resolve to do our best during this time of prayer, to really listen to God, and be open to His truth and to what He asks of us. A prayer before the Divine Office applies well to preparation for any type of prayer: "Open, Lord, my mouth so that I bless your holy Name; purify my heart from all vain, perverted, or wandering thoughts; enlighten my mind, inflame my affections; so that I worthily, attentively, and devotedly pray."

We cannot, before each little prayer during the day, spend time recollecting to this extent, but we need to acquire the habit of quickly putting aside our current activities and turning to the Lord. If we are praying at home, it helps recollection if one reserves for prayer some little quiet corner with a crucifix and an image of Our Lady, maybe one of St. Joseph or of saints you are particularly close to.

Now, let us consider major moments of formal prayer.

Liturgy in general

I want to mention a couple of principles concerning liturgical life, then we will look over praying the Divine Office and Holy Mass.

The liturgy is the Church's full and official prayer, the prayer of the High Priest in His Church, of Christ's entire mystical body united to its Head. It strives to give honor and praise to God and help us grow closer to Him. In the Church's worship, we have God's own inspired word as well as prayers grown out of the Church's meditation and experience of encounters with God. The liturgy is a school of prayer. The Church teaches us how to speak to Our Lord. In all liturgy, we find the four "steps" mentioned previously, in varying degrees. There is *oratio,* of course, and also a fair amount of *lectio,* with some *meditatio,* and opening to *contemplatio.*

The faithful of old lived very much by the liturgy. Liturgy pervaded their lives like the radiance of Christ on Mt. Tabor shining out. It lifted up all the little activities of the day. We need to restore that habit in our lives, thinking more in terms of the feasts, fasts, and saints' days than of the secular calendar, and praying around the Church's worship. A family should have traditions that follow the liturgical year.[6]

The *Catechism* presents the liturgy's sanctifying role and its link to private prayer: "The Liturgy proclaims, makes present and communicates the mystery. Personal prayer internalizes and assimilates the liturgy during and after."[7]

---

6 For all this, see Dom Proper Gueranger's *Liturgical Year.*

7 No. 2655.

The liturgy *proclaims, makes present, and communicates* Christ's mystery of salvation. The liturgy brings us the seven sacraments, but it is itself sacramental, effectuating Christ's mystery in us if we are open to grace. Liturgy is not, first of all, catechism but a work of art in which mysteries are reenacted so that we enter into them. Thus, in Advent, we relive with the Old Testament the awaiting of Christ, then in Christmastime, the mystery of the Incarnation with Christ's childhood. We begin His public life in His baptism and go with Him into the desert. We listen to Him in His preaching; we are called with the apostles to follow Jesus; we witness His glory at the Transfiguration. We are there in the moving moments of the Last Supper for the gift of the Eucharist. We are with Mary at the foot of the cross and rejoice in the riches of His resurrection and the coming of the Spirit. During the time after Pentecost, we are in His presence as our King, and we participate in the special features of one saint after another.

The liturgical year, going successively through the seasons, the fasts, and celebrations is a masterpiece. Year by year, we intensify our participation in these mysteries; we deepen our sense of the Incarnation, of Redemption, of Our Lady's role in our salvation. The Christian mystery is greater than what we can embrace at once, but living the different aspects tends to establish in us a synthetic view of the whole. We begin to see the oneness shining through the parts. Each mystery has its special teaching and beauty, and these teachings and beauties converge, entering into relation to one another. Through them all, we naturally advance toward the Absolute Mystery of God's rich silence. Celebrating these mysteries leads us to a silent, intuitive gaze on Christ's infinite treasures.

We are to *internalize and assimilate* the mystery, says the *Catechism*. We reflect on the texts and make our own the teaching and the prayers. Much of our personal prayer life normally and naturally revolves around the liturgical year. The Church helps the assimilation as it chooses among Scripture and texts written by Christian authors, bringing them together to enlighten one by the other. We have seen how this assimilation is also assisted by the fact that the mystery is richly and beautifully presented so that we are led to the interior attitude by which we should respond to God's initiatives.

The Divine Office

The Divine Office, or the Liturgy of the Hours, consecrates the parts of the day. It is the religious' and cleric's bread and butter, their regular contact with God during the day. It fosters an atmosphere of prayer all day long, cultivating our habit of being in relationship with God. A priest friend told me once that when a priest falls away, the first step is nearly always abandoning the Office. It is good when the faithful can also participate in this prayer of the Church.

The Office nourishes our contact with the liturgical year. The antiphons, the hymns, and the readings basically follow the seasons and the feasts. The hymns are beautiful, some more devotional, some more doctrinal. Here are lines, for example, from the moving hymn of Vespers for the feast of the Holy Name of Jesus:

Jesus, of sweet memory,
Joy of our heart,
But above honey and all
Is the sweetness of your presence.

Nothing can be sung so sweet
Nothing heard more joyful,
Nothing more delightful to think,
Than Jesus the Son of God.

Jesus, the hope of the repentant,
How devoted you are to those who ask,
How good to those who seek,
What will you be for those who find?

No tongue is able to say,
Not letters express,
Only those who have experienced can believe
What it is to love Jesus.

Jesus, be our joy,
Who is to be our reward;
May our glory be in you,
For ever and ever.[8]

The Divine Office is substantially made of psalms, a rich and sure path to God. When we pray the psalms regularly, we spontaneously adopt their views on creation, on history, on life, on good and evil, on God and man. Father Louis Bouyer proclaims this to be a sweet, simple way to rise from created beauties to God's beauty: "If the Bible is a world

8 My translation.

brought into the perspective of the divine plan, the psalms fit into it as a microcosm which condenses all its beauty in the translucid crystal of their praise. The splendor of the psalms will guide . . . spontaneously and better than any laborious industry along the journey one must make from those beauties which are only a reflection to the Beauty beyond compare of the one and only Source."[9]

The psalms also inscribe in us the habit of presenting everything to God, of living all events in reference to Him, of being simple with God by opening up to Him the details of our life, crying out to Him from our heart, finding Him in everything. "You are great, you made the world, I'm miserable, help me!" they say. They give depth, intensity, and amplitude to our essential sentiments before God, to our pain, our joy, our worry, our aspirations, our repentance, our trust, our gratitude. A well-known French poet tells us: "The psalms express in exquisite terms the relation that our heart strives to bond with the supreme, faithful, living God, praying he be our protector and friend."[10]

Listen to some of these verses: "To you I lift up my eyes, O you who are enthroned in the heavens!" "From where does my help come? My help comes from the LORD who made heaven and earth." "O LORD, my God, I cry for help by day; I cry out in the night before you, incline your ear to my cry! O LORD, why do you cast me off? Why do you hide your face from me?" (Ps 123:1; 121:2; 88:1–2, 14) How

---

[9] Louis Bouyer, *The Meaning of Monastic Life* (London: Burns and Oates, 1955), 188.

[10] A. de Lamartine, quoted in *Les Psaumes*, Louis Jacquet (Belgium: Duculot, 1975), 159. My translation.

movingly, beautifully they express yearning for God: "O God, you are my God, I seek you, my soul thirsts for you; my flesh faints for you, as in a dry and weary land where no water is" (63:1) They praise him: "Make a joyful noise to the Lord, all the earth; sing the glory of his name; give him glorious praise! Say to God, 'How awesome are your deeds'" (66:1–3). They hope: "For God alone my soul waits in silence; from him comes my salvation" (62:1). And on and on. There are no lines of prayer like the ones found in the psalms.

The psalm is a ladder to God we use to lift our heart. We need to let the text direct our gaze toward God, keeping the underlying meaning of the psalm present, and then savoring here and there a particular phrase. We usually need to be somewhat active with the psalms because, in reciting someone else's text, we can easily let the words fly by without paying attention to their meaning, especially if the text is in Latin. The New Testament accomplishes the Old, and we should transpose the psalms fairly often into Christ's mysteries. For example, psalm 119 celebrates the Law, and we know that the New Testament is the law of love. Also, many of the psalms deal with Israel's struggles with other peoples or with the psalmist's enemies, but we can shift that into our Christian life as battles against evil and the devil.

We can appropriate the psalms as our own desires and joys, and also pray them in the person of the Church. In Advent, I sometimes pray them with Mary and Joseph, who sweetly knew the secret that the hopes of the psalms were being fulfilled with the Child Mary was expecting. I pray them with Christ during Holy Week, as He is confronted with the attacks of evil. In general, throughout the year, I pray them in and with the Church, in Christ as Head of the Church, according to my needs and desires, but even more to the Church's, as she lifts her heart up to the Lord in praise, thanksgiving, and desire, but also interceding notably for her persecuted and suffering members.

Those who recite the psalms often need to renew their acquaintance with them by taking the time to study them, read a commentary on them, meditate on them.

Holy Mass

All the Church's life flows from the Holy Sacrifice of the Mass because it is the presentation and communication of the Easter mystery, which is the source and center of all the rest of Christian life. All Church activity leads up to and flows from the celebration of Holy Mass.

Holy Mass carries a high *lectio* with the solemn actualization of God's word; it is a *meditatio,* notably through the various chants, and it is a summit of *oratio* as we pray in union with Christ in His sacrifice and with the Church. It naturally leads to an eminent *contemplatio* as we adore Our Lord in His Sacrifice and enter into communion with Him. Holy Mass is often the main place where one really learns to pray, especially to adore and contemplate.

The silent, recollected Low Mass concentrates on the sacrifice and the Real Presence. The sung High Mass brings in more adornment to help us penetrate the mystery of the season and the day. For pieces that are sung, it is advisable to give a glance over the whole before it begins, then follow it word by word in the chant with this whole in mind. It is helpful sometimes to think about how the music emphasizes this or that view, why the melody ascends here and goes down there to underline an aspect of the text. For those who sing, if they do so in a prayerful way, the chant will have its proper effect of inclining others to prayer.

We awaken our faith before the tremendous event in which we are about to participate. We have to think because we do not see the mystery. The Introit opens the celebration with a pertinent view. The Church, for example, so fittingly launches the new liturgical year in the first Sunday of Advent: "To You I lift up my soul." "I have risen and I am still with You," we say with Our Lord to the Father on Easter morning. "A great sign appeared in Heaven," we sing at the feast of Our Lady's Assumption. In the Kyrie, with great reverence, we lift up our intentions; I usually pray these invocations in a general way for all the Church's needs at Low Mass, but attach an intention to each Kyrie in the High Mass—for the Church, for the monastery, for my country, for my family and friends, for those who live around the monastery, for special intentions of the time. Then we often praise the Lord in the Gloria, notably for His beauty: *gratias agimus tibi propter magnam gloriam tuam*. We join with the priest as he prays the Collect—that is, a prayer that brings all our intentions into its petition. They are rich and fruitful for meditation. We should then be disposed to hear what God has to say to us in the first reading.

The chants after the reading usually take up verses of psalms in such a way that we consider them more in depth and better taste them; they ordinarily go back over the reading or the theme of the day. These chants aim at achieving a common state of recollection, of receptive silence, for listening to Jesus in the Gospel. For the Gospel, we stand out of respect, which is a sort of prayer with our body. All has built up to hearing the very words of Jesus. What does He want to teach us in and through this proclamation?

The meditation on God and Christ's mystery in the chants and readings of the first part of the Mass leads to awe before God and so prepares us for the more silent and contemplative adoration of Christ's sacrifice. In the Offertory, we offer bread and wine as a symbol of all our labors being lifted up by Christ to the Father, and even more as an expression of our recognition that all should be for God's glory, that all belongs to Him. We place ourselves and those for whom we are praying on the paten and in the chalice and unite ourselves to Christ as He offers Himself to the Father.

In the Preface, we praise and thank Our Lord in union with the whole angelic company as we begin the central act of the sacred mysteries. The Sanctus proclaims that nothing is comparable to God, and then we enter into the bright cloud. It is understandable to want to hear the priest's prayers in the Canon to pray along with him, but the silent Canon marks the action as especially sacred.

We can silently pray with the priest during the Canon. My master of novices suggested for the High Mass that, with the Virgin Mary, we spiritually place ourselves in adoration at the foot of the cross. For the Low Mass, he recommended that we follow the liturgical text the priest prays. At our High Mass, where I usually do not celebrate, I sometimes pray the Canon, but rather in my own words. I sometimes discreetly pray some of the Rosary, the decade on the Agony during the Offertory, and one on the Crucifixion during the Canon. In any case, we should strive to enter into Christ's sentiments, into His passage to the Father beyond all created things. We pray for all our loved ones, for those whose intentions we especially carry, and for the Church. We priests, when we are celebrating, must be very aware of the One to whom we are speaking, as well as what we are saying, of the meaning of our gestures. Witnesses tell us how carefully St. Padre Pio pronounced the words of Holy Mass.

All builds up to the Consecration. This passage from the novel *Judith's Marriage* describes the impressions at that moment of a young non-Catholic lady attending her first Mass. The bell of the Consecration has just rung:

> It was the consecration, the Real Presence. There fell a silence like the primeval silence before ever the world came to be. It was colossal. . . . It had nothing to do with particular theological arguments; it concerned the whole orientation of man's outlook. Was religion centered around man or was it centered around God? . . . The Mass gave a peremptory answer: the religious act was theocentric; it was an act of adoration. All those strange folk . . . quite unconsciously were attempting to adore. The object of their adoration, too, was perfectly clear: it was the Real Presence.[11]

[11] Bryan Houghton, *Judith's Marriage* (Evanston, IL: Credo House, 1987), 20–21.

Having united with Christ in His sacrifice, we are ready for the third part of the Mass, where we receive the fruits of the sacrifice. First, thanks to Christ's sacrifice, we are able to pray with Him to God as to our Father. Then, we ask for mercy from the Lamb of God as we prepare to approach Him. Finally, in Holy Communion, we nourish our union with the Incarnate Son. We receive Christ in the intimacy of our soul. The priest distributing Holy Communion should gaze with Christ on each faithful he encounters at the rail; he should deliberately and consciously want to give Our Lord to the person before him.

After Mass, in the silence of thanksgiving, we come to Jesus to take on His sweet yoke and find rest in Him. We have deep respect and gratitude for this Lord who deigns to come to us. I was taught in the novitiate that this is not the time for intercession but for adoration. We go beyond all creatures in faith, hope, and charity, letting Christ invade us, grasp us, and assimilate us in such a way that He transforms us into His living images. We remember that this Host was offered in sacrifice, and we pray that Our Lord take us with Himself to the Father. We are in communion with Christ, with all the Trinity, and with all those who are in communion with the Trinity. Sometimes, I adore in communion with the others who have just received Holy Communion at that Mass.

This Presence in us may well overwhelm any thought. My Father Master suggested that if attention slackened, we slowly, sweetly recite some prayer we know well, such as the Gloria of the Mass, or an Our Father, as we adhere to Our Lord. We could pray a *Magnificat* in thanksgiving with Our

Lady. We do not try to excite our feelings, but we rely on faith. Feelings will come on their own. We pray that our communion with God be constant during the day, that we continue to be attentive to Him, that He be with us.

Confession

In all liturgy but especially in the sacraments, Christ is present, touching us in order to give us participation in His life. When we attend a baptism, a wedding, or a priestly ordination, we should not be so taken by the social event that we forget to awaken our faith, to look to the invisible, and participate in the prayers. We must be attentive to what is really happening. Baptism and Confirmation are often accomplished with some liturgy, with readings and prayers. Marriage and Ordination usually take place at Holy Mass. Confession is more distinct from such liturgical celebrations. It should, nevertheless, be an intense moment of prayer. Since we come so often to this sacrament, I think it would be worthwhile to say a word on it.

Everyone should accomplish a daily examination in the light and love of our Father who wants only our good. The monks at Clear Creek do a two-to-three-minute examination of conscience in the evening. We recognize where during the day we have been unfaithful to Our Lord, when we acted against our conscience, and were not good children for our Father. We regret damaging our friendship with Him. We repent having not been loyal to Him and now want to return fully to Him. For this to be a real regret, we must be resolved to amend our lives. We have to have a firm resolution to avoid any mortal sin. We need to want to correct our venial sins, avoid them more and more, and take measures to do so. Sorrow for our sins does not necessarily have an echo in the sensibility. It is in the will; it is a deliberate choice. With this regular examination of conscience, it will be easy to prepare immediately for confession when the time comes. We monks are taught that one should always be ready to go to confession. We need to approach confession with a greater awareness of what it is—namely, a sacrament in which we encounter the Lord and which communicates to us the power of His cross and resurrection. We need recollection, with a view enlivened by faith, hope, and charity. We must remember that the priest is a veil for Christ's presence and an instrument for His action. Our gaze should go beyond the priest to the Lord.

We come to this sacrament to draw from the source of purity and mercy, to put our sins in contact with Christ's purifying blood. We present ourselves as we are to our Father, like a leper before the one who can heal him. We remember that He sees the bottom of our soul, but also that He is the merciful Father in whom we trust. We believe in His love. We tell all, courageously, simply. We want to put everything in God's light so that He will heal us. We must not mask over the more humiliating sins—it is probably best to mention them first in confession. We speak to the priest, but as the intermediary for Our Lord. The priest has special graces for his advice and exhortation, and we should listen and try to put into practice what he says. In the absolution, he is a pure instrument of God's grace.

When we leave the confessional, we must not throw ourselves immediately back into ordinary preoccupations but hold onto our recollection for a moment. It is best to do the penance right away. We show the sincerity of our regret by the earnestness of our penance. When we offend a friend, even after forgiveness, we want to make it up to him, give him a special token of our affection, prove to him we really do regret having offended him. We can never compensate completely for the offense against the divine majesty, but our satisfactions united to Christ's become worthy. A sacramental penance has special value.

Rosary

The Rosary, over the past eight centuries, has proven itself. It is a gift from God to His Church, an excellent, simple way to learn to pray and even attain to contemplative prayer. We learn to live our joys, our luminous moments, and our pains with the Lord in hope of eternal glory. It is said that Padre Pio prayed Rosaries continually. I have known monks that prayed several each day. When I have been able to do so, I have always profited markedly.

We monks of Clear Creek pray the Rosary generally in the evening after dinner, often while strolling in the cloister or the garden. It is, for us, rather a relaxing, enjoyable moment with Our Lady. We usually pray the Rosary alone, partly because we have so much common prayer.

The Rosary teaches us to live in Mary's company, to sweetly think about our heavenly mother, and better realize how near she is and attentive to us. During our Rosaries, we should strive to enter into a communion of thought and love with her. If we are attentive to Our Lady, she will teach us her ways of looking on the Father, on her Son, on the mystery at hand, on our neighbor, and all things.

While reciting our Paters and Aves in the Rosary, with Our Lady, we consider Christ's mysteries. We know the Our Father and the Hail Mary very well; we have reflected on the meaning of the words. We can then lift them up into our attention to the mystery of each decade, with a flexible awareness of the words that become like a rhythmed and relaxing background to the mystery. This does not mean that we reason much. We look toward the scene, with maybe a thought or an image as our perspective, relying on Our Lady to help us consider and taste the mystery's beauty. For example, in the Annunciation, we could have in mind Mary's deep simplicity in responding to the angel and try to say a total *ecce* with her. We could think about Christ's love in coming to us in the Incarnation. Little by little, as we say our beads over and over again, Mary will teach us about the great mysteries of her Son. We will draw closer to them both.

Mental prayer

I use the term "mental prayer" in the sense of a quiet, undisturbed time set apart to be alone with the Lord, totally occupied with Him, heart to heart, whatever be the style of prayer, more vocal, more meditative, or more contemplative. We are there to share intimately with the One who we know loves us, St. Teresa told us. Monks of former times had no official daily period prescribed for this private prayer. They spent the day celebrating the Divine Office and Holy Mass, in prayerful reading of Scripture and the Fathers, living in God's presence, pondering His words all day long, and turning to Him more intensely from time to time. Dom Delatte wrote: "[The ancients] thought that the word of God, of the saints, and of the liturgy, meditated and repeated without ceasing, had a sovereign power of withdrawing the soul from anxious self-consideration, in order to possess the soul wholly and introduce us into the mystery of God and His Christ."[12] The Church and monastic tradition have nevertheless recognized that it is prudent to require at least a continuous half hour a day consecrated to mental prayer.

In the novitiate, I received no instruction on a method for this prayer. My Father Master told us that if we are really seeking God in our life, then our prayer will be real; we can go about it naturally, as it were. He wanted to leave the Holy Spirit free to work with us, for only the Holy Spirit can teach us to pray. I was even instructed to do during this quiet time what I was attracted to—like a child in a candy store, my master of novices said, who chooses what he likes!

We were, however, given a few directives. We could reflect, for example, on a couple of lines from Scripture or from the liturgy. We would read a little if need be, without turning our prayer time into a reading. We might recall a line or two we had appreciated during our earlier reading time. But if we were content simply to be in God's presence, like a puppy at the foot of his master or a lizard warming in the sun, so much the better. That is, from the very first of our time in

[12] Dom Paul Delatte, *Commentary on the Rule*, 308.

the monastery, we were invited to enter into contemplative prayer if the Lord led us there.

When we monks come to our mental prayer, after so much praying of the Divine Office and a good amount of *lectio divina*, after the celebration of Holy Mass and reception of Holy Communion, and living in God's presence during the day, we find it easy to pay attention to God. Most formed monks in my monastery come to their prayer time in later afternoon or early evening, mainly to actuate their presence to the Lord, probably with an idea or two they are pondering, or some liturgical text or a line from Scripture.

For the faithful, supposing that one has half an hour for quiet prayer sometime during the day, one could mainly or at first engage in spiritual reading, stopping a little sometimes to reflect and pray, but generally going forward in the text. Or one might read at the beginning of mental prayer, then think and pray about it for the remaining time. Or again, especially if one has reading at another time, one could rather aim at meditating from the first, drawing from a reading just what is needed for reflection and prayer, and taking up the text again only when that thought has been completed or if one falls into daydreaming or inertia.

I might suggest, as an ongoing basis for the meditation, the Sermon on the Mount, or the Lord's farewell discourse at the Last Supper, Romans chapter eight, or the first epistle of St. John. There are, of course, many other possible scriptural passages. One can also reflect on a few phrases from a spiritual writer. Some writings are more apt for meditation than others. For a while, I used *The Imitation of Christ*, whose dense phrases lend themselves well to prayerful meditation.

Our Father Abbot at Fontgombault used to reflect especially on the rich Collects of the Mass, which furnish so much to think about; for example: "Almighty and everlasting God, give to us an increase of Faith, Hope, and Charity: and that we may deserve to obtain what Thou dost promise, make us love what Thou dost command."[13] I especially like the intense invocations of the Litany of the Sacred Heart: "Heart of Jesus, of infinite majesty, house of God and gate to Heaven, full of goodness and love, center of all hearts . . ." In my first years as a monk, I found it fruitful to meditate on prayers from saints such as Elizabeth of the Trinity's famous invocation of the Three Divine Persons, or St. Augustine's "Lord, to know myself, to know Thee."

No matter what we use or do, in such a time of prayer, we should be attentive to the Lord. We meditate in His presence, and we pray to Him. We enter more into the domain of contemplative prayer when our regard is rather on God's presence than on our thoughts or words. The *Catechism* tells us that "contemplative prayer seeks him 'whom my soul loves.' . . . In this inner prayer we can still meditate, but our attention is fixed on the Lord Himself."[14] We do not necessarily feel Him, but by faith, we dive into His reality. As a last word, let's consider more closely how to exercise ourselves in a silent contact with the Lord.

---

[13] Thirteenth Sunday after Pentecost.

[14] No. 2709.

From silence to Silence

There are three conditions for this deep contact with God: interior silence, desire, and habit of purity in our exercise of the theological virtues. These conditions correspond to the first three parts of this book.

Interior silence

In the first part of the book, we recognized we must be receptive. Louis Lavelle gives an account of our needed attitude: "God is hidden. . . . He escapes all the words which try to designate him and grasp him. . . . He reveals Himself to us only in solitude, in the deepest and secret domain of our heart. He requires of us this perfect interior silence . . . where there remains of myself only a pure attention to his presence. . . . This religious silence testifies that the soul can't do anything except receive. It is respect, recollection, expectation."[15]

We have considered how *God is hidden*, how no idea of Him is adequate. St. John of the Cross wrote: "You do well, o soul, to seek him ever as one hidden, for you exalt God and approach very near him when you consider him higher and deeper than anything you can reach."[16] Anything that we can clearly seize is not Him. And He is deeper in us than we can dig.

Yet He *reveals Himself* if we have a *perfect interior silence*, a *pure attention*, "*respect, recollection, expectation.*" We strive to enter into the place of thickest silence in ourselves, beyond

---

15 Louis Lavelle, *La Parole*, 153.

16 St. John of the Cross, *The Spiritual Canticle,* first stanza, no. 12.

any multiplicity, any thoughts of this or that, in order to come in contact with His mystery. This attentive silence presupposes the realization in our heart that God indeed transcends all, that He is the absolute. It is a profound awe in His presence, an awe that knows that any contact with God can only be a gift. With this *pure attention*, we become something like the eternal Son in a pure relation to the Father. The heart of the attitude is looking and listening, with mind and heart ready to receive God's action.

Desire

Our interior silence is enriched by meditations, as we tried to do in our second part. We know much about the One who is present. We know that He is our Creator, from whom we come and on whom we depend. He is of surpassing beauty and love, goodness and wisdom. By grace, He is our Father, who calls us into His own life. This knowledge arouses our desire for Him. We are from Him and going back to Him; we want to be all His, we want to be His friend, His loving child.

As we read, Fr. Haggerty describes the primordial role of desire in contemplation: "Contemplative prayer has its source in an intense passion for God. The strain of wanting God begins to permeate a life, overwhelming other desires. . . . Prayer becomes a steady, unrelenting passion for someone not possessed, not near enough to be permanently enjoyed, someone who disappears again into hiding after every closer approach."[17]

---

[17] Haggerty, *Contemplative Provocations*, 63.

Purity of the theological virtues

In the third part, we considered the theological virtues, which aim directly at God. To attain Him, we must consent to go beyond all creatures. In the night of faith, the silence of hope, and the solitude of divine love, we know, trust, and desire the One we are looking toward. We know that He is there, that He lovingly holds us in being right now and perceives the depths of our hearts. We fix our trusting, desiring gaze on Someone who fixes His loving, fatherly gaze on us.

While always fostering these conditions, when we come to the time of our prayer, we should normally, at least part of the time, make an effort to be simply with the Lord, practice looking toward Him. For years, much of my time of prayer consisted in considering God's presence in my soul in order better to realize it and reach a silent adherence, like with someone in the room whom we do not see. Our meditation and prayer can be like eyes looking at someone's silhouette in the dark, where we try to make out the features of the beloved person; our contemplation may be like a bride who seeks in her loved one's eyes his tenderness, tries to glimpse the bottom of his heart.

Instead of reasoning, we could have one simple, rich thought, such as "I must diminish so that He increase," or "Blessed are the pure in heart for they shall see God," where we mainly let the thought resonate in our soul as we look in the direction of Our Lord. We might take up another thought in a few moments to nurture that gaze. We can make simple acts which sustain our attitude, maybe just murmur from time to time an invocation, such as "my Lord and my God." As the *Catechism* says: "Words in this prayer are not speeches; they are like kindling that feeds the fire of love."[18] A witness who happened to sleep near to him once said that St. Francis prayed all night, only saying from time to time "My God and my all."

If we begin generally to pray without meditation, to seek a silent contact almost from the first of our quiet time in order to be sure that we are not being lazy or taking the wrong path, one can refer to two main signs: we are content to being silently alone with the Lord, and we are faithful in our life. Our Father Abbot of Fontgombault gave as main criteria of fidelity that we are truly obedient and given over to fraternal charity. We indeed must judge the quality of prayer not by sensible effects but by its influence on our activity. We could check if we are growing in the fruits of the Spirit—charity, joy, peace, patience, kindness, goodness, generosity, gentleness, faithfulness, modesty, self-control, and chastity—linked to an increasing hunger for God. If we are, then we can proceed peacefully in dark silence and abandon ourselves to a simple attention to the Presence.

Eventually, with the theological virtues especially blossoming in contemplative prayer through the gifts of the Holy Spirit, we can become aware of our participation in God's life. In any case, in this silent expectation, we know that the life is in us. The Father is there giving birth to the Son, and the two are breathing the Spirit of love. The *Catechism* describes contemplative prayer as an involvement with each of the Three Divine Persons: "Contemplative prayer is

[18] No. 2717.

silence . . . or silent love. . . . In this silence, unbearable to the outer man, the Father speaks to us his Incarnate word. . . . In this silence the Spirit of adoption enables us to share in the prayer of Jesus." Fr. Marie-Eugène explained to us that we should turn to where the Father gives birth to the Son in us. Dom Guillerand spoke similarly. After alluding to a "bed of silence" in our soul, he wrote: "It is from this ground that is born for each the One who is the eternal Word. All our vocation is there: to listen to the one who begets this Word, and live by this begetting. The Word proceeds from Silence, and we strive to attain it in its Principle."[19] All these authors are doubtless thinking of John of the Cross's line quoted in our preface about hearing God's eternal Word in the silence of our soul.

We listen to the Father saying the Son, but the *Catechism* text also tells us that the Spirit unites us to the Son's prayer, gives us to share His filial relationship to the Father. Something like the Son, we come from the Father, and we go back to Him in Christ by the Holy Spirit breathed into our souls by the Father and the Son. Thus, indeed, we participate in Christ's prayer, by the Holy Spirit, as both John Paul II and Benedict XVI taught us to do in the texts at the beginning of this part. In union with the Son and by the movement of the Holy Spirit, we cry out "Abba, Father."

With this silent, loving gaze toward the mysterious Presence, we are on the threshold of the Sanctuary of Silence. God may lift us up into the experience of the contact with Him or even of our participation in the life of the Three

---

[19] Dom Augustin Guillerand, *They Speak by Silences,* 5.

Persons, but on our side, the main work is to expect God, like a mother who waits for her son to come home late in the evening, like the father of the prodigal son intent on the point in the road where his son might appear. Our prayer is the cry of someone calling for his friend in the silence and solitude of the night. St. Teresa of Calcutta, for example, in the last years of her life, totally given over to the service of her neighbor, was one pure yearning for God. All our life is this expectation of God, which finds its most intense and pure moment in focused, contemplative prayer.

Conclusion

Entering the Sanctuary

"You lavished your fragrance, I gasped, and now I pant for you; I tasted you, and I hunger and thirst; you touched me, and I burned for your peace."

—St. Augustine[1]

With meditation and contemplative prayer, we can dimly perceive, at least from the outside, some of the beauty of the Sanctuary of Silence. We can perhaps guess how splendid the inside might be with the sunlight shining through the stained-glass windows, how ornate the stone and woodwork could be, how handsome the colors of the tile. Sometimes a peek in the obscurity enables us to distinguish some features. Perhaps we distantly hear a hint of music coming from the Sanctuary, and we catch a little of the fragrance of incense.

The goal of our interior silence is that the soul can listen and receive but also concentrate all its energies with the help of God into perfect love so that God be loved in and above all things. The soul, then, without distraction, can yearn with all its being for Him. The soul turned totally toward God aspires to Him in faith, hope, and love. As the divine light,

1 St. Augustine, *Confessions* X, ch. 27.

the fire of God's gaze, penetrates more and more the soul, as the soul becomes pure, it understands better and better His infinite beauty and also her own malice and nothingness. Like someone in purgatory, in the night, in the silence and solitude, the soul cries out to its God. Let me quote St. Teresa describing a high experience of contemplative prayer, a rapture:

> All at once the soul feels within itself an indescribable longing for almighty God. . . . Although, at those times, God seems to be very far removed from the soul, yet often He reveals to it His supreme glories in a manner so extraordinary as to surpass anything we can conceive. . . . The end of this sublime communication is not to comfort the soul, but to show her how justly she afflicts herself at beholding herself absent from a good containing all other goods. . . . She knows well that she wishes for nothing but her God, but there is no special characteristic that she loves in Him; she simply loves all that He is, without knowing at all what she loves.[2]

Even such experiences are not yet heaven. God remains hidden. One day at last, by God's grace, we will enter for good, lucidly and completely, into God's Sanctuary of Silence. St. Augustine, at the end of his book on the Blessed Trinity, after decades of meditation, rising in many words from the consideration of creatures toward their cause and

---

[2] Quoted in *Life and Teaching of Jesus Christ,* Jules LeBrfeton (Burns and Oates: London, 1933), vol. 2, 293–294. The quotation is from St. Teresa's autobiography, ch. 20.

exemplar in His absolute simplicity, lifted his heart toward heaven where all will be said in one Word: "A certain wise man, when he spoke of You in his book which is now called by the name of Ecclesiasticus, declared: 'We say many things, and fall short, and the sum of our words is, He is all' [Sir 43:29]. But when we come to you, these 'many things' which we say 'and fall short' shall cease; and You as One shall remain, You who are all in all; and without ceasing we shall say one thing, praising you in the one, we who also have been made one in you."[3]

We say many things about Him who is *all.* Created, finite perfections point to His infinite perfection. Here below, we must multiply our ideas and approaches to better express His ineffable and infinite perfection, but *all falls short.* The ideas are helpful, but they are not adequate. They are only limited refractions of God's fullness.

We shall say one thing; that is, in heaven, we no longer will need to think about God by multiple, finite creatures, by reflections and images. We will know God in His Word. The Beatific Vision is the creature's highest possible union with God. In that Vision, we will join in God's perfect expression of Himself, which is His Word, and also in His loving joy, which is His Spirit. We will take part in the Father's pronouncing of the Word and the Father and Son's breathing of Love. We will share in God's own joy, in His knowledge and love.

3 St. Augustine, *De Trinitate,* trans. Stephen McKenna (Washington: Catholic University of America, 2002), XV, ch. 28.

Although, in that vision, we will be taken up as it were into God's own gaze and love, we will never be more truly ourselves, more human, than when at last we receive the grace of seeing God. We are made in the image of God, and this union with Him will bring all our depths to total, unspeakable fulfillment and, therefore, perfect repose and silence.

We will be *praising [God] in the one*. There will be a summit of silence by our repose in the infinite and by the convergence and union of all our powers in our loving gaze, but also an expression of our gratitude, praise, and wonder in participation in the Son's relation to the Father. Our praise will be perfect silence.

We have been made one in you. The supreme communion of all with the Trinity is the end of the whole economy, the reason for all God does outside Himself—Creation, Incarnation, Redemption. Father Ratzinger wrote about community life in heaven: "In their being together in the one Christ . . . the whole creation will become song."[4] The whole universe, all of creation, will come to its completion when men and angels are thus united to its and their Principle. The noise brought into creation will be over. All will be perfect music and harmony again. This symphony will be the supreme manifestation of God's beauty, the perfect, created unfolding of His Silence. God will be "all in all." We will have one life, vibrant with a common love, knowledge, and joy. We will all take part together in the Father's perfect

4 Ratzinger, *Eschatology*, 238.

repose and silence, in His pure act, in the eternal communion of the Three.

> Jesus! Whom for the present veiled I see
> What I so thirst for, oh, vouchsafe to me:
> That I may see Thy countenance unfolding,
> And may be blest Thy glory in beholding.[5]

St. Joseph and Our Blessed Father, St. Benedict, men of silence, pray for us. Our Lady of Silence, pray for us.

Amen.

5 This is the last stanza of the hymn "Adoro Te."